KU-447-669

An Atlantic "Rue de la Paix"

Shopping in the long gallery of
the *Aquitania*

PENGUIN BOOKS
THE LINERS

Terry Coleman went to fourteen schools, read Law at London
University and is now chief feature writer of the *Guardian*.
His first book, *The Railway Navvies*, won the *Yorkshire Post*
prize for the best first book of 1965 (published in Pelicans
1968). He was co-author of *Providence and Mr Hardy*, a
biographical study of Thomas Hardy, and recently edited the
first edition in England of Hardy's unpublished first novel. He
has also published *The Only True History*, a collection of
interviews and other journalism, one novel, and *Passage to
America*, a history of emigrants to the United States in the
mid-nineteenth century (Penguin, 1974).

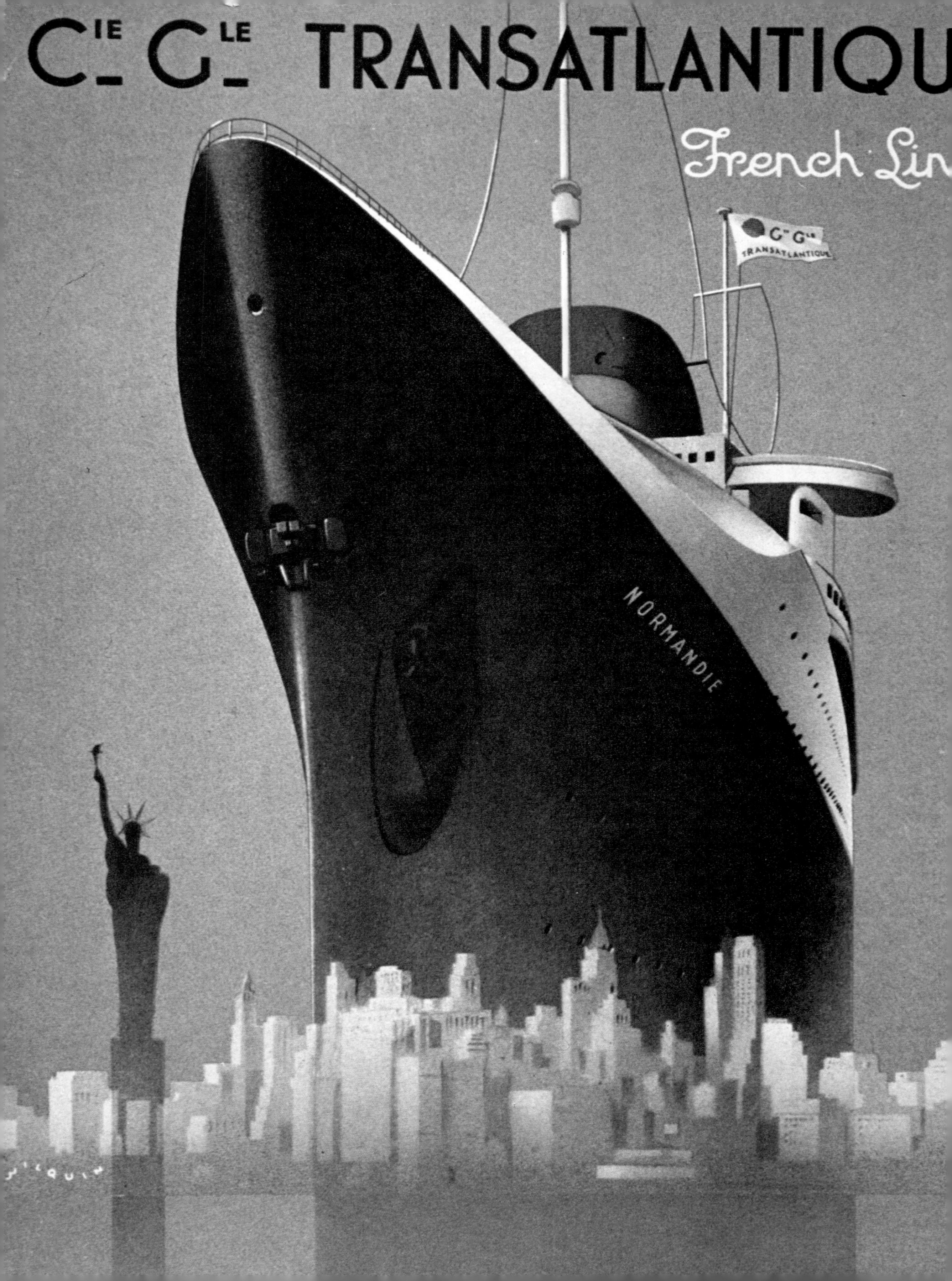
Cie Gle TRANSATLANTIQU
French Lin
NORMANDIE

The Liners

A History of the North Atlantic Crossing

Terry Coleman

Penguin Books

Penguin Books Ltd, Harmondsworth,
Middlesex, England
Penguin Books, 625 Madison Avenue,
New York, New York 10022, U.S.A.
Penguin Books Australia Ltd, Ringwood,
Victoria, Australia
Penguin Books Canada Ltd, 2801 John Street,
Markham, Ontario, Canada
Penguin Books (N.Z.) Ltd, 182–190 Wairau Road,
Auckland 10, New Zealand

First published by Allen Lane 1976
Published in Penguin Books 1977
Copyright © Terry Coleman, 1976
All rights reserved

Made and printed in Great Britain by
Fletcher & Son Ltd, Norwich

Set in Monophoto Photina

Designed by Fred Price

Except in the United States of America, this book is
sold subject to the condition that it shall not, by
way of trade or otherwise, be lent, re-sold, hired out,
or otherwise circulated without the publisher's prior
consent in any form of binding or cover other than
that in which it is published and without a similar
condition including this condition being imposed on
the subsequent purchaser

Frontispiece: A French Line representation of the *Normandie* and New York, which as one Paris newspaper remarked, had shown itself to be a city on the scale of the great ship

In happy recollection of Voyage 124 (West)

'The Liner She's a Lady'

Kipling

CONTENTS

ACKNOWLEDGEMENTS

I wish to thank the following people and institutions whose kindness
and encouragement made possible the writing of this book. In England:
the Cunard Steam-Ship Co., in particular Mr Stephen Mitchell, public
relations officer, and also the officers and some of the crew of the *QE2*,
for generous help; at Liverpool University, Mr Michael Cook, archivist,
and Mr Dennis E. Glover, keeper of the Cunard archive there; the
Reading Room of the British Museum and the newspaper collection at
Colindale; the National Maritime Museum, Greenwich; Professor Leslie
Young; Mr Roy Anderson, the authority on White Star history; the
newspaper library of the *Guardian*, and Mr Ken Murphy, London
librarian; the London Library; and the Deptford Branch of Lewisham
Public library. In America: the Mariners Museum, Newport News,
Virginia, and particularly Mr John L. Lochhead, librarian, and his staff,
for the most open and kindly help; the New York Public Library,
magnificent as always, and its newspaper collections; the Library of
Congress; the Museum of the City of New York; and the Titanic
Enthusiasts of America, particularly Mr Ed Kamuda and Mr Ken
Marschall. In France: La Compagnie Générale Transatlantique, and
particularly M. René Bouvard, historiographer, who lent generously
from his splendid collections. 'The Convergence of the Twain' by Thomas
Hardy, and the lines by Kipling, are quoted by permission of Macmillan
and Co., London, and the passages from *The Queens and I* by permission
of the author, Commodore Geoffrey Marr, and of Adlard Coles, London.
I should particularly like to thank Stephen Moreton-Pritchard for his
photographic work.

CHAPTER ONE

'Lights Burning Bright and All's Well, Sir'

To begin, for the moment, with the *Mauretania* and *Lusitania*. They were sister ships, of 31,000 tons, with four raked funnels. They were the first Atlantic liners in which it was the invariable rule to dress for dinner in first class. They both made their maiden voyages in 1907, but the date does not matter because they express, more than any other ships, the *idea* of the ocean liner. It is very strange to look at a photograph of the *Lusitania*'s arrival in New York after her maiden crossing and see that the Cunard dock is crowded with horse-drawn cabs. Her passengers, who had made a sea-crossing of the Atlantic in a style that did not essentially much change ever afterwards, and in a beautiful piece of machinery that was essentially never much improved on, then had to rely on horses to take them to their Manhattan hotels. To say this of the *Lusitania* is not to say there was no progress from then on. Liners were built more than twice as big. But the last of the Atlantic liners, the *Queen Elizabeth 2*, generally steams only a couple of knots faster than the *Mauretania*. The crossing is still five days. With those Cunarders of 1907, the modern express liner had suddenly appeared, and the tenor of the times, with its belief in the inevitability of progress, made much of this. The *Philadelphia Inquirer* said, 'Just now the man who came over in the *Lusitania* takes precedence of the one whose ancestors came over in the *Mayflower*.' Hearst papers had their own correspondent on board, and ran headlines like:

MRS POTTER PALMER
REPORTS OCEAN RACE

A CHICAGO SOCIETY LEADER
SENDS WIRELESS MESSAGES
FROM THE LUSITANIA

Mrs Potter Palmer said there had been no seasickness (which means either that the passage was a miracle or that she was not an observant reporter) and described the ship as 'an ocean greyhound, as it were, with open fireplaces'. From New York Mrs Palmer went by train to Chicago, and claimed the Liverpool–Chicago record, saying she had left Liverpool at nine on Saturday evening, 7 September, and had reached home at nine the following Saturday morning. The Hearst press also reported that, upon her arrival, Chicago's social queen took occasion to deny that she was to marry King Peter of Servia. This, rather more than Mrs Potter's own reportage, catches the right tone of a fashionable crossing.

By 1907 the Atlantic crossing was well established as the voyage of voyages. Money was in it, and so therefore were the best and fastest ships anywhere. Here were the two greatest civilizations of the world, and the liners were the only way to cross. The Atlantic is the roughest and hardest of seas,

◀ The Cunarder *Lusitania* at her New York berth after her maiden crossing in September 1907. She was in essence the first of the modern super-liners, but her passengers were taken to their Manhattan hotels in horse cabs

If You Fell Overboard From the Lusitania

"MY HAT!"

OH—

—LORDY!

SPLASH!!

Cartoon on the maiden voyage of the *Lusitania*, from the Louisville, Kentucky *Times*, 14 September 1907

especially in winter; and even in summer, and even for the steadiest of liners, the Atlantic was never a pond. This was something the shipping companies played down, even though they knew perfectly well that their officers put on oilskins and seaboots the moment they left the Irish coast behind. The crossing west was the only way to the new world. The *Mauretania* and *Lusitania*, like generations of liners to come, made their American landfalls and sailed up the bay into what H. G. Wells called 'the hard, clear vigour of New York, that valiant city which even more than Venice rides out upon the sea'. And from America, the crossing east was the only way to the old world. It was already the custom, and remained so, for the big liners to sail at midnight from their North River piers, with farewell parties continuing to the last moment and the liner easing out of her berth festooned with paper streamers. 'I heard the *Queen Mary* blow one midnight,' said E. B. White, 'and the sound carried with it the whole history of departure, longing, and loss.' The *Queen Mary*'s siren was pitched two octaves below Middle A, and so was the *Mauretania*'s.

Western Ocean steamships had always been grand. As soon as they attained any size at all, say by 1870, it had become customary to remark that they were as well appointed as the best Swiss hotels, but by the *Mauretania*'s time they were grander than that and it was usual to call them floating palaces. They were island palaces, where the lookouts called, 'Lights burning bright and all's well, Sir.' This sense of a sea-going abstraction from ordinary things, of an exacerbated sensibility, of feeling everything more intensely, was written about not only by novelists but also by sea captains in their memoirs. Harry Grattidge, Commodore of the Cunard line, grieved when 'the subtle spell of the voyage was broken'. Sir Bertram Hayes, Commodore of the White Star, wrote on his retirement: 'Hull down! The ship on the horizon, outward bound. A thousand times I have stood on that ship, thought of those on the shore watching us disappear over the edge, then turned to the company of travellers and, with

Grand saloon of the *City of New York, c.* 1890

them, lost myself . . . [Now] I have the feeling that also the ship of my affairs is hull down too. The adventures of the sea, most of the adventures of life, are behind me . . . I shall never again have under my hand the control of what is a young city afloat.'

North German Lloyd, applying themselves with German thoroughness to an analysis of the intangible feeling of voyage, said it was akin to what a great actor might call the illusion of the first time. In the theatre the actor's art hypnotized each member of the audience into

'Drawn by like-feeling'. (Left) Woman passenger and ship's officer on a British ship; engraving 'The Old, Old Story', by Julius M. Price, 1888. (Right) Man and woman on deck on a French ship *c.* 1880, from a painting by L. Sabattier

believing that the actions he saw taking place on stage had never happened before, and that now, as he saw them, they happened only for him. In the same way, if a sea voyage was happy, you would always feel that the ship had never sailed before you sailed on her, and would never sail again until the next time you were on board. This was the illusion of the ship. In the mind of the passenger, nothing existed except himself and one or two of his fellow passengers to whom he was drawn by like-feeling and with whom he shared this intensity of isolation. The ship on which they sailed was for the moment their only piece of land. Those drawn together by like feeling were often of opposite sex. Steamship companies knew this

and often advertised erotically. Here is Cunard being unsubtle: 'Passengers will remember how romantically the glowing phosphorescent waves curled back in the ship's wake, falling forever in flakes of diamond and pearl. They will remember how readily the damsel of their choice could be persuaded to a secluded spot in order to observe this poetic phenomenon. They will remember quite a lot of things, we have no doubt.' Ivan Bunin, in a short story translated from the Russian by D. H. Lawrence, describes an exquisite loving couple on board a liner, whom everybody watched curiously because of their unconcealed happiness. *He* danced only with *her*, and sang, with great skill, only to *her* accompaniment, and everything about them was so charming, and only the captain knew that this couple had been engaged by the steamship company to play at love for a good salary, and that they had been sailing for a long time, now on one liner, now on another.

It seems an unlikely story. What would the need be? Why should a steamship company pay such people when, as Sinclair Lewis noticed, at night, on deck, there were always honeymooners quickly unclasping as the pestiferous deck-circlers passed. Comedies could be written about shipboard life, and not the least of them would be that suggested by the remark, first made of the *Mauretania*, that she was so big that a man and his wife could unknowingly take passage on her separately, and never meet.

To go back to the photographs of the *Lusitania* and *Mauretania* and the horse-drawn cabs: there is a real sense of anachronism. The horses do not belong. And yet it is also true to say that if anyone had had the foresight and the courage to demand it, those ships could feasibly have been built almost twenty years before. They would have lacked the turbine engine, which would have made them a knot or so slower, but the state of the shipbuilding art was such that they *could* have been built. There still exists a sketch made before 1888 at the suggestion of Sir William Pearce of Fairfield's yard on the Clyde. He had begun as a labourer in the yard, worked his way up to design the biggest of the Cunard ships, and been made a baronet. In 1888 he was working on plans for yet larger ships, which could cross the Atlantic in five days, but then he died suddenly with his work uncompleted. The

drawing of his that remains is the spitten image of the *Mauretania*. The largest ships Sir William had designed and seen completed were the Cunarders *Umbria* and *Etruria*, and it is with them that this history of the north Atlantic passenger liner must properly start. The *Lusitania* and *Mauretania* were the first of the huge express liners, but the *Umbria* and *Etruria* were the first to be built whose silhouette even now would not seem archaic. It is no good calling them the first liners or any such thing, because a liner is merely a ship which runs regularly on a particular line, making the same passage, and plenty of others did that before them. But they are probably the first vessels to be built which could show their noses in port today, and be recognized as liners. The typical hull, funnels, and superstructure are there.

And yet, at the same time, they still retained the vestiges of what had gone before them. They carried three masts and enough sail to continue their passage should mechanical power fail. They were the last passenger steamers to do so on the Atlantic. They are thus at a divide – the last of the old, the first of the new; the first of the real Atlantic liners. Before them, in the years since the American *Savannah* had partly steamed but mostly sailed across the Atlantic in 1819, there had been many years of experiment and then solid achievement. Wooden hulls had at last, only in 1865, given way to iron, and then to steel; paddle-wheels had at last, only in 1867, completely given way to propellors. Passenger berths had at last been placed amidships, where the ship pitched least, rather than in the

Steamship designed to cross the Atlantic in five days – a sketch by Sir William Pearce of the Fairfield yard, as early as 1888

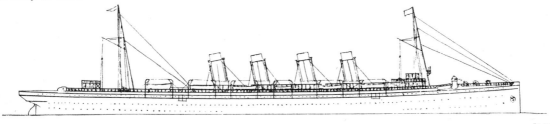

The captain at Sunday service, probably in the saloon of the *Campania*. A very early stunted publicity picture, *c.* 1893

stern, which was the old sailing-ship tradition. There were separate state-rooms, rather than communal cabins, and these cabins were heated by steam and lit by gas or even electricity. By the time of *Umbria* and *Etruria* the Atlantic crossing was still an adventure but could no longer be called by any stretch of the imagination a calculated risk of one's life. By the 1880s the advice given in 1878 by an American woman, Kate Ledoux, in a guide called *Ocean Notes for Ladies*, had an archaic sound. She advised lady saloon passengers to dress sensibly but well, because she had always felt that a body washed ashore in good clothes would receive more respect and kinder care than if dressed in clothes only fit for the rag bag.

This history of the liner and its passengers begins then, at a time when such pioneer days are over, but it is first necessary to give the briefest sketch of that pioneering. Samuel Cunard was not the first man whose steam-

ships crossed the Atlantic, but his were the most regular, they got the first large mail contract, and they did not sink. The Cunards were Quakers who came from Redditch, Shropshire. The family emigrated to Philadelphia in the seventeenth century and then, on the American Declaration of Independence, patrioti- cally moved north to British North America where Samuel was born at Halifax in 1787. He went into banking, lumber, whaling, fire insurance, and the militia, in which he became a colonel. As early as 1819 he had a British government contract to carry mails in sailing brigs down the east coast of America from St John's, Newfoundland, to Boston and Bermuda. When in 1838 the British government asked for tenders to carry transatlantic mail by steam, he went to London and offered the services of three steamers each of 300 horsepower and 800 tons, to carry the mail to America and back twice a month, all for the sum of £55,000

The Cunarder *Etruria*, 1884, surrounded by the house flags of the principal international lines and the international code of signals.

Samuel Cunard: a miniature in oils still in the Cunard archive

The Inman steamer *City of Rome*, the first three-funnelled liner and said by many to be the most beautiful steamship ever to cross the Atlantic. She was a commercial failure and Inman's got rid of her

La Normandie, of the French Line, 1886, under steam and sail

La Touraine, of the French Line, 1891. Oil painting by Antonio Jacobsen

A Cunard departure from Liverpool, 1881

per annum subsidy. He won the contract, and was received back home in Halifax by a ceremonial procession of Hammermen, Mechanics, Master Shipwrights, Caulkers, Blacksmiths, Joiners, Riggers, and Sawyers, and a guard armed with adzes and axes. He had the contract but he did not yet have the ships; and when these were built it was not by the master shipwrights and joiners of Halifax but by those of the Clyde. He commissioned a fleet of four ships, of which the first was the *Britannia*. They were wooden paddle boats, of about 1,150 tons and capable of 9 knots. They were not the fastest and nothing like the biggest ships of their day. The rival *British Queen*, for instance, was half as big again. The *Britannia* made the first crossing from Liverpool on 4 July 1840, Independence Day, an auspicious day for an American service, and reached Halifax in twelve days and Boston in fourteen. The Cunard company used later to assert that if

an examiner were to ask a student to name one of the greatest events in the marvellous history of the nineteenth century, and he were to answer the first voyage of the *Britannia* in 1840, he would be able to justify his reply with very good arguments: it was peaceful revolution of the whole commerce of the world. By 'world', Cunard naturally meant Britain and America, which was something very proper for a north Atlantic steamship company to assume. When the *Britannia* arrived in Boston, Cunard was fêted at a banquet for 2,000, and told in a formal toast that he had a head to contrive, a tongue to advocate, and a hand to execute. Someone then shouted another toast from the crowd – 'Samuel Cunard – the only man who has dared to *beat* the British Queen.' This was 1840, the year the new Queen Victoria married Prince Albert, and there were many jokes current about beating or being aboard the British Queen. The next year Fanny Kemble met Cunard in London at

[21]

dinner, and such was his reputation even by then that she described him in her diary as a sort of proprietor of the Atlantic ocean between England and the United States.

Even though Cunard was a Canadian, and often thought of as an Englishman, he was made much of in the United States, and Bostonians were proud that their city and not New York was chosen as his second port of call after Halifax. There was profit in it for Boston. In the winter of 1844, the *Britannia* was frozen into Boston harbour, and the mayor and businessmen, anxious that this should not persuade Cunard to go south to New York on subsequent voyages, contracted for ice ploughs to cut the *Britannia* a passage to the open sea at the city's cost. This was done. The ice was cut from the harbour in cubes and carted away by teams of horses. The *Britannia* proceeded on her

eastbound passage through the canal out in the ice and was accompanied, for the first part of the way, by half the population of Boston skating by her side.

There is no use pretending that these first Cunarders were anything other than profoundly uncomfortable. They were the size of seaside-resort steamers. The paddle-wheels and machinery took up all the space amidships, so the passengers' quarters were fore and aft, where they got the worst of the movement. The saloon was a gigantic hearse with windows at the sides, one stove, and one solitary long table. The state-rooms are familiar from Dickens's description of the one in which he and his wife crossed for his first American tour. When he had been shown its picture in the shipping office it had indeed been a state-room. When he entered it, he found two berths one above the

The *Britannia* in the ice of Boston harbour, 1844

Dickens's state-room on board the *Britannia*, 1842

other, the upper being an inaccessible shelf than which, he said, nothing smaller for sleeping in was ever made than a coffin. And apart from these berths, the remaining space was no bigger than a hackney cab. A special deck-house with padded sides sheltered the ship's cow whose milk was kept for women, children, and invalids. Fresh vegetables were stored beneath overturned lifeboats. Dickens made the return passage by sailing packet.

But from the start Cunard was likely to succeed. He was not an adventurer but a most experienced merchant, broker, and shipping owner. He was fifty-three years old before he embarked on steamships, and then they were conservative ships. But he *sounded* as if he had dash: there are names which have dash in the very sound of them, and Cunard is such a name. That is a great advantage, particularly when it is allied to a cautious nature, and Samuel Cunard was by nature cautious. This shows in his orders to the master of the *Britannia*:

The *Britannia* is now put under your command for Halifax and Boston. It is understood that you have the direction of everything and Person on board.

Good steering is of great value.

In navigating of our vessels we have great confidence in the ability of our captains, but in the matter of fog, the best officers become infatuated and often attempt to push through when prudence would indicate patience.

In the 1890s Henry Fry, Lloyds agent at Quebec, recalled that in fifty-three years Cunard had never lost the life of a passenger,* and in the previous forty-four years never a letter, and no other company could say that. He had watched every Atlantic steamship for fifty-six years, and crossed the Atlantic himself thirty-seven times. He remarked that someone at the head of the Cunard company was an excellent judge of character. Never, he said, was discipline more perfect or order more complete. Such captains as Lott, Judkins, Leitch, and Harrison were the very *crème de la crème* of the British mercantile service, brave, bold, watchful, cautious, and stern, and also, with perhaps one or two exceptions, accomplished gentlemen. Lott had been given a public banquet in New York on completion of his 500th trip. Anderson had been knighted, but poor Harrison, after braving Atlantic storms, had been drowned in a ditch at Southampton by the upsetting of a rowing boat.

The advantage of steamships on the Atlantic was that they were not only faster than sailing ships, but also more reliable. The Cunard passage to Halifax was twelve days and a bit, with very little variation from passage to passage. In a sailing ship the best westward passage could take say twenty-two days, but the worst thirty-eight, God willing. The eastward passage back to Europe, with the prevailing winds, was easier, and could be as short as seventeen days. This is why Dickens, having been badly shaken by the vibration of the *Britannia*'s paddle-wheels on the passage to America, chose to return in the comparative smoothness of a sailing packet since, in that direction, it would take only a few days longer. The American packets of the 1840s and the succeeding decade were, along with the Ameri-

* And this is a record that has lasted to this day. In peacetime, discounting the *Lusitania* sinking, Cunard have never lost a passenger by shipwreck, though one woman is said to have died of terror and seasickness on the *Queen Mary* in a storm.

can far-eastern clippers, the finest sailing vessels ever built, fast, the largest of their day, and commonly admitted, even by Englishmen, to be very much the superior of all their rivals in sail. It is all the more extraordinary, then, that the Americans should have allowed Britain almost immediately to build up and maintain such a distinct superiority in steam, but that is what happened. Perhaps the Americans' superiority in sail was so evident that they relied on it longer than they should. However, there was one early exception to this American complacency, and he was Edward Knight Collins. He was himself an owner of sailing packets, and of one of the most famous lines. The packet lines of those days bore names like the Black Ball, Red Star, Blue Swallowtail, Red Swallowtail, and the Dramatic, whose vessels were called *Garrick*, *Siddons*, *Roscius*, and the like. Collins owned the Dramatic packets. He was an adventurous man. His family had come over from Ireland as early as 1634. When he was fifteen he became a clerk in a shipping firm in New York. In 1836 he started his Dramatic line and prospered mightily, so much so that by 1846 his name was appearing in a paperbound booklet called *The Wealth and Biography of the Wealthy Citizens of New York*, an alphabetical list of the most prominent capitalists whose fortune was estimated at $100,000 or more. In real values, they would today be millionaires many times over. His fortune had come from sailing packets, but he suddenly sold the lot out of a belief in steam and in hope of a federal subsidy.

He was right that steam was the future, only it was not his. He enjoyed, of course, the enthusiastic support of a not unreasonable American jingoism. Americans did not like a Nova Scotian being regarded as a sort of proprietor of the Atlantic. Congressman Bayard of Delaware said in the House of Representatives that American shipowners should be given a free hand 'to proceed with the absolute conquest of this man Cunard'. He did not mean a free hand; he meant a subsidized hand. Collins then built the four finest Atlantic steamships of their day, each of 2,800 tons,

much bigger than their Cunard competitors, and much faster. They were called *Atlantic*, *Pacific*, *Arctic*, and *Baltic*, Collins explaining that he had to take the oceans since Cunard, with *Africa*, *Asia*, *America*, and *Europa*, had already taken the continents. Like the Cunarders, his were wooden paddle-boats. He wanted iron hulls but American shipyards were unable to build them. But his ships were much faster, up to $12\frac{1}{2}$ knots, and they had the straight stem which was later to become so familiar on the Atlantic. They were not beautiful. The Cunarders were pretty and rakish and had clipper bows, but they shipped water. The Collins liners were ugly but drier. And Collins so prospered at first that after twenty-eight round voyages his boats had carried 4,306 passengers against Cunard's 2,969. But he had lost two-and-a-half million dollars doing so, and if it had not been for the federal subsidy this loss would have been nearly three-and-a-half millions. The rivalry with Cunard was strangely friendly. When Nathaniel Hawthorne, the novelist, was American consul at Liverpool after 1853 he said that the Mersey was alive with steamboats whizzing industriously along. But the principal steamers were the Cunarders and the Collins. When a Cunarder came in with her red funnel whitened by the sea spray she would lie for several hours after mooring with smoke and steam coming out of her, as if she were smoking a pipe after her heavy Atlantic passage. Once a fortnight an American Collins steamer passed a Cunarder in the river, and they saluted each other with cannon, all the more ceremoniously because they were rivals and jealous of each other. Hawthorne got to know Captain Luce of the Collins line, whom he thought a sensitive man, courteous, quiet, with something almost melancholy in his aspect. This was the Luce who went down with the *Arctic* in 1854. Hawthorne said he had seldom been more affected by anything. The *Arctic* was the first of the Collins fleet to founder. She was run down by a small French ship in thick fog only sixty miles from Cape Race. She ran for land but foundered within twenty miles. Heavy seas smashed her boats, and only a quarter of the 365 souls on board survived. The crew saved themselves and abandoned the passengers. On board her, Collins lost his own wife, son, and daughter. One passenger in the sea offered £30,000 if the boats would put back and save him. They did turn back, but he sank before they could reach him. Next year Collins launched the *Adriatic*, which was even bigger, 4,114 tons, but in 1856 another of his fleet, the *Pacific*, disappeared and was never heard from again. He lost his federal subsidy, and what was left of his fleet was sold to pay creditors. The last of his vessels to survive was the grand *Adriatic*, and she was sold first to Ireland and then to even more dubious owners who first converted her to sail and then let her rot as a hulk off the coast of Nigeria. Collins had failed, but he had in his time taken the blue riband of the Atlantic from Cunard. This was a notional honour invented for themselves by the steamship companies. The expression did not exist when the sailing packets were racing each other. Perhaps it comes from the ribbon or riband traditionally given for excellence, or for coming first, as at horse shows. There are those who assert that the colour at least is derived from the ribbon or sash of the Order of the Garter, and that this is one reason why British ships considered they had a prescriptive right to the blue riband. At any rate, it became the colour of the long pennant that a claimant to the record flew from the topmast. Collins had taken this honour at a most delightful time for American pride, in 1851, during the Great Exhibition in London, when the *Baltic* crossed in 9 days 10 hours. The Americans said John Bull took it like a gentleman.

Collins failed, but he established three things. First, that wooden hulls, hard-driven, would not stand the wracking of the Atlantic. His ships were constantly being strengthened one way and another. Carpenters and mechanics often worked all night in New York to get them ready for sea. Second, that American shipowners were going to have to pay high American wages, a thing which was to hamper the American mercantile marine ever afterwards: he was obliged to pay his American stokers $30 a month against Cunard's $15 for their Irishmen, and his captains $6,000 dollars a year against Cunard's $2,500. Third, *he* more than anyone else created the idea of opulence on the north Atlantic. Early Cunarders were sparse. Collins's liners had steam heating, ice rooms, barber's chairs, and even carpets which were however prudently rolled up and stowed away at sea. Cunard's steamers, inside, resembled English and Irish channel ferries which were then as sordid as most of them still remain. Collins's steamers derived their interiors from American river steamers, which were palaces.

Another of the pioneers was William Inman, who had no intention at all of going into the express Atlantic passenger trade. In 1850 he was twenty-five, a partner in the Liverpool merchant house of Richardson Bros., where he had formerly been a clerk. His business was emigrants. He had run the Richardsons' line of sailing packets to Philadelphia, but by 1850 most emigrants were going to New York and preferring the newest and largest packets, which were all American. In the summer of that year he happened to see the Clyde steamer *City of Glasgow*, 1,600 tons, which had been built speculatively, and he persuaded his partners to buy her. On December 17 she made her first voyage for Richardsons' out of Liverpool for Philadelphia with 400 steerage passengers. She was an immediate success. The immigration movement of the mid century was then at its height. In sailing ships it was sordid, unhealthy, and dangerous, and it was the steamship, and not the reforming, humanitarian, or self-interested motives of any government which made the Atlantic passage in steerage for the first time tolerable. Nobody in the emigration business was a philanthropist. Inman was not. He wanted to pack 1,000 in the steerage and the British government allowed only 600, but he still made a profit. At his first ship's arrival, a Philadelphia magazine talked fatuously of time being annihilated, and of there being such luxury and elegance on board as in the most princely mansions ashore, which was rot. But simply by cutting the passage-time in half, and feeding his emigrants decently so that they

STEAM COMMUNICATION
MONTHLY FROM
LIVERPOOL
TO
NEW YORK, BALTIMORE,
PITTSBURGH, CINCINNATI, CHARLESTON, HAVANA, &c.
BY WAY OF
PHILADELPHIA.

THE LIVERPOOL AND PHILADELPHIA STEAM SHIP COMPANY
INTEND SAILING THEIR NEW IRON SCREW STEAM SHIPS AS FOLLOW:—

CITY OF GLASGOW,	- - - -	Captain K. MORRISON - - - -	1610 Tons.
CITY OF MANCHESTER,	- - - -	Captain WILLIAM WYLIE - - -	2125 ,,
CITY OF PHILADELPHIA, (building) -		Captain ROBERT LEITCH - - -	2189 ,,
CITY OF BALTIMORE, - (building) -		Captain R. LEITCH - - - - - -	2472 ,,

FROM LIVERPOOL.
CITY OF MANCHESTER	..Captain LEITCH....	,,	..	1st February, 1854.
CITY OF GLASGOW	......Captain WYLIE....	,,	..	1st March, ,,

FROM PHILADELPHIA.
CITY OF MANCHESTER	..Captain LEITCH....	Saturday	7th January, 1854.
CITY OF GLASGOW	......Captain WYLIE....	,,	..	4th February ,,
CITY OF MANCHESTER	..Captain LEITCH....	Thursday	..	2nd March ,,

RATES OF CABIN PASSAGE
FROM LIVERPOOL.

After Saloon State-rooms, (2 berths in each,) - - **21 Guineas each berth.**
Ditto, and Midship, (3 berths in each,) - - **17** ,, ,,
Ditto, Ditto, Forward State-rooms - **15** ,, ,,
Including Provisions and Steward's Fee,
ALL HAVING THE SAME PRIVILEGE, AND MESSING TOGETHER.

A limited number of Passengers to Philadelphia will be taken at Eight Guineas; to New York at Eight Pounds Sixteen Shillings, and supplied with Provisions of a superior quality, properly cooked, and as much as is required; and these Passengers are hereby informed, that, in order to satisfy the requirements of the Government Officers, the Date filled into their Contract Tickets will be, in every case, the date of the day preceding the fixed day of sailing, and those Passengers booked for New York, will, on their arrival in Philadelphia, be provided by the Agents of the Steamers with a Ticket entitling them to a Free Passage by Steam-boat or Railway to New York.

THESE STEAMERS CARRY PHILLIPS' PATENT FIRE ANNIHILATORS.
AN EXPERIENCED SURGEON IS ATTACHED TO EACH STEAMER.

Passengers will find PHILADELPHIA the most central Port, BEING ON THE DIRECT MAIL ROUTE from New York to the Western and Southern States.

RATES OF FREIGHT.

Freight £4 per ton, with 5 per cent. Primage, with the exception of Unmanufactured Produce, &c. which will be taken, subject to agreement, payable here or in Philadelphia, at 4 dols. 80 cents per pound sterling. Private arrangements have been made by the Agents to transport fine goods to New York, by Steam-boat (including insurance) and Canal, at four cents per foot, or about 6s 8d per ton measurement, and by steamer to Charleston eight cents, and to Norfolk and Richmond Va., at six cents per foot.

Goods intended for the interior of the United States, if consigned to the Agents at Philadelphia will be forwarded without charge for commission. Dogs at Three Pounds each.

Apply in Philadelphia, to SAMUEL SMITH, 43, Walnut-street; in Belfast, to RICHARDSON BROTHERS and CO.; in Dublin, to CORNELIUS CARLETON; in London, to EDWARDS, SANFORD and CO. for Passengers, and PICKFORD and CO. for Goods; in Paris, to FRED. REDFERN, 8, Rue de la Paix; in Havre, to W. DAVIDSON; in Manchester, to GEO. STONIER; and to

RICHARDSON BROTHERS & CO.

Liverpool, 12 Mo. 10th, 1853.   12 13, Tower-buildings, LIVERPOOL.

J. MAWDSLEY & SON, PRINTERS, LIVERPOOL.

Advertisement for Richardsons' of Liverpool (later Inman's) for their steamships. 1853

should be reasonably fit on arrival and not so starved and diseased as to cause his vessels to be held up at quarantine in America, Inman was a great benefactor to the immigrants. He had also, quite accidentally, made two discoveries. The *City of Brussels*, which he had not commissioned at all but bought practically off the stocks, happened to be iron-hulled, and he found very early what his competitors learned only by long experience, that iron hulls stood up much better to the combined strain of the Atlantic outside and of the steam engines pounding away inside. The *City of Brussels* was also a screw ship. Up to that time the screw had always been reckoned a slower means of propulsion than the paddle-wheel. This did not matter to Inman. He was not after a record-breaker. A ship which could cross in fourteen days against the Cunarders' twelve was good enough for him and for his emigrants. Within a few years the screw, which he had not minded being a little slower than the paddle, had turned out to be, in its slightly more developed state, not only distinctly more economical but also faster. By 1866, when his *City of Paris*, crossed the Atlantic at $13\frac{1}{2}$ knots, Inman found himself holding the blue riband.* By then it also happened that the emigrant business had fallen off from its peak of the mid century, and so he was carrying much the same class of passenger as Cunard. Inman was a little unlucky in one way. He lost five ships at sea within thirty years which is perhaps a record for any single company, though only two took their passengers with them, those of the other three being rescued from wrecks off Cape Race, off Cobh, and in the Mersey. It was probably the crews who had been victims of these disasters that Inman's loyal employees had in mind when, in 1872, they presented him with an illuminated testimonial saying they could not find language wherewith adequately to express

themselves, but calling him an earnest-minded, zealous servant of God who had often acted generously to those who, in the mysterious providence of God, had found a grave in the mighty deep. Inman had shown the great value he attached to the immortal souls of those of his employees who still lived by erecting for them a handsome and commodious mission-hall. The signatories to this testimonial, who were led by an engineer, a shipwright, and a missionary, added that they hoped it would be many years before he would have to respond with rapture to His Saviour's welcoming words of 'Well done, good and faithful servant: enter ye into the joy of your Lord.' Inman did not enter into this joy until 1881, a few days after the launching of the ship which was intended to be the greatest he ever possessed, but which would in the event have given him no pleasure.

She was the *City of Rome*, very big for her day at 8,400 tons and also intended, at $18\frac{1}{2}$ knots, to be the fastest. But she never did more than 16 knots, never did the Liverpool–New York crossing in much less than ten days, and after only six round voyages was handed back to the builders, who resisted her return but lost the ensuing lawsuit and had to take her. She was sold from line to line, once survived striking an iceberg, was requisitioned for Boer War trooping, and eventually foundered at her scrapping berth. But on one thing almost all marine historians seem to be agreed — that she was the most beautiful liner ever to cross the Atlantic. This is puzzling. She was, as it happens, the first liner to have three funnels, and in this sense she created an image of power that was to last for eighty years. But she was a long ship, in the sense that her beam was very narrow, only one-eleventh of her length, which did not long remain a typical liner characteristic, and she is almost always pictured flying along with a full spread of sail. Beautiful she may be, but her beauty is rather that of the one and only three-funnelled clipper ship.

Of the other two lines to be noticed in this period of pre-history, one, the Guion, is now little more than a footnote though at the time it

* He also found himself owning the ships outright. He had been a lucky young man. In 1855 the British government wanted to hire Richardsons' two steamers to transport soldiers to the Crimea. But the Richardsons were Quakers and had religious doubts, of which Inman relieved them by buying out the ships and making a large profit on the charter.

promised much. The other is the White Star, which was the beginning of greater things than could have been guessed. Guion also had its beginnings in emigrant packets. Towards the very end of the days of the American sailing packets the largest of them were those of the Black Star line out of New York, not to be confused with the much older-established and respectable Black Ball line. Black Star were huge packets, well-made, dry, sound vessels, but crewed with the riff-raff and dive sweepings of New York, and consequently suffering from a richly deserved reputation for beating and defrauding helpless emigrants. These packets were run by the firm of Williams and Guion, who, when the emigrant trade fell off in the late 1850s and 1860s, took to steamers and adopted the name of the Guion line. The sailing packets had been American built and owned and flew the American flag. The steamers were still American owned, but because they were British built, and because Congress decreed that no ship built elsewhere than the United States could fly the Stars and Stripes, they were registered in Liverpool and flew the Red Ensign. Guion were not without distinction. In 1879 their *Arizona* crashed full into an iceberg at 15 knots and survived with twenty-five feet of the bow beaten in. This did nothing but breed a sadly-wrong belief that modern construction could make ships almost unsinkable. It was in the *Arizona* that Oscar Wilde later crossed and announced to the New York customs that he had nothing to declare but his genius. In 1877 and 1880 the company contrived a double which must be unique, wrecking two ships near Anglesey within a few miles of each other. Then, with *Alaska*, they took the blue riband at $16\frac{1}{2}$ knots. She became the first ship to cross from Ireland to New York in under a week. Their new ship *Oregon* did even better but by then the company was unable to pay for the ship, which was seized by the builders and resold to Cunard. She lasted another two years before she too was sunk, rammed by an unknown vessel in the approaches to New York. All on board survived, and so did Cunard's record of never losing a life.

So much for Guion. White Star was another matter. This was the company formed by T. H. Ismay, who was really interested in the Australian trade until he was persuaded by the new Belfast shipbuilding firm of Harland and Wolff that the ships they could build for him would do better on the American run. He took their advice, and between them they produced ships that played their part in the making of the mature Atlantic liner. Ismay was the first to put his first-class passengers amidships, the first to allow the dining-saloon to go the whole width of the ship, and the first to provide large cabins, much larger than anything Cunard had at that date. The relationship between shipping line and shipbuilder was and remained so close that, throughout White Star's long history, no other yard ever built a ship for them.

White Star, like so many other companies in these early days, had their shipwrecks. In 1873 their *Atlantic* found herself, at the end of a crossing, with less than enough coal to make New York, tried to make for Halifax instead, and there stranded and broke up in sight of land with the loss of 546 lives. Patrick Leahy, an Irishman, said: 'Then I saw the first and awful sight . . . a large mass of something drifted past the ship on the top of the waves, and then it was lost to view in the trough of the sea. As it passed by a moan — it must have been a shriek but the tempest dulled the sound — seemed to surge up from the mass, which extended over fifty yards of water; it was the women. The sea swept them out of the steerage, and with their children, to the number of 200 or 300, they drifted thus to eternity.'

It was ships of the *Oceanic* and *Atlantic* class that were first described as having all the comforts of Swiss hotels. Their smoking-rooms — rooms and not just the deck awnings Cunard offered at the time — were described as narcotic paradises. And it was over cabins in a slightly later White Star liner, the *Britannic*, that two American railroad millionaires came into dispute. Both William Henry Vanderbilt and John Pierpont Morgan wanted the same state-rooms. Vanderbilt thought he settled the matter by booking the same cabin for five years in advance, only he died soon after doing so. Morgan, having won there, also made sure of getting what he wanted elsewhere by reserving several cabins on several dates on several ships, also for years ahead. He survived, but there arrived a time when he had no need of advance bookings since he came, in the course of his later business career, to own half the Atlantic shipping lines.

This, then, is what had happened, in very brief review, by the mid 1880s, by the time *Umbria* and *Etruria* were beginning their long careers, and by the time the ocean liner was approaching its maturity. Other lines than Cunard, Collins, Inman, Guion, and White Star had made a mark, or promised well, or even for a time flourished, but they had added nothing to the development of the liner. There was the French Line, but that early it had done little out of the ordinary, except achieve a renown it never lost for its cuisine. There were the German lines, but in those days their passengers were mainly emigrants, and their vessels nearly always built in Britain.

So there, in 1886, were *Umbria* and *Etruria*, and in the time between them and *Lusitania* and *Mauretania* were twenty years of the most rapid but straightforward development. But before pursuing this story it is necessary to look for a moment at a vast hulk which *Umbria* and *Etruria* often passed on their way in and out of the Mersey. It was a hulk which retained four funnels of its original five, it looked five times the size of the passing Cunarders, and on its black hull was painted the slogan, 'Ladies Should Visit Lewis's Bon Marché'. It was a fairground and a floating advertisement hoarding, and it was the remains of Brunel's *Great Eastern*, a ship never intended for the Atlantic at all, a ship which had bankrupted everyone who tried to sail it on the Atlantic, a ship which had had no conceivable influence to that date on the development of the Atlantic liner, but a ship that was nevertheless a masterpiece, built by a man who had a vision which later ships, many years later, would show to have been a right one.

Menu for *La Normandie* of the French Line, 1889

The designer was Isambard Kingdom Brunel, one of the great engineers of the century, who had built the Great Western Railway, Clifton suspension bridge, and, before the *Great Eastern*, two smaller liners. One of these, the *Great Britain*, was a successful contemporary of the earliest Cunarders, a steamship propelled by a screw and with an iron hull that lasted so well that although at the end of a long career she was abandoned in the Falklands as a hulk, she was in 1970 towed back to England where she is now on show at Bristol. But the *Great Eastern* was greater than these, and greater than anything else. She was launched in 1858, and her tonnage of 22,500 was not exceeded until 1904. Tonnage figures give little idea of her size. At her launching she was six times the size of the next biggest ship in the world, and she looked much more massive than a modern ship of 20,000 tons. She had no superstructure. All her capacity was within her hull, whose sides towered like black cliffs. She never had a chance.

The *Great Eastern* awaiting launching at Millwall, 1858

She had been built for the Far Eastern run to Ceylon and perhaps on to Australia, and had to be built as big as she was to take enough coal for the long voyage, there being then no coaling-stations on the way. She bankrupted her first owners, and Brunel died during her trials, having warned her new owners that she would be unsuitable for the Atlantic. On the Atlantic in those days there was no cargo to fill such a ship, but she had been designed principally as a cargo carrier. Nor were there then enough passengers. She had berths for 2,986 people. On her maiden voyage in 1860 she carried thirty-eight paying passengers. Once she got to New York, in a respectable eleven days, she was exhibited to curious crowds at twenty five cents and took trippers on coastal passages, which helped to cut the loss. Her one and only successful Atlantic crossing was in 1861. That year, when Canada was vaguely fearing American invasion, she took 2,500 soldiers and 470 women and children to reinforce the garrison at Quebec. This passage was completed in eight-and-a-half days, and made a profit of £10,000. But this was in fair weather. In a gale she was unseaworthy.

The *Great Eastern* arriving at New York after her maiden crossing, June 1860

Her paddle-wheels smashed, and her single screw, even though it was much bigger than those which were many years later to be fitted to the *Queen Mary*, could not give her enough power to maintain way in a heavy sea. Brunel had designed her with steam-powered steering, but this had been one of the economies made by her builders. The result was that this ship, two-thirds the length of the *Queen Mary*, had to be steered by the force of men's hands on a wheel. In a heavy sea, with ten men's hands at the wheel, she was unmanageable.

She was sold from company to company and in 1867 was chartered by a French concern to take American visitors from New York to the Paris world exhibition of that year. She attracted only 191 passengers, but one of them was Jules Verne who, if the great ship had not existed, might well have invented her, and in any case wrote a book about the voyage, called *A Floating City*. Because there was no superstructure, she had a vaster expanse of open deck than was ever seen again on such a ship. American children ran about throwing ball and bowling hoops. To go and look over the stern was known as walking in the country. In the saloons, Verne listened to the tones of an organ and three pianos. The *Great Eastern* still relied partly on sails, but on Sunday the captain would not allow them to be hoisted, though the weather was fine, saying it would be improper on the Sabbath. Verne wondered why, in that case, the machinery was still allowed to continue. 'Sir,' replied the captain, a fierce Puritan,

'that which comes directly from God must be respected; the wind is in His hand, but the steam is in the power of man.' On the Sabbath the captain assumed the position of pastor. No pianos, cards, chess, or billiards were played. At a holy concert in the grand saloon, passengers sat on the side sofas or glided about from time to time, catching hold of one another silently but almost without talking. Once the

Jules Verne, who could have invented her if she did not exist, aboard the *Great Eastern*

Sabbath had passed, the captain himself organized a race between sailors, three times round the deck, and there was betting on the result. Verne sat in a deck chair. When the French charterers got her into Brest they abandoned her without even paying off the crew.

What the *Great Eastern* did achieve was to lay the transatlantic cable, but then she was put up for auction. There was talk of using her as a coal hulk and as an exhibition ship in New Orleans — like the *Queen Elizabeth* later — but not even these poor plans came to anything. She advertised Lewis's Bon Marché for a while, and then was scrapped. She was an idea hopelessly before her time. Her length was so great that orders could not be shouted from one end to the other; and since the telephone had not been invented, the only means of communication from stern to bow was by semaphore. The simple and fundamental idea she contributed to marine architecture was that a ship *could* be built that big, and moreover that a ship might, with more powerful machinery, be feasibly and profitably built that big. She had proved that big ships would not of their very size disintegrate, which was an idea fixed in the minds of many of the more timid. And the construction of her hull was among the strongest ever seen in a passenger liner, even though she was of iron and not of steel. Brunel had given her both transverse and longitudinal bulkheads, which rose six feet above her water line, and she had a complete double bottom. The *Titanic* was built with no such unsinkability. In 1862, fifty years before the *Titanic* disaster, the *Great Eastern* struck an uncharted rock off Montauk Point. Next morning she steamed into New York with what seemed to be a trifling list, but divers discovered she had a hole eighty-three feet by nine feet. Only the double hull had saved her.

The *Great Eastern* was genius, which did not work. The Cunarders were talent, and did. The tone of the Cunard company in talking of their *Umbria* and *Etruria* was, to say the least of it, satisfied. Until their launching, the company hinted, perfection had not been reached. They were with the exception of the *Great Eastern* the largest vessels afloat, and without any exception the most powerful — 'for size does not always represent power, as stout men are aware'. They were, in fact, long-lived and very successful ships, which stayed in service until just a few years before the 1914 war, and they very nearly deserved all that the company could say of them, even the company's New York office. The steamship companies were beginning to realize their dependence on American passengers. The prosperity of the cabin* (first-class) business was very largely determined by the number who travelled from the States to Europe either on business or on pleasure, or to recuperate their health at some European watering place or on the Riviera. Shipping companies found themselves relying on the attractions of the London season and the Paris fashion shows. In the transatlantic shipping business, America was evidently the giving and Europe the receiving party. Four out of five passengers were American. As early as 1875 a Captain Charles Chapman published a book saying the time was fast approaching when going to the seaside would with some pleasure-seekers be quite out of the question. The fashion would be to take a trip across the Atlantic for the summer holiday, as well as for a change of climate. To advertise the *Umbria* and *Etruria*, a booklet appeared entitled *An Aristocrat of the Atlantic*, by Maev, a lady of fashion, and a close inspection reveals that it was published by Cunard. The text would soon have revealed that anyway. 'The Cunard,' it said, 'has something. It has a name. Half the pleasure of doing a thing really well consists in letting the other people — the people who are not doing the thing at all but would like to if they could — know that one is enjoying the very best that can be had.' If one said one was crossing by Cunard, the sleepiest inhabitant of a duck-ridden village would know what that meant.

* The terms 'saloon', 'cabin', and 'first class' almost always meant the same and are used interchangeably in this book, though company usage varied from time to time. As late as the 1930s the *Queen Mary*'s best class was called cabin, but it meant first.

Maev then reported a conversation between a young American girl and her mother, who were returning from Europe. 'Say, Momma, don't you think the sofa-covers and curtains in the music room just like the brocaded Court trains we saw in London? I tell you, I'd like a Watteau train of that myself; it's a real elegant colour that sea-green Genoese velour. Do you think that the purser would know where they got it and how much it was?'

The only jarring note on board, said Maev, not apparently thinking the wretched girl and her green velour at all jarring, was that provided by passengers. Rough tweed ulsters, plain inexpensive tailor-mades, and heavy boots such as people would wear at sea, were all shown up by the coquettish elegancies of the vessel, just as a lady's boudoir might intensify the roughness of a shaggy-coated retriever. She gave other advice on dress. The skirts chosen for deck wear should be very heavy, as sea breezes were no respecters of persons, and draperies behaved embarrassingly at gusty corners. It was a good plan to sew dress weights at intervals round the hem or three or four inches up. Little coins in packets of three apiece could be used instead. Coloured underskirts, if such were worn, were preferable to white. Maev said ten meals a day would be provided, and regretted that even the necessity of 'paying with one's person' did not prevent some people, who had paid their money in advance, from eating right through their ticket, so to speak. Here is a summary of the ten meals a day Cunard offered to first-class passengers in the 1890s.

Before breakfast: grapes, melons, etc.
Breakfast: 'Almost anything on earth'
11 am: Pint cup of bouillon
Noon: Sandwiches carried about the decks
1 pm: Lunch
3 pm: Trays of ices
4 pm: Tea
5 pm: Toffee or sweets carried round on trays
7 pm: Dinner
9 pm: Supper

In the matter of food, Maev advised ladies to 'moderate their transports, you know'. In other matters, she remarked that lady passengers, especially those travelling alone, should not sit out on deck in the dark. She quoted Mark Twain as saying that Cunard were such hard-headed, practical, unromantic people, that they would not take Noah himself as first mate until they had worked him up all the lower grades. Then Maev gave the company's telegraphic code for the use of passengers. Here are a few examples:

AMEN — Arrived all well, stormy passage
BACK — Baggage has gone astray
CACKLE — Your cable has been received and understood
FADE — Am out of funds
HOOK — Seriously ill, no hope of recovery

The passage was still taking eight days, which made it reasonable to say, as another travellers' guide did, that chief among the opportunities within reach of those who crossed the ocean was that of learning to receive enjoyment from meagre sources. Some idea of these sources is conveyed by the *Etruria's* ship's newspaper, the *Daily Bulletin*. On one Thursday evening, it reported, a court sat in the saloon to hear a case in which Miss Cora Truheart, a young American, sued Will E. Flint Esq., an Englishman, for £10,000 for breach of promise. Evidence was given of tender exchanges alleged to have occurred on the deck of the *Etruria*. The witnesses included a private detective named Padlock Holmes. The jury found for the girl, but awarded only five shillings damages to be put into the poor-box. On another voyage the ship's bulletin reported that two large whales kept company with the ship for nearly a quarter of an hour, and were named Dorothy and Nina, in honour of two little girl passengers.

At the beginning of the 1890s the steamship companies were, for the moment, making a profit, and looking for business. Dr A. W. Thorold, Bishop of Rochester, published it as his opinion that given three good things — five weeks of holiday, a wholesome liking for salt water, and fifty pounds — you could not do better than take a trip to Niagara Falls. On the voyage you would have invigorating and pure air and the amusing and by no means unprofitable opportunity of studying human nature among numerous fellows. Once in north America, the visitor would everywhere hear his native language spoken, and would have seen what all his life afterwards he would be glad to have seen. The bishop probably did not know that the White Star line, for one, considered that clergymen were less amenable to discipline aboard ship than any other class of person. The line thought this was perhaps because they were so accustomed in the exercise of their calling on land to telling people what to do, that they resented any restrictions being placed on themselves at sea.

Broadly, there was a profit to be made on the passage because both in America and England there was prosperity. Profits bred competition, and competition, enhanced by a new American maritime chauvinism, produced bigger and better liners from Cunard, White Star, and Inman. All had one important thing in common. All, looking for extra speed and hoping to reduce vibration, installed twin screws. They were thus able for the first time to rely absolutely on mechanical power, even if one screw should be disabled. They at once discarded the remains of canvas which had been, on *Umbria* and *Etruria*, the last vestiges of the sailing ship. Yard-arms disappeared, and masts became flagpoles. In 1888 Inman produced the *City of Paris* and *City of New York*, and in the next year or so White Star put into service the *Teutonic* and *Majestic*. All these ships were of about 10,000 tons and capable of 20 knots, though the Inman liners almost always maintained the slightest edge. These four in their turn were eclipsed by the new Cunarders *Campania* and *Lucania* of 1893, vessels of 13,000 tons and 22 knots. The *Teutonic* held the blue riband for two months in 1891, but, after her, White Star never again held or tried to hold the record, settling for size and comfort rather than absolute speed. The

New York, formerly *City of New York*, in American ownership, seen from the *St Paul* in New York bay

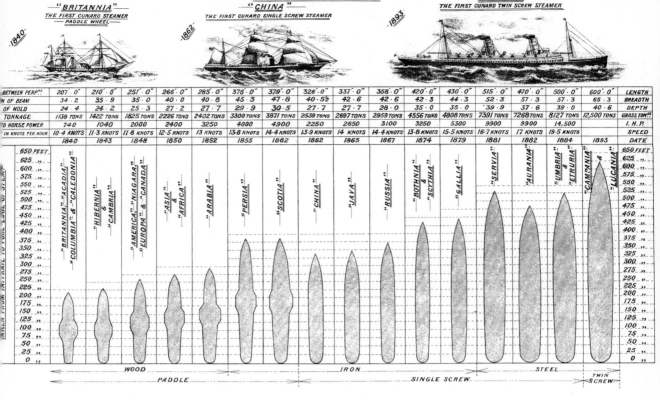

The growth of Cunarders, 1840–93

French Line's new *La Touraine* was slower, but beautiful, and the first liner to offer cabins *en suite*. The new Cunarders were the most brilliant. Of the two, the *Campania* was completed in time to take visitors to the Chicago World's Fair of 1893. She was fitted with electric light throughout, but still had coal fires with Anglo-Persian tiles round the hearths, an organ with gilded pipes, ottomans, and revolving chairs. A stenographer was on board. A company brochure which devotes 108 pages to the *Campania*'s interior appointments gives only one sentence to the steerage, which it says to be in every way excellent. As for weather, it was well known that Atlantic storms moved in circles, so that a fast modern steamer soon sailed right through the most severe gale. So far from a gale of wind being a thing to be dreaded, it formed a pleasant incident in an Atlantic voyage, and few passengers would like to cross without seeing what Cunard called one of the grandest and most beautiful sights of ocean travel, an Atlantic storm.

The tempests were enjoyed by fewer passengers than had been expected, because the Chicago traffic was very slack. Few Europeans yet considered Chicago worth travelling more than three thousand miles to see, even with grand gales thrown in, and most of those who did go travelled second class. And what the companies had forgotten was that far from being any help to them, the Fair was bound to ruin business. Visitors to the Chicago World's Fair tended to be American, and among them were many of the rich who might otherwise that year have gone to Europe.

Though the new Cunarders were the most brilliant ships, the new Inman liners were the most interesting, and this is because they were to be the beginning of a brief renaissance of the American maritime marine. They were the first pair of liners to fly the Stars and Stripes on the Atlantic since Collins's failure nearly forty years before. *City of New York* and *City of*

Grand saloon of an Inman steamer, probably the *City of Paris*, 1890

Paris were Inman ships, but were finished after Inman's death and after his company had been sold into American ownership in 1886. From the time of their first voyages in the late 1880s, until 1893, they continued to fly the Red Ensign because, as with the Guion ships of a few years earlier, they were British built although American owned, and Congress said only American-built ships could fly the American flag. Then Inman's American owners did a deal with Congress. They changed the name of the company to the American Line, and, in exchange for a Bill permitting them to fly the Stars and Stripes and in consideration of a U.S. Government contract to carry the European mails at four dollars a mile, agreed to build two extra liners in all-American yards. The names of the ex-Inman ships were abbreviated to *New York* and *Paris*, and the British port of call was changed from Liverpool to Southampton, from where it was easier for their predominantly

American passengers to get to France, which was the destination of many.

New York and *Paris* were striking ships, three-funnelled like the poor *City of Rome*, retaining a clipper bow, and inside very grand. Their state-rooms had patent fans which admitted fresh air but excluded the sea. Both single and double beds closed up in the daytime as in a Pullman car. There was hot running water. There were fourteen suites on the promenade and saloon decks, each with its own private bath and lavatory. The dining saloon was more than fifty feet long, and the height from the polished floor to the roof of arched glass was twenty-five feet. The library was lined with stained glass windows inscribed with poems about the sea. The kitchen was isolated in a steel shell, and odours carried off by ventilating shaft to a funnel. At each end of the saloon was an oriel window. On Sundays one became a pulpit, and the other contained

[36]

the organ. The ships had of course been ordered when Inman's were British owned, and were built on the Clyde, but they were already all Yankee dash. Their transfer to the American register and their hauling-up of the Stars and Stripes were effected on 22 February 1893, Washington's birthday. President Harrison himself raised the flag at the stern of the *Paris*. A cartoon embellishing on this ceremony showed it being accomplished by a woman dressed like the Statue of Liberty and assisted by an eagle, while John Bull and an animal meant to be a British lion were kicked overboard into New York bay. The New York *Evening Telegram* carried the headline: MERCHANT MARINE REVIVED. 'For the first time in a generation [though it was really more like two generations] the American flag floated over an ocean greyhound, the peer of any craft afloat.' This was true, because with the two *Cities* the

John Bull and the British lion being thrown overboard as the former Inman liners *City of New York* and *City of Paris* are brought under the American flag, on 22 February 1893

HOMEWARD BOUND.

PURSER (*making "dinner-talk"*): "Glad you made up your mind to come back with us, Mr. Venu. Did you go everywhere you intended?"

PA VENU: "Yep, didn't miss nothin'. Went all through Italy, 'n' all over."

PURSER: "You spent some days at Venice, of course?"

PA VENU: "Nop. Meant to, but when we got thar, ther' was a flood or somethin', and the hull place was under water. Everybody goin' round in boats. So we cleared right out."

MA VENU: "We was *so* disappointed."

Above and right: Two cartoons, both from a Hamburg–Amerika line guidebook of the 1890s, the first deriding *nouveau-riche* American tourists and the second an English lordling in New York

U.S. register had also acquired the blue riband, though only until May of that same year when the *Campania* came along and took it from them. After the flag-raising the two liners went on little celebratory cruises, but it was deep winter, and when the *New York* returned she found her berth iced up and had to wait for it to be cleared. The New York *Commercial Advertiser* said dryly; 'The *New York*'s plight this morning might be, and not inaptly, compared to the lamentable situation of a gentleman who after a night of celebration returns home to fail to find his latchkey, or that the door is bolted and that he is frozen out.'

It remained to build the two new ships that had been agreed. This was done at Philadelphia, and the two liners were named *St Louis* and *St Paul*. They were the first express Atlantic

liners to be built in America for thirty-eight years; and no more, afterwards, would be built for another thirty-seven. In 1894 the new president, Grover Cleveland, launched *St Louis* with a bottle of American champagne and quoted the words of John Paul Jones, the American Nelson of the War of Independence: 'We are just beginning to fight.' Although *St Paul* and *St Louis* were never the record-breakers it had been hoped, the American line was fighting indeed. In three years after 1893 it came up from nothing to be the second-biggest carrier of cabin passengers to New York. Cunard might own the very largest and fastest, although that was not going to last for long, but the American Line had the third-, fourth-, fifth-, and sixth-biggest liners in the world. Cunard carried 18,000 cabin passengers a year, American 14,000, and White Star was third with 12,000.

These last two competitors, American and White Star, strangely permitted the guidebooks issued in their companies' names to be written by the same man, John H. Gould, and published by the Ocean Publishing Company of New York. Both contain the same features, including chapters of impertinent hints for passengers, meant to be amusing:

'Don't carry on a flirtation with girls who are travelling to get married.'

'Don't be too uppish.'

'Don't seek to establish acquaintanceship by sending wine at dinner to celebrities.'

'Never quarrel in your state-room. Sounds emanate from there in several ways.'

Apart from this stuff there is some useful information. An American, says Gould, could expect to do Europe in three months for $500 inclusive. Then there are some more telegraphic code words. These are some of White Star's:

AWATCHA — Await letter; it will explain matters

MYDAVS — My draft on you for the amount of — — is returned unpaid. Why is this?

RAPIDO — Sinking rapidly [Probably a person dying and not the ship foundering]

YOUTHFULLY — You have misunderstood my telegram

So in the middle of the last decade of the nineteenth century, there was this plain Anglo-American ascendancy. The Americans, it is true, had only recently done well, but it was said to be in the nature of John Bull to be generous to inexperienced Americans, as John Bull had been a gentleman when Collins took the blue riband in the middle of the Great Exhibition of 1851. Cunard still ruled the Atlantic. And did not Britain own five-eighths of the steamship tonnage of the entire world?

One of the greatest British shipyards was Harland and Wolff at Belfast, and a young apprentice there was Thomas Andrews, who happened to be a nephew of Lord Pirrie, who owned the yard. Andrews was diligent. He read no novels and wasted no time on newspapers, but applied himself to mathe-

AMERICAN HOSPITALITY.
(*M' Lord, who wants to paralyze an American hotel clerk.*)
M'LORD (*pompously*): "I'm Lord De Lacy Shortmoney Starvedale, of Starvedale Abbey, England, y'naw."
CLERK (*sympathetically*): "Oh! that's all right! That's no fault of yours. We'll see that you are treated as well as the rest of the guests."

matics and marine architecture. By the mid 1890s, when he was in his early twenties, he was one of the yard's chief designers, and there were stories of his insouciant British heroism. 'Or,' said an admirer, 'he kicks a red-hot rivet, which has fallen fifty feet from an upper deck, missing his head by inches, and strides on laughing at his escape . . . Or just in time he snatches a man from falling down a hold; or, saying that married men's lives are precious, orders back another from some dangerous place and himself takes the risk.' Andrews went on to great things. Years later he designed the *Titanic*. But in 1897 he was kicking red-hot rivets, and lengthening a German liner simply by cutting her in two and inserting a new section amidships. They were high days, but Andrews, being a shipbuilding man, would have guessed the days of British supremacy on the Atlantic were already over for at least ten years, and he would have been right.

[39]

CHAPTER TWO

The Kaiser, J. P. Morgan, and the *Mauretania*

Wilhelm II was Kaiser, Emperor of all Germany, and John Pierpont Morgan was a millionaire from Hartford, Connecticut. Being more or less equals, except that J. P. Morgan had slightly the larger yacht, they occasionally dined together. At one dinner the Kaiser introduced into the conversation the political idea of socialism, but found that his guest was more interested in railroads, steamship companies, and beautiful vases, all of which he liked to collect. Both men unquestionably had a great influence on the Atlantic passenger trade. Morgan's was the greater, but the Kaiser's came first.

Wilhelm became Emperor in 1888, when he was only twenty-nine. He was the son of Queen Victoria's eldest daughter and had therefore been brought up in part to be an English gentleman, but had preferred to become a Prussian. He was the nephew of the Prince of Wales, who later became Edward VII. Wilhelm II was to become that Kaiser whom the British jingoists wanted to hang after the 1914–18 war. But in 1889 England and Germany were natural allies, besides which there were all the ties of royal blood; except that it was mostly bad blood. Edward, being then aged forty-eight and being after all the young Kaiser's uncle, treated him as an uncle would a nephew. It was then officially made known to the Prince of Wales, through the German ambassador in London, that Wilhelm expected to be treated not as a nephew but as an emperor. Queen Victoria was incensed. In letters to the Prime Minister, Lord Salisbury, she described the Kaiser's notion, underlining the words, as '*perfect madness*' and 'really too *vulgar*'. The

man wanted to be treated not only in public but in private as His Imperial Majesty? '*If* he has *such* notions, he had better *never* come *here.*' The Queen went on to call him hot-headed, conceited, wrong-headed, and devoid of all feeling. It might, at ANY moment, become *impossible* for the political relations of the two governments not to be affected. So much from the Queen, who did tend to write emphatically. But the Prime Minister himself, who was not given to be emphatic, told the Prince of Wales that the Kaiser appeared to be 'a little off his head' and 'not quite all there'. He also mentioned that the Kaiser had expressed a strong wish to pay a State visit to England soon.

After much bickering, the goodwill visit was arranged. The new diplomatic exchanges were entertaining. The young Wilhelm, who demanded that he himself should be addressed as an emperor, pointedly referred to the Prince of Wales as Uncle Bertie, but the Prince of Wales, after first exclaiming that he had his own dignity to uphold, magnanimously received his insufferable nephew. In August 1889 he took him to see the naval review at Spithead. Both wore the uniform of British admirals of the fleet, the Kaiser just having received this honorary rank, which pleased him. When he was shown round, he did not seem nearly so interested in the torpedo boats and dreadnoughts as in HM Armed Cruiser *Teutonic*. And nor, when he looked round her, was he much interested in the bits of armour plate tacked on to her hull for the occasion, or in the few small guns disposed around her superstructure. He saw her for what she was, the

White Star's new liner *Teutonic*, which, according to the cant of the time, and in order to attract a subsidy, was supposed to be able to double as a merchant cruiser in wartime, and was displayed in this role. As soon as the review was over, the naval geegaws were stripped off and she promptly embarked on her maiden voyage to New York as a liner. The day the Kaiser saw her, he spent almost two hours wandering around, looking at ceilings, leather armchairs, electric lights, and decorated woodwork, and then he remarked, 'We must have some of these.' In the next few years, Germany did.

It would be wrong to suggest that the German marine came up from nothing. Both North German Lloyd and Hamburg-Amerika had large fleets, but they were scattered worldwide and not concentrated on the Atlantic, and most of what tonnage they did have on the Atlantic was given over to emigrants. They had possessed fast ships, though never the fastest. The food was good. The ships' bands were famous. Only musicians were employed as second-class stewards, and they played on deck every morning at eleven. One American passenger said even the seasick were reheartened. Who, he asked, would ever forget the sweet, deep pleasure of being wakened on Sunday morning by the playing of 'Nearer, my God to Thee'? It was the German lines who first introduced winter cruising in the Mediterranean. On the Atlantic there was little competition with the British lines. And, there being no rivalry, there was something in the behaviour of British and German lines to each other which might be called chivalric. When in 1892 the North German Lloyd *Eider* stranded in fog off the Isle of Wight all of her 393 passengers and crew were saved by British lifeboatmen. The Kaiser sent £200 to the Lifeboat Institute and gave gold watches to the lifeboatmen. A few years earlier the *Eider*'s sister ship, the *Fulda*, had saved 824 passengers and crew from the Cunarder *Oregon* when she was rammed by a schooner near New York. When their New York agent cabled asking what compensation he should require of Cunard, the directors in

H.I.M. The Emperor of Germany
and
H.R.H. The Prince of Wales
inspecting the
"TEUTONIC"
at Spithead on August 4ᵗ 1889.

Emperor and Prince inspect the *Teutonic*, 1889. Part of a White Star publicity card issued much later, probably in 1897

Bremen cabled back, 'Highly gratified having been instrumental in saving so many lives. No claim.'

But then in the 1890s, Germany began to lay down ships that would dominate the Atlantic. The reason was, partly, that the large ships of both German lines were becoming worn out and needed replacing anyway. Also, and more important, Germany had decided to become not only a land but a sea power. This policy was openly stated in the German Fleet Law of 1897, whose preamble said that to protect German trade and commerce only one thing would suffice — a fleet of such strength

The *Teutonic* departing from New York

that even the most powerful adversary (which could only mean Britain) would think its own supremacy uncertain. By implication not only a battle fleet was needed. The German merchant marine too would have to be as good as anybody's, and the ocean on which marine powers showed off their best ships was the Atlantic. Germany, most of whose merchant tonnage had previously been built in Britain, began to build her own best vessels. The first to astonish everyone was the North German Lloyd's *Kaiser Wilhelm der Grosse*, 14,350 tons, $22\frac{1}{2}$ knots, four funnels. The British were a little wounded that in 1897, the year of Queen Victoria's diamond jubilee, Germany should bring forth not only the largest but also the fastest ship in the world. The name was a little derided. The ship was named after Wilhelm I,

[42]

King of Prussia, who in 1871 had become the first emperor of the newly-united Germany. He was not traditionally known as 'the Great', but his grandson Wilhelm II, with his sense of grandeur, thought that this tradition ought to be created. It did not take hold on the imagination of even the German public, who sometimes changed the name to *'Der Dicke Wilhelm'*, the Big Billy. But the ship herself was not derided by anyone. She was beautiful, and had great dash about her. The shipyard had built her as a calculated gamble. North German Lloyd gave the Vulkan yards at Stettin an almost free hand to build what they liked, with this proviso, that if the resulting ship did not take the blue riband they would hand her back and not pay for her. On her maiden voyage she did take the blue riband easily from the old *Lucania*. For ten years no British ship regained it. There was a second North German liner, ordered at the same time on the same speculative terms from a Danzig yard, but that ship, which was at the time certainly one of the fastest in the world, was not *the* fastest and she simply was handed back. For twelve years she lay a dead loss at Kiel, and was then sold to an obscure French company at a third of her cost to work the South American route.

In 1900 Hamburg–Amerika eclipsed the *Kaiser Wilhelm der Grosse* with their last record breaker, the *Deutschland*, who nearly shook herself to pieces but added a quarter of a knot to the Atlantic speed record. Thereafter, North German Lloyd had everything their own way with a whole royal family of liners. The Kaiser, sailing on one of these vessels, said his only canopy was the starlit firmament of the Almighty, and the only limit of his vision the boundless seas. There was the *Kaiser Wilhelm II*, named after the emperor himself, the *Kronprinz Wilhelm*, after his son, and the *Kronprinzessin Cecilie*, after the crown prince's wife. Wilhelm II's own empress was a little unfortunate in her ship. One had been named after her a little too early, before the new German ascendancy, and not only was it no record-breaker but her name was incorrectly spelled on its bows as Augusta Victoria, and remained uncorrected for ten

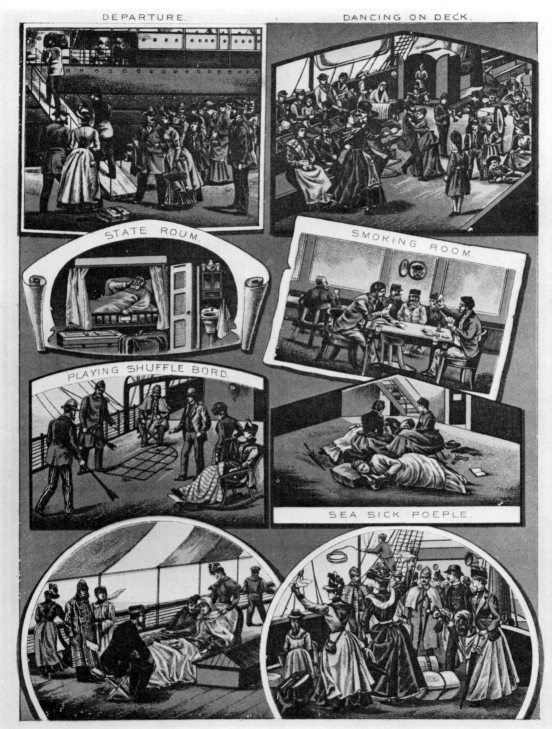

North German Lloyd advertisement, 1885

years until Augusta was at last changed to Auguste.

The commercial results of these splendid ships were spectacular. Their speed advantage over the old Cunarders was only a knot or so, but they were new, they had flair, and within a year of the *Kaiser Wilhelm der Grosse*'s maiden voyage, North German Lloyd had almost a quarter of the entire Atlantic passenger trade, and more first-class passengers than Cunard. Cunard had no new ships to offer. White Star did in 1899 launch the *Oceanic*, which was the first ship to exceed the *Great Eastern* in length, and was briefly the largest in the world. White Star declared a holiday in Belfast in her honour, and said she was a sybaritic ship, which was the truth. She had lavatories of 'costly marble', and resembled 'a Hotel Cecil afloat'. The Hotel Cecil was then the grandest in London. White Star also claimed, which was not the truth, that it went without saying that they could have built a ship to cross the Atlantic in five days, and said that the *Oceanic*, were she driven, could steam at 25 or 26 knots. This was absurd, as the company perfectly well knew. They then said, with classic impertinence, that they did not *want* a five-day voyage, but aimed at leaving Liverpool on Wednesday afternoon and reaching New York the following Wednesday morning. Briefly, White Star had chosen to sell comfort, and to leave expensive speed to the Germans.

The only way, in this period, in which English or American ships kept any sort of lead was in the use of wireless. The German liners had it of course, but it was an American liner, the *St Paul*, which on 15 November 1899 first published a ship's newspaper carrying reports which had arrived by radio. *The Transatlantic Times* published on board, price one dollar per copy in aid of the Seamen's Fund, carried, by the courtesy of Mr G. Marconi, bulletins broadcast by his transmitter on the Needles in the far west of Cornwall. It was a small sheet, printed on one side only, and said, 'As all will know, this is the first time that such a venture has been undertaken. A Newspaper published At Sea with Wireless Telegraph messages received and printed on a ship going twenty knots an hour!' The messages included:

1.50 pm. First signal received. 66 miles from Needles.
2.40 pm. 'Was that you, St Paul?' 50 miles from Needles.
3.30 pm. '40 miles. Ladysmith, Kimberley, and Mafeking holding out well.'
4.00 pm. 'Sorry to say the U.S.A. Cruiser *Charleston* is lost. All hands saved.'

In 1903 another American ship, the *Philadelphia*, which was the old *City of Paris* renamed, carried on a chess game in mid Atlantic with the *Etruria*. It lasted five hours until the *Etruria* asked to close the game as a draw after the forty-first move, with honours even. The same year another Cunarder, the *Lucania*, became the first vessel to be in wireless touch with both sides of the Atlantic at once.

But, wireless apart, the Germans owned the Atlantic. The German express steamers, starting with the *Kaiser Wilhelm der Grosse*, had four funnels, and this influenced fashion for years. They did not need four. They could have done with two. Three years later the Cunarder *Saxonia*, of much the same tonnage, though slower, made do with one. But four looked powerful, and for ten years remained a German peculiarity. Four was even a disadvantage, in that the designer had to break up his interior space with four descending pipes, but the Germans minimized this difficulty by placing four funnels not equidistantly but in two pairs, with the larger gap between the second and third funnels used to accommodate the dining saloon. After 1907 the Germans built no more four-funnelled liners, but between then and the beginning of the 1914 war the French built one and the British six. The last of all was the

◄ 'The Steerage'. This celebrated photograph was taken by Alfred Stieglitz (1864–1946). He wrote that on an Atlantic crossing on a German liner he stood for four days looking at the steerage, disliking the first-class way of travel and wanting to change places. Then he took this single photograph

Aquitania in 1914. The fashion for great liners then became three, though one of these was often a dummy, used for dog kennels or the like, and this fashion in its turn was taken up by even tiny liners. Little Anchor Line ships of 7,000 tons had three. One was enough, but two would have looked asymmetrical, so three it was. On the great ships, the nuisance of huge great pipes piercing the height of the vessel was avoided by deviously leading the flues not through the centre of the decks but in a sort of tuning fork shape with one prong descending at each side of a vast public room. Later the fashion became two funnels, as in the *Queen Elizabeth* of 1940 and the *United States* of 1952, and then finally one, as in the *QE2*. But in the 1890s the German four-stackers had distinction, and first-class passengers on the Atlantic always wanted that.

In the 1890s it was also the turn of the German lines to put out the preposterous publicity that goes with truly extravagant success. In one brochure, a young woman, Eleanor, is leaving New York for Europe on a German steamer, in company with her father:

ELEANOR: 'I want to go to the Imperial Yacht Races at Kiel, and around the British Isles and to Norway by way of Iceland. I want to go wherever these beautiful boats will take me, if we are a whole year about it.'

At this she concludes with a gay little gesture of her white hands. A man called Burroughs approaches, who has already made the father's acquaintance.

FATHER: 'By Jove, let me introduce you to my daughter.'

ELEANOR: 'Isn't this a night of nights, Mr Burroughs?'

It turns out that it is indeed. They talk. She says she met a man out west who fell off a horse and killed himself. His last act was to pull a ring off his finger and ask her to wear it for his sake.

BURROUGHS (*in low, eager voice*): 'His name?'

ELEANOR: 'Leveret.'

Astonishment. Leveret had been Burroughs's brother, whom he had unsuccessfully been trying to find.

BURROUGHS: 'Eleanor, my dearest, I love you. Marry me next fall, and we'll engage passage on the *Deutschland* for the Mediterranean in January. Let it be the initiatory cruise to that long and happy voyage of life, which, please God, we will make together.'

ELEANOR (*murmuring*): 'Of course, if father says I may.'

About this time Marian Lawrence Peabody, who was real, and one of *the* Peabodys, was thinking and writing in her diary that to be young was very heaven. 'It is so pretty,' she wrote, 'to hear the watch in the fighting top call out 'All's well' in German; the bow watch answers him and then the bells ring out. I try to hear this every evening after dark. Oh I do love a life at sea.'

The French Line, with *La Savoie*, were elegant as ever, but, at 20 knots, too slow. And at this time Cunard were definitely down-market. There is a letter in the company archives, apparently intended as a general instruction, which says, 'We now have some people who travel Second Cabin but should really go Saloon, and they specially request that their names do not appear on the Second Cabin Passenger List.'

And yet Cunard had been, admittedly for devious reasons, the only great English company to resist the intention of an American corporation called International Mercantile Marine, I.M.M., to buy up the Atlantic in 1902. I.M.M. was really J. P. Morgan, known as one of the Lords of Creation. He or his banks, corporations, and cartels had at one time or another bought the Chesapeake and Ohio Railway, the Erie and Reading, the Northern Pacific, and the Baltimore and Ohio. If it is agreed that a nation may rank itself with the great money powers when its mere bankers become the creditors of other nations, then Morgan made the United States a money power because he *was* a creditor of other nations. He was also a creditor of the United States, to which in 1896 he had supplied $62 millions in gold, to restore the U.S. treasury reserve to $100,000. After railroads he went into steel. When Andrew Carnegie tired of making money and steel and wished to

The French, like the Germans, were all style in their publicity handouts. By day, *La Savoie* enters New York with the Statue of Liberty (a French gift to America as it happens) behind her, and at night, two women aboard a French Line ship watch the receding skyline of New York as they leave for Europe. The day scene is by Le Quesne. The departure, by Gabriel Nicolet, formed the cover of *Le Journal de l'Atlantique*, the French Line's shipboard newspaper, which received news daily by wireless

embark on his later career of philanthropy, it was J. P. Morgan who, in the largest private financial transaction in American history, bought him out. He then tossed in a few steel mills he already owned himself and created U.S. Steel, the first billion-dollar corporation in the world. When he wanted something he was direct about getting it, which sometimes delighted the vendors. There were once some men who came to him with only a small steel mill, which they knew he wanted. They hoped for $5 million and thought they would start by asking $10 million, but before they could say a word Morgan himself began, 'Now I don't want any talk from you men. I know all about your plant and what it's worth; I haven't time for any haggling; I'm going to give you $20

millions. Now take it or leave it.' He was a much-travelled man, who had been educated partly in Germany. He had suites at the Hotel Bristol in Paris and the Grand Hotel in Rome, and a house in Prince's Gate, London, which he filled with unpretentious Rubens, Rembrandts, Holbeins, Gainsboroughs, and Turners. He had great confidence in his judgement. An art dealer came to him with an exquisite Vermeer. 'Who is Vermeer?' asked Morgan. It was a good question. Vermeer was very little known at the time. The dealer told him. Morgan bought the painting for $100,000. He was a man who not only dined with the Kaiser; he also took snuff with Pope Pius X in the Vatican gardens. In London in 1902 street peddlers were selling documents called 'Licenses to

[47]

Live', signed J. P. Morgan, price one penny.

As early as 1893, on an Atlantic crossing, someone asked him whether it ought not to be possible to bring together the north Atlantic steamship companies so that they could make a profit rather than cut each other's throats. 'Ought to be,' he said. When he had finished for the moment with both railroads and steel, he looked into shipping. What American shipping there was, he bought. Then in 1902 he formed I.M.M. with a capital of $120 millions and bought the Red Star lines, the Mississippi and Dominion lines, the Leyland line, a few others, and the entire capital stock of White Star, which was the jewel in his crown. It was the first international corporation of its kind. He considered that the sums of money he paid were not, according to modern standards, very large. White Star cost him $25 million in gold. Then, without buying the least control, because the Germans would not sell it, he came to an agreement to stagger sailing dates with the German lines. He then approached Cunard, offering them 80 per cent above the market value of their shares. Cunard appeared not altogether reluctant, though the British government and public were. The legal position was and is this. A ship is not an ordinary piece of property to be bought and sold anyhow. A ship is in the eyes of English law a piece of the realm which happens sometimes to be at sea. To maintain jurisdiction over this travelling territory, it is necessary that it shall be owned by British nationals. No British ship or any share in it may be owned by an alien, and even if an alien were fortuitously to come into purported ownership of a British vessel, as by having it bequeathed to him, he would forfeit it to the Crown, although he would be paid compensation. Furthermore, no alien may even be an officer of a British ship, let alone own it. Morgan knew all this. But the loophole in the law through which, as the lawyers said, you could drive a coach and four, was that by 1902 all the big ships were owned not by individuals but by companies, which had a quite separate legal identity from their shareholders. So long as the company remained nominally British with its headquarters in Britain, there was nothing to prevent all its shares being bought by an American holding company, I.M.M. The British company would then indeed be controlled by I.M.M., who for instance had eight out of thirteen directors on the White Star board. But in the eyes of the law, they owned the company's shares, not its ships. White Star ships continued to be British registered, to have British crews, and to fly the Red Ensign. To a lawyer this is tidy, plain, and unexceptionable. To anyone else it is a blatant fiction.

Letters were written to the London *Times*, fearing that America would soon 'close the door' on Britain in the Atlantic, remarking that Americans were not philanthropists, and pointing out that the merger was inimical to the best interests of British shipowners and therefore to those of the nation at large. 'Suppose,' said a correspondent, 'that we are at war with France, and this "British" (but really American) vessel is pursued by a French man-of-war; it is British blood and treasure which would have to defend it.' The writer suggested that the Companies Act should be amended so that no more than a quarter of the shares of a steamship company could be held by a foreigner, any contravention to be punishable as a grave offence. 'In this way,' he concluded, 'I imagine the Morganization of the Atlantic would be nipped in the bud.'

It was not forgotten that White Star vessels were notionally British armed cruisers. But, said another correspondent, they were now as much American ships as if they flew the Stars and Stripes. Did the government suppose that if Britain got into a 'European difficulty' in which America wished to remain neutral, the White Star steamers would be available? No. 'They would conveniently find themselves in an American port and there they would remain . . . We have lost the great north Atlantic trade, the only trade which can support ships of great speed and tonnage so essential as cruisers in time of war.' Only one correspondent saw any hope. He proposed that Atlantic supremacy could be regained by running a service from Galway to Halifax in four days at

Women passengers boarding a French ship at Le Havre about 1905. The French Line did not at the time have the resources to build the biggest or the fastest, but never even considered selling out to Morgan, and always asserted its individuality and chic. Painting by L. Sabattier

24 knots. The effect of crowds of passengers disembarking at Galway and crossing through Ireland in different directions would, he felt sure, be most beneficial to Ireland. So it might. But this letter must, to many steamship people, have been a reminder of the farcical efforts made in the mid nineteenth-century to promote Galway as an Atlantic port. It is certainly the nearest European port to America, and vast sums had been spent to build a huge and handsome railway hotel for all those Atlantic passengers. It still stands, utterly out of proportion with the decrepit town, and the only memorial of those grand plans of the 1860s. In 1902, as in the 1860s, nobody wanted to leave from Galway and nobody wanted to go to Halifax.

The Times itself, in a leading article, took a less chauvinistic view than its readers. There was over-competition on the Atlantic. Demands for rapidity and luxury had produced magnificent fleets of steamers which did well only in the high season. At the moment there was no proper return on the capital invested. If there were a merger, and therefore less competition, the exacting passenger would miss some opportunity for making disparaging remarks to the purser about the alleged superiority of other lines, but on the whole he would still get his money's worth, and would not be quite helpless so long as Cunard maintained its attitude of splendid isolation.

But Cunard was not maintaining any such attitude. When Morgan made an offer, Cunard simply said it was not enough. The British government became apprehensive that higher offers might be made and accepted, and Cunard let the government think this might happen. What Cunard was doing, with perfect propriety, was playing off one against the other, seeing from whom the greatest financial advantage might come, from Morgan or from the government. Put bluntly, Cunard would sell unless it got a large government subsidy. The outcome really did depend on the will of the British government. German shipping interests saw this clearly, and expected Morgan to win unless

A section of the *Caronia*, a second rank Cunarder built only two years before the *Lusitania* and *Mauretania*. She spent a long life, until 1932, either acting as relief on the Liverpool–New York run, or sailing from Mediterranean ports to America

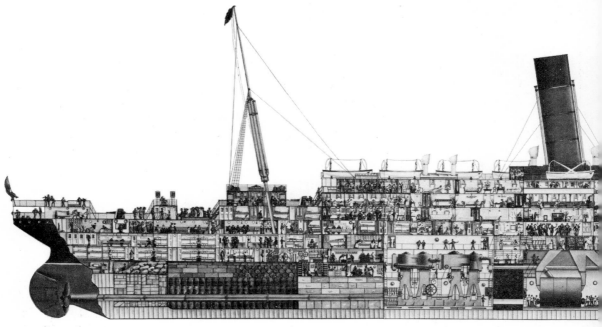

the British pulled themselves together at the eleventh hour. As the Germans saw it, the British government was playing the whole affair down, and representing the deal as no more than an Anglo-American shipping consortium, but really knew perfectly well that what was at stake was the control of the north Atlantic.

In the middle of the controversy the *Etruria*, by then a very ancient Cunarder, broke down in mid Atlantic and was towed to the Azores by an I.M.M. tramp steamer. This put the whole issue only too clearly, and it was too much. For years the German express liners had shown their evident superiority; then an American called Morgan had come along and bought more than half the British Atlantic tonnage; and now one of the Cunarders that had once upon a time held the blue riband,

before being so badly beaten by the Germans, had got into such a state that it had to be towed to safety by a tramp steamer owned by that same Morgan. The British government capitulated to Cunard. The company would receive a state loan of £2,600,000 to build two new ships that would beat the Germans, would also continue to receive a mail subsidy of £150,000 a year, and in return would agree to remain British for twenty years and not sell out to the Americans. The secretary of the Admiralty explained to the Commons that the cost to the government was less than half that of building a third-class cruiser for the navy.

Morgan had lost, but he had a third of the Atlantic passenger trade.* He enjoyed what he had. Whenever he returned from Europe in one

* Here are the numbers of passengers carried for 1902:

Morgan's I.M.M.		German Lines		Other Lines	
American Line	16,083	Hamburg–Amerika	34,068	Anchor	8,141
Atlantic Transport	4,197	North German Lloyd	32,770	Cunard	26,786
Red Star	14,625			French Line	24,579
White Star	29,833				
Total	64,738	Total	66,838	Total	59,506

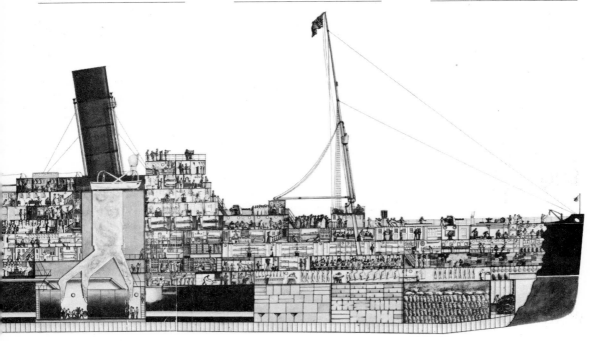

of his White Star liners she would be approached and greeted in New York bay by his own yacht dressed stem to stern with pennants, and he would respond by leaning over the rail and swinging a handkerchief from side to side. Once, when his wife had gone to Europe and he had stayed at home, he met her off the *Oceanic* in the bay. He had his launch swung alongside, seized a rope ladder, and climbed the full sixty feet to the liner's deck with a cigar in his mouth and a straw hat on his head. He was then well over sixty.*

The two new Cunarders which were then planned, laid down, and built were by intention the largest, most powerful, and fastest ocean liners ever constructed. The English magazine *Engineering* thought that not only the British Empire but the whole world owed a debt of gratitude and a tribute of admiration to the Cunard Steam-ship Company for the great enterprise and courage they had showed in the inception of two such ships.

Gratitude? Admiration, yes; because Cunard had been very sharp. And the two ships were very beautiful. They were half as big again as any vessel ever built or planned before, and had three-quarters more power. Their engines were steam turbines, which were inherently more efficient and smooth than the old kind with reciprocating pistons. It was the first time such engines had been fitted to express liners. Both carried 7,000 tons of coal in bunkers in the double skin along their sides, which was designed to protect them against shell-fire. For the same reason, the 25 boilers and 192 furnaces of each ship were placed below the water line. They were designed for $24\frac{1}{2}$ knots, but both comfortably exceeded that. When *Engineering* exclaimed that their superiority in speed over other ships was so great that

it was unlikely to be challenged for many years, it could not conceivably have foreseen how many years that would be. For twenty-one years they were the fastest liners in the world. They were built simultaneously, one in Scotland on the Clyde and the other in England on the Tyne, in a shipyard on the site of the old Roman fort of Segenudum at the easternmost end of Hadrian's wall from the Solway to the Tyne.

What were the names of these two ships to be? As always with Cunard, this was not something to be decided lightly in a moment. Lists were drawn up and submitted to successive meetings of directors. One list contained 461 names, beginning with *Acarnania* and *Alpis Julia* and ending with *Xanthis* and *Zenobia*. *Britannia* was suggested, but there were already twenty-three ships of that name afloat, and one director pencilled a note on the list saying that the company should in any case adhere to its old principles and not repeat names. *America* was proposed, but there were already thirteen vessels of that name. *Victoria* was suggested, but there were already thirty-nine of them. The Board of Trade of Saskatoon City, Canada, wrote suggesting that *Saskatonia* would be 'euphonious, catchy, and easily remembered'. The Chairman of Cunard recalled that someone had suggested the name of 'a district in China called Cambodia'. *Aquitania* was considered, and there was found to be no such name on Lloyd's register, but for the moment that too was rejected. *Cynuria* and *Cytheria* were considered as a pair. Professor G. G. Ramsay of Glasgow University gave his written opinion. He suggested that the provincial names of ancient Italy had quite a distinct character, and had provided the names of successful ships like *Umbria*, *Etruria*, *Campania*, and *Lucania*. If Cunard took *Apulia* they would have included in their fleet all the ancient provinces of Italy as they were named in the best classical times. Ramsay then suggested, alternatively, that the company might like to consider the names of Roman provinces of the east, including *Mauretania*, which he pointed out had five syllables. 'Perhaps,' he said,

---

* I.M.M. did not prosper. It was the only venture of his that did not. One of his last public appearances was at the launching of the *Titanic*, which was of course an I.M.M. ship. He died in Rome in 1913, aged seventy-five, and his body was shipped home on the *France*, which was not one of his own, the French Line always having remained utterly unbuyable, even for ready money. But in America the coffin was carried on his own railroads, and the New York stock exchange closed for a day.

VOL. XXXIII.—No. 835.   PUCK BUILDING, New York, March 8th, 1893.   PRICE, 10 CENTS.

Copyright, 1893, by Keppler & Schwarmann.

Puck

Entered at N. Y. P. O. as Second-class Mail Matter.

IT CAME HIGH, BUT WE HAD TO HAVE IT!
FEBRUARY 22ND, 1893.

Uncle Sam riding high, having acquired the bankrupt Inman liners and with them, briefly, the blue riband.
Puck, New York, 8 March 1893

Kaiser Wilhelm II, far left, and, centre, with his back towards his troublesome German nephew, the Prince of Wales, at Cowes before the Naval review. A Spy cartoon from *Vanity Fair*

The North German Lloyd *Kaiser Wilhelm der Grosse*, the first four-funnelled liner, which took the blue riband ▶ for Germany in 1897. This is from a menu cover. Those of the German lines were often most beautiful

ELDREDGE COLLECTION

AMERIKA-
ASIEN-
AUSTRALIEN.

Norddeutscher Lloyd

Bremen.

Dep. 1407.

D. „Kaiser Wilhelm der Grosse"

La Savoie of the French Line leaving Le Havre about 1901 at the beginning of a long life of twenty seven years on the Atlantic. Painting by F. Le Quesne

AUT CÆSAR AUT NIHIL

J. P. Morgan, the American millionaire who tried to buy the Atlantic, and did buy White Star. Cartoon from the French magazine, *Rire*, 1902

The newly-fitted-out *Mauretania* with the tiny *Turbinia* alongside. *Turbinia* was the first turbine vessel, and it was she who proved the superiority of the turbines over ordinary reciprocating engine by racing through the assembled British fleet at Spithead in 1897, leaving far behind those naval vessels which tried to intercept her. *Mauretania* was the first huge liner to be powered by turbines

'these new monsters deserve an extra syllable.'

Cunard thought they did deserve it. The new steamers were named *Mauretania*, after ancient Roman Morocco and Algeria, and *Lusitania*, after Roman Portugal. When the *Lusitania* reached America after her maiden crossing, a newspaper called the New Orleans *States* explained that the ship's name was to be pronounced to rhyme with Pennsylvania.

According to Cunard, the interiors of the ships were restrained. The restraint consisted in the following. The grand staircases were on the fifteenth-century Italian model. Public rooms were treated either in the Italian or French Renaissance styles, and this work on the *Mauretania* was carried out under the supervision

of Mr W. C. Phipps, the shipbuilders' head foreman joiner, who thought the work worthy of beautiful palaces. To save weight, the grille round the electric lifts was of aluminium, but in the style of fifteenth-century wrought ironwork. The dining rooms were panelled in straw-coloured oak in the style of Francis I, and each had a dome in cream and gold reminiscent of the Chateau de Blois. There were Adams, Sheraton, and Chippendale state-rooms. The first-class lounges were treated in a style of which perhaps the Petit Trianon at Versailles was the best example. In the smoking room the fire-basket and firedogs were reproduced from originals at the Palazzo Varesi, and this room also had a waggon-headed roof rather in the style of an English barn, and a frieze of old New York. Where there was wood veneer it was of the best, and the forests of both England and France were searched for the great quantity needed. Where there was carving, it was always cut back from the face of the solid wood. All lavatory fittings were of white metal, which in the first-class state-rooms and the royal suite was heavily silver-plated.

There were at first a few little troubles. The chief steward of the *Lusitania* reported that steam escaped through the third-class drinking fountains every sailing morning from Liverpool. The staff captain of the *Lusitania* recommended that the type-writing room should be moved, since in its present position it was a source of annoyance to passengers in A deck cabins, not only on account of the ticking of the machine but also because people's voices were audible when they dictated to the typist.

In spite of this, first the *Lusitania* and then the *Mauretania* took the blue riband easily, both ways, and kept it. They were the latest things there were. And yet, extraordinarily, Cunard included the following testimonial in every copy of a free guide they gave to passengers on the *Mauretania*:

'For what is comfort, and more than comfort – luxury – and the certainty of safety – we come into an understanding of the significance, which is assurance, certified by this hall-mark: CUNARD' – Gladstone

It was fourteen years since Gladstone had been Prime Minister, and by the time the *Mauretania* made her maiden voyage he was almost ten years dead. But then, Cunard would say, what was the mere blue riband – for the sake of which the company had, nevertheless, finagled with Morgan and subtly soft-talked the British government – compared with Gladstone's assurance that everything was safe? That the ships were marvels could be taken for granted. Cunard did not need to say so. Kipling did it for them. He wrote, in a poem called 'The Secret of the Machines':

You can start this very evening if you choose,
And take the Western Ocean in the stride

Of seventy thousand horses and some screws.
The boat express is waiting your command!
You will find the *Mauretania* at the quay,
Till her captain turns the lever 'neath his hand,
And the monstrous nine-decked city goes to sea.

Kipling probably did not know that for eighteen hours before she went to sea her firemen and trimmers would be raising steam. They were Liverpool Irish, who often arrived on board more or less drunk. At sea, they worked two four-hour spells in each twenty-four, lifting five tons of coal each a day. The trimmers brought coal from the bunkers and wheeled it to piles handy for the firemen to shovel into the furnaces. They worked in twenty-one minute spells. There were seven minutes to feed coal into furnaces whose heat scorched the firemen, then seven minutes for cutting and clearing clinkers with long slicers, and then another seven for raking over. A man who was behind in any seven minutes could not escape being seen by his fellows to be weaker, and so the weak drove themselves to keep up with the strong. After the three periods of seven minutes there was a short pause, and then a gong announced the beginning of another twenty-one minutes. This was the fireman's work for four hours on end, scorched by furnaces and choked by coal dust and by gases from white-hot clinkers and ashes. When they had finished their watches they often took the air with chests open to the cold Atlantic wind. They worked, and ate, and then slept exhausted. They could not obtain drink aboard, so when they did get ashore they made up for this by getting and staying drunk. As firemen, only the Hungarians were as good as the Liverpool Irish. The *Mauretania*, like all other express liners, was converted to oil-burning after the 1918 war, which relieved the firemen of their intolerable work.

And this work was generally done on a moving, rolling platform. *Mauretania* and *Lusitania* were lively in a sea-way. The dive and swoop of their pitch became famous. Steaming hard into a head sea they could lift their bows sixty feet and then dip and bury them, cleaving a way through the water, thrusting it to either side, but not all of it. At speed, their logs often read,

The *Mauretania* at her North River pier in New York ▶

'Pitching and spraying forward', or 'Pitching, lurching, and spraying all over', or 'Labouring, pitching, lurching, spraying all over'.

Ships so lively as that in a sea-way do not endear themselves to some passengers. Franklin Delano Roosevelt did not like the movement, but said he never failed to realize that if ever a ship possessed a soul, it was the *Mauretania*. And the New York waterfront reporters never failed to realize that her sister ship *Lusitania* had the best purser on the Atlantic. As soon as she docked, the reporters went straight down to Purser McCubbin's cabin on B deck, the port side, where they were welcomed by two quarts of Cunard Scotch whisky and a passenger list. McCubbin asked whom they would like to interview. They told him. 'Go find Mr Hoggenheimer,' McCubbin would say, and soon in his cabin, in tow of brass-buttoned cabin boys, there would appear for interview captains of industry, movie queens, statesmen, soldiers of fortune, the idle rich, and the principals in the latest divorces.

They were both famous and remembered ships, the *Mauretania* the more beloved of the two because she lasted so much longer. There are many famous liners, but very few that have achieved immortality – the *Queen Mary*, the *Titanic*, the *Normandie*, and the *Mauretania*. One autumn afternoon, making an eastward passage, homeward bound in clear seas, the *Mauretania* at 25 knots sighted on the horizon first the royals, then the top-gallants, and then the upper topsails and gaff topsail of a three-masted barque, a Norwegian. The captain of the *Mauretania*, Rostron, had been in sail, and so had her first officer, Bisset. As soon as they came near enough to read her signals, they saw the barque was flying F-G-L, 'I need a doctor.' The *Mauretania* replied that she was coming. The barque was put about and her main yards backed to bring her to a standstill. Bisset's heart went out to her. She was almost a replica of the ship in which, seventeen years before, on three voyages round the world, he had served his apprenticeship in sail. The *Mauretania* stopped her engines, went full astern, and made a graceful turn round the

[60]

barque, coming to a stop three hundred yards away. Rostron sent Bisset and the doctor in the sea boat, and also a hundredweight of fresh beef, some potatoes, onions, and cabbages, and a case of oranges, with his compliments. 'She's probably a hundred days out from the West coast (of America) – you know what that means, Bisset.'

The Norwegian crew were astounded that the *Mauretania* should have stopped for them. The provisions were handed up and accepted with joy. On board the barque, Bisset felt out of place in his brass-bound uniform. The first mate said a man was ill in the poop, and that he would lead the way.

'Mister,' said Bisset, 'I could find my way there blindfolded.'

'Old Cape Horner?'

'You've said it.'

At the break of the poop the Master was waiting, also in brass-bound uniform and cap. Bisset saluted him. 'Very good of you to come,' said the Master.

In the saloon the decks were holystoned and the bulkheads panelled with bird's eye maple, and over the polished table hung a swinging tray holding red Venetian wine-glasses. Bisset felt like a boy apprentice again, allowed to enter the captain's holy of holies. The sick man was in a cabin. For two days he had not spoken, eaten, or drunk. After a while the doctor came back and said the man had died perhaps half an hour before, of pneumonia.

The captain said: 'We sighted no steamer for many days. Then came your big steamer and so kindly stopped.' Bisset replied that it had been their duty. As he returned to the *Mauretania* he looked up at the liner silhouetted against the sky, stopped in mid ocean, with smoke pouring from her four funnels and spreading away in the breeze, and her deck rails crowded with three thousand people.

'Resume the voyage,' said Rostron. Bisset rang the engines to full ahead and set course. As the liner gathered way, both vessels dipped their ensigns in salute and then brought them to half mast, and the *Mauretania* blew three long blasts.

CHAPTER THREE

The Greatest of the Works of Man

The White Star liner *Titanic*, 46,328 tons, the largest liner in the world, bound for New York on her maiden voyage, glanced against an iceberg after dinner on 14 April 1912, a Sunday. She was unsinkable, liners having been built for some years before to be quite unsinkable, with bulkheads and waterproof compartments through which the water could not pass, but it was not generally realized that even a great ship's hull plating, in relation to her size, was less than half as sturdy as the shell of an ordinary soup can. As she foundered, the purser, looking down into the Atlantic from B deck, said to his companions, 'Boys, it will be sand for breakfast in the morning.' The story of the *Titanic* is the most famous, and best documented, of all stories of ocean liners, and it is most certainly known to have happened between 11.40 pm, when she struck, and 2.20 am, when she sank, on that April night in 1912. And yet so much of it is almost surreal. She was four days out of Southampton, and had sailed for those four days on a glass-calm sea. The Atlantic is never that calm for four days at a time. On Sunday evening, before she struck, a stoker said that in twenty-six years at sea he had never known so calm a night. It was also a night so black and so clear that you could see stars set. Where the sky met the sea the line was so clear and definite that as the earth revolved and the water's edge came up and partially covered a star, it simply cut the star in two, the upper half continuing to sparkle as long as it was not entirely hidden, throwing a long beam of light across the sea. When this was later described to Ernest Shackleton, the polar explorer, he said he had never in all his experience known such a night. It was all uncanny.

And it is made the more uncanny by something an American short story writer had written fourteen years before. In 1898 Morgan Robertson, a prolific writer about the sea, had published in New York a story called 'Futility'. It is the story of the liner *Titan*, the largest craft afloat and the greatest of the works of man, 800 feet long, capable of 25 knots, and carrying 2,000 passengers, two brass bands, two orchestras, and a corps of physicians. She had nineteen watertight compartments. With nine of them flooded she could still float, and as no known accident of the sea could possibly fill this many, she was considered practically unsinkable. Because she was indestructible, she carried as few lifeboats as would satisfy the laws. The events of Robertson's story are these. One of the first-class passengers is a young sunny-haired American woman, said to have the blue of the sea in her eyes. She is called Myra Selfridge, and is travelling with her husband. She sees a sailor on board whom she recognizes as an old flame of five years before. Then he was Lieutenant Rowland, United States Navy. Since then he has sunk, through unrequited love and drink, to be no more than a drunken common seaman. The *Titan* ploughs on. In mid Atlantic the lookout shouts a warning, 'Hard a port, sir — ship on the starboard tack — dead ahead.' But it is too late, and the liner runs down a sailing ship, from whose foundering wreckage a voice cries upwards, 'May the curse of God light on you and your cheese-knife, you brassbound murderers.' The *Titan* goes ahead, does not stop, and makes no attempt to rescue the crew of the small ship. Orders are given to clear the wreckage from the *Titan's* bows, to say nothing, and put nothing in the log. The captain calls the look-out to his cabin, and mentions that when they make port he will receive a packet containing £100 in bank notes. The look-out is Rowland. He says he is a graduate of Annapolis, declines the bribe, and declares that he will speak out when the time comes. Later, in fog, the *Titan* strikes an iceberg and sinks. Rowland saves Myra Selfridge's child, fights off a polar bear on an ice flow with a penknife, is rescued, and restores the child to its mother. He becomes a dock lounger, but then, improving himself, attains first a clerkship and then a lucrative post under the government. Myra, having lost her husband in the *Titan*, watches Rowland's advancement with interest and, when he achieves the lucrative post, writes inviting him to come to her.

If you put aside the contrivances of Robertson's story — the running-down of the sailing craft, the gallant Rowland, the sunny-haired Myra, and the polar bear and the penknife — the resemblances are close. The *Titan* was 800 feet long, the *Titanic* 883. The *Titan* had nineteen watertight compartments, the *Titanic* fourteen. The *Titan* was carrying 2,000 souls, the *Titanic* 2,201. Both ships were considered unsinkable. Both foundered after striking an iceberg. Both carried only as many lifeboats as the law required, enough for about half their passengers. It is only fair to say that there are details in which the events of the stories are different. The *Titan* was a new ship, but on her third and not her maiden voyage, and was sailing east and not west. The *Titan* struck her iceberg in a fog, and she rammed it and wrecked herself. There is none of the stillness of the *Titanic* disaster, when she struck glancingly and almost without impact, and then lay quiet on a still sea. The *Titanic's*, in short, is much the better story, but the coincidences are many, and much the most telling is that of the names. *Titan* became *Titanic*, but that much change was inevitable since all White Star

ships bore names ending in -*ic*. And *Titanic* was a name which, though it might have seemed a natural one for any of the large White Star liners of the previous couple of decades, had in fact been held back for a special occasion. At her launching, the magazine *Scientific American* asked, in an article, why that particular moment should be considered critical for bringing out this 'loaded treasure of nomenclature'. Actually, it was a former United States consul at the Court of Siam, of all people, one David Banks, who had suggested the names *Titanic* and *Gigantic* to White Star, and when in the first decade of the twentieth century the company decided to build three great steamers, the largest in the world and capable of running between them a weekly transatlantic service, those were two of the names they chose. The third name was *Olympic*, and it was she that was launched first, in 1910. The second, launched in 1911, was *Titanic*. The third, launched in 1913, was due to be called *Gigantic*, but never was so named. After the *Titanic* disaster it was thought that to name her sister ship *Gigantic* would be hubris, and asking for trouble. She was called *Britannic* instead.

These three sister ships were all built by Harland and Wolff at Belfast, and two of them at the same time, on adjacent slips. This was a very grand plan. No three sister ships of this size or anything remotely like it had ever been built before, or ever were afterwards. At the time of their launching they were the world's largest by a long way, half as big again as the *Lusitania* and *Mauretania* which had for four years been unapproached in size. The White Star liners were not intended to race. They were designed for a steady 21 knots, and never had a thought of the blue riband. That was left to Cunard and to the German companies. White Star wanted liners that were the most luxurious and steady on the Atlantic. The luxury was obvious, and meant to be. The first-class dining-room simulated the decorations of Hatfield, and the walls of its annex were covered with Aubusson tapestries. The first-class lounge took its style from the Palace of Versailles. The style of the palm court was

The *Titanic* at Belfast, after fitting out ▶

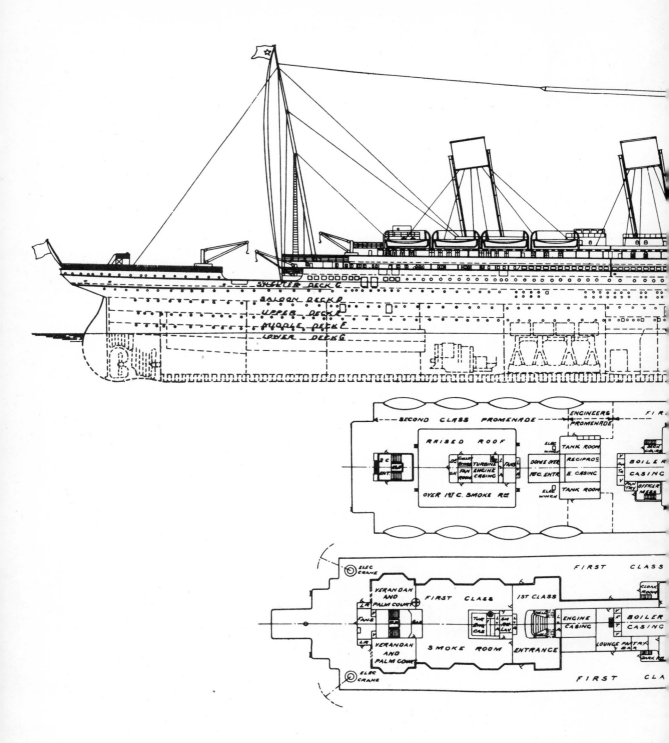

Section of the *Titanic*. The *Shipbuilder*, special number, Midsummer 1911

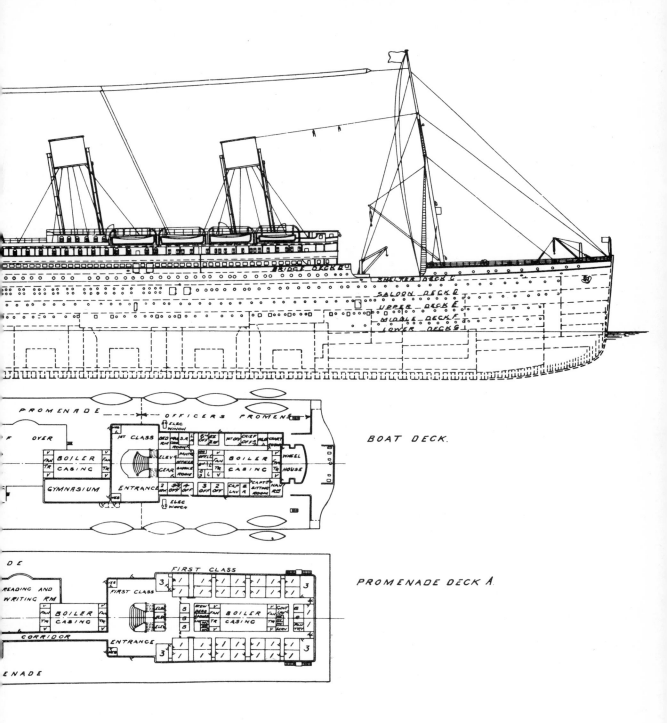

BRIDGE DECK B
SHELTER DECK C
SALOON DECK D
UPPER DECK E
MIDDLE DECK F
LOWER DECK G

PROMENADE   OFFICERS PROMEN

BOAT DECK.

F   OYER
1ST CLASS
ELEC WINCH
BOILER CASING
GYMNASIUM
ELEV
GEAR
ENTRANCE
BOILER CASING
WHEEL HOUSE
CHIEF OFFS
CAP. SITTING ROOM
ELEC WINCH

FIRST CLASS

DE
READING AND WRITING RM
FIRST CLASS
3
BOILER CASING
BOILER CASING
CORRIDOR
ENTRANCE
3
ENADE

PROMENADE DECK A.

The *Titanic*'s swimming-pool, open to men and women, but at separate hours

treillage of the period of Louis XVI; that is to say, trellis, so that ivy and climbing plants could curl round it and reassure passengers that they were not at sea at all but on dry land. The ship's Turkish baths were Arabian, with Cairo curtains and suspended bronze lamps and a marble drinking fountain. There was a gymnasium, an idea taken from the German ships, and for the first time an Atlantic liner had a swimming-pool and a squash rackets court complete with professional. State-rooms came in eleven styles, from Italian Renaissance to Old Dutch. Even the single beds were four feet wide. Everything was handled with great panache, and White Star must take the credit for the grandest single day in the history of British ocean liners. That was 31 May 1911 when at Belfast the guests of the company watched the *Titanic* launched at 12 noon, and then boarded the *Olympic* which had been launched seven months before and had been fitting out there. At 4.30 in the afternoon she sailed from Belfast with the company's guests for Southampton, there to begin her maiden

voyage. The maiden voyage of the *Titanic* was still eleven months in the future.

She remained for the moment at Belfast, where the purser of the *Oceanic* and Dr W. F. N. O'Loughlin, the senior surgeon of the White Star Line, wrote some lines of verse about her:

'Neath a gantry high and mighty she had birth.
And she'd bulk and length and height and mighty beam.
And the world was only larger in its girth
And she seemed to be a living, moving dream.

Next year the moving dream had also been fitted out, and she began her maiden crossing from Southampton to New York on 11 April 1912, a Thursday. For use of the first-class passengers she carried a dinner service of 10,000 pieces of plate made by the Goldsmiths and Silversmiths Company of Regent Street. Among those passengers were ten millionaires. When they all died a few days later their fortunes were computed and published. Colonel John Jacob Astor, a member of one of the wealthiest families in the world and a gallant

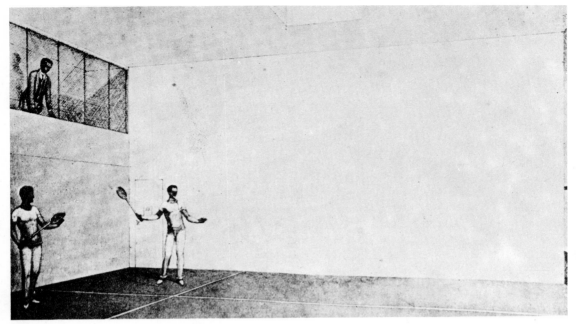

The rackets court, for hire at two shillings an hour, including the services of the professional

man who had served with honour in the Spanish American war, had £30 millions. Benjamin Guggenheim had £20 millions. Isador Straus, merchant and philanthropist, had £10 millions, and so had George D. Widener, son of the Philadelphia millionaire who had just bought a Rembrandt painting called 'The Mill' from Lord Lansdowne. There were also the Presidents of the Pennsylvania and of the Grand Trunk railroads, the *aide de camp* of President Taft, and W. T. Stead, editor of the *Pall Mall Gazette*. As the passengers assembled and met each other for the first time, it was the subject both of observation and admiration that there were so many beautiful women aboard the ship. Among them were Miss Elizabeth Shutes, and the Countess of Rothes. Miss Shutes was always to remember the strange odour of the air, as if it came from an ice cave on the Eiger, which, on the night the *Titanic* foundered, just before the ship struck, came to her so vividly that she could not sleep. And many years later the Countess of Rothes, while dining with friends, was to feel coming over

her the awful sense of cold and horror she always associated with the *Titanic*, and to realize it was because the orchestra was playing 'The Tales of Hoffman', the last piece of after-dinner music played the night the *Titanic* went down.

The commander of the Titanic was Captain E. J. Smith, the very type of a British sea captain, strong in command but gentle in social converse, and with shaggy eyebrows. He had started his career in sail, taken his master's certificate at the age of twenty-five, and had commanded seventeen White Star liners in succession. As commodore of the line he had taken the *Olympic* on her maiden voyage. As commodore he was also taking the *Titanic*. He was sixty-two. J. Bruce Ismay was on board, the chairman of the White Star line and the son of its founder. He survived, but the wreck of his ship was the wreck of his career and he lived in seclusion for the remaining twenty-five years of his life. Thomas Andrews, the marine architect who had designed the *Titanic*, was on board. He did not survive. The band-

[67]

The gymnasium, where McCawley, the instructor, remained until the liner foundered, still encouraging passengers to ride his mechanical horses

master was a musician called Wallace Hartley, who was going to be famous. He normally worked on Cunard liners and had returned to England only a few days before the *Titanic* was due to sail. He was thirty-three, and about to leave sea life because he was engaged to be married, but the musical director of the White Star line persuaded him to sign on with the *Titanic*. Before she sailed, he wrote to his fiancée, 'This is a fine ship. We have a fine band, and the boys seem very nice. We are due back here on a Saturday morning [that would have been the 27th of the month] and I hope to be home on Sunday.'

Each of the 322 first-class passengers was given a passenger list of twenty-eight pages, in which were also printed details of the ship's routine. The bars opened at half past eight in the morning, and closed by half past eleven at night. Lights were extinguished in the saloon at eleven. Even the smoke room closed at midnight. By the standards of the liners of the 1920s and 1930s, these were early hours. Deck chairs could be hired at four shillings for the voyage.

Wireless Marconigrams could be sent at sea to the United States via Cape Cod at 8s. 4d. for ten words, extra words sixpence each, but the address and signature free. The squash court could be hired for two shillings the half hour, which included the services of the professional. The company also took the opportunity of intimating to passengers that gamblers were on board, who were said to be 'in the habit of travelling to and fro'. In bringing this to the knowledge of passengers, the managers of the company, while not wishing in the slightest degree to interfere with the freedom of action of its patrons, nevertheless invited their assistance in discouraging games of chance, as being likely to afford those individuals (the gamblers) special opportunities for taking unfair advantage of others. On the back cover of each passenger list was a map of the North Atlantic to enable passengers to plot the ship's course. There was also the information that the *Titanic* would complete thirteen round voyages that year.

On great liners, it is commonly only the first-class passengers and their pleasures that

The electric lifts

get remembered and described. Because the *Titanic* sank, and because her sinking was the most widely reported maritime disaster there ever was, a great deal is also known about the steerage passengers, and even those of the second class, who were usually the most anonymous of all. The best single account of what her passengers did on board is given by Lawrence Beesley, a science master at Dulwich College, London, who was travelling second and observed passengers of his own class and in the steerage. In the steerage there was a Scotsman who often played on his bagpipes something which faintly resembled an air. Also, standing aloof from them all in the steerage, generally on the raised stern deck, was a man of about twenty to twenty-four years, well dressed, always gloved and well groomed, and obviously quite out of place. He never looked happy, and Beesley classified him at hazard as a man who had been a failure in some way at home and had received the proverbial shilling plus his third-class fare to America: he did not look resolute enough or

happy enough to work out his own problem. Then there was another man who was himself travelling steerage but had placed his wife in the second class. He would climb the stairs leading from the steerage to the second deck and talk affectionately with her across the low gate which separated them. Beesley never saw him after the collision, but thought his wife was among those rescued. Whether they even saw each other on the Sunday night was doubtful. The man would not have been allowed on the second-class deck, and if he had been, the chances of seeing his wife in the darkness and the crowds would have been small.

In the second class were two Catholic priests, one Irish, who read a lot, and the other, dark and bearded and wearing a broad brimmed hat, who talked earnestly to a friend in German, explaining some verse in the open Bible in front of him. There was a young photographer with a French wife who was fond of playing Patience, and two young American women, one returning home from India by way of England, and the other probably a school-

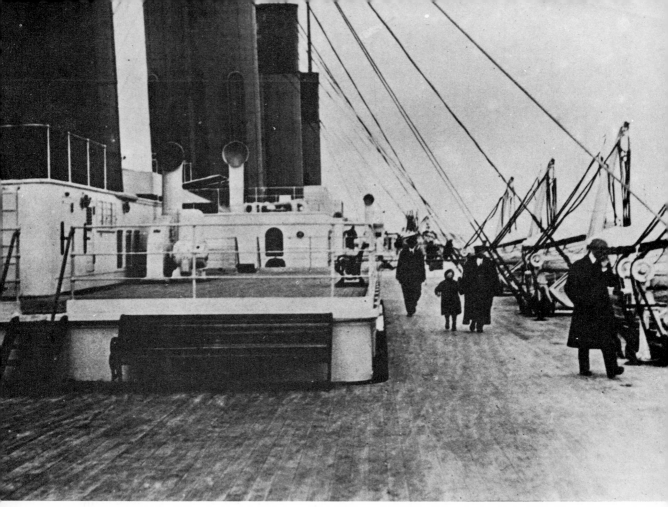

Second-class promenade deck of the *Titanic*. One of the last photographs, taken at Queenstown

mistress, a graceful girl in white who wore pince-nez. There was a young Scots engineer going out to join his brother fruit-farming in the foothills of the Rockies, and another engineer going out to Mexico. There was a man calling himself Hoffman, travelling with two children, Lolo and Louis. It was to turn out that his real name was Navatril, that he had parted bitterly from his wife and kidnapped the children from her in Nice and was taking them to the United States. He did not survive. The children did, and were returned to their mother. There was a clergyman of the Church of England, the Rev. Ernest Carter, with his wife Lillian. He said he could not have got through half his parish work without her constant help. None of

these men survived. Mrs Carter died too. The *Titanic* had an electric lift even for the second class. This was in charge of a boy who could not have been more than sixteen. He loved the sea and the games on the deck and the view over the ocean, and he did not get any of them. Beesley once saw him look through the vestibule windows at a game of deck quoits and heard him wish he could go out there sometimes. He was not seen after the collision.

From Thursday noon to Friday noon the *Titanic* ran 386 nautical miles, Friday to Saturday 519 miles, and Saturday to Sunday 546 miles. She was making 22 knots. Everyone agreed she was the most comfortable ship they had travelled in. There was, though, a vibration, which was most noticeable as one lay in the bath. The throb of the engines came straight up from the floor through the metal sides of the tub so that one could not put one's head back with any comfort. Throughout her voyage, the *Titanic* slightly listed to port, but it was nothing. As the second-class passengers sat at table in the dining-room they could, if they watched the skyline through the portholes, see both skyline and sea on the port side but only sky to starboard. The purser thought this was probably because more coal had been used from the starboard bunkers.

When some passengers went on deck on Sunday morning they found the temperature had dropped so rapidly that they did not care to stay outside, although there was no wind, or only that artificial wind created by the passage of the ship. Both the French liner *Touraine* and the German *Amerika* had wirelessed the *Titanic* reporting ice, and the *Titanic* had replied thanking them. Sunday dinner was served, and then coffee. Thomas Andrews, the shipbuilder, strolled down to the kitchens to thank the baker for making some special bread for him. The passengers went to bed with the presumption, perhaps already mentally half-realized, as Beesley put it, that they would be ashore in New York in forty-eight hours time. At the evening service, after coffee, the Rev. Mr Carter had caused the hymn 'For Those in Peril on the Sea' to be sung, but he had brought the service to a close with a few words on the great confidence all on board felt in the *Titanic*'s great steadiness and size. At 11.40, in Lat. 41° 46′ N Long. 50° 14′ W, Frederick Fleet, the look-out in the crow's-nest, saw or sensed an iceberg ahead. The *Titanic* veered to port, so that it was her starboard plates which were glanced open. The engines were stopped. There was a perfectly still atmosphere. It was a brilliantly starlit night but with no moon, so that there was little light that was of any use. She was a ship that had come quietly to rest without any indication of disaster. No ice was visible; the iceberg had been glimpsed by the look-out and then gone. There was no hole in the ship's side through which water could be

seen to be pouring, nothing out of place, no sound of alarm, no panic, and no movement of anyone except at a walking pace.

Within ten minutes the water had risen fourteen feet inside the ship. Mail bags were floating about in the mail room. The passengers had no idea of danger. Beesley, who was in bed, noticed no more than what he took to be the slightest extra heave of the engines. What most people noticed first was the sudden lack of engine vibration. This had been with them so constantly for the four days of the voyage that they had ceased to be conscious of it, but when it stopped they noticed the supervening silence and stillness. The only passengers who saw an iceberg were a few still playing cards in the smoking room. They idly discussed how high it might have been, settled on an estimate of eighty feet, and went back to their cards. One pointed to a glass of whisky at his side and, turning to an onlooker, suggested he should just run along on deck to see if any ice had come on board. If so, he would like some more in his whisky. They laughed. In fact, as the crew discovered, the decks were strewn with ice, but even then, so unaware were they of danger, that Edward Buley, an able seaman, picked up a handful of it, took it down to his bunk, and turned in again. There was no panic because there was no awareness. The *Titanic* was assumed to be unsinkable. The shipbuilders had said so. Practically everyone believed she was as unsinkable as a railway station. A Rothschild, asked to put on his life-jacket, said he did not think there was any occasion for it, and walked leisurely away. Stewards rode bicycles round and round in the gym. She was in fact sinking very fast, and by midnight was a quarter sunk already. There was something unusual about the stairs, a curious sense of something out of balance, a sense of not being able to put one's foot down in the right place. The stairs were tilting forward and tended to throw your feet out of place. There was no visible slope, just something strange perceived by the sense of balance. The *Titanic* was settling by the head. The first real indication of disaster was the letting off of distress rockets. Suddenly the

The grand staircase in the first class

decks were lit up, showing men and women in all states of dress and undress, and the flash of the rockets illumined at the same time the faces and minds of those who until then had only been curious. The rockets were being fired to attract the attention of a ship which the look-outs saw lying five or ten miles away, but she did not respond. Captain Smith ordered the second officer, Lightoller, to put the women and children into the boats and lower away. He knew that Andrews had found the ship to be ripped open on the starboard side ten feet above the keel for a distance of 300 feet, one-third the length of the vessel, and that she could not survive. His officers may have known this too: his crew and the passengers did not. Many women declined to leave the security of the decks to get into lifeboats and be lowered, merely as a precaution, seventy feet into the darkness. Stewards were engaged in locking

state-rooms so that nothing should be stolen during their occupants' temporary absence in the boats. One man had somehow got locked into his cabin and was shouting and banging so loudly that passengers who had casually gathered in the cabin outside thought him afflicted. Still, one of them smashed the door down and released the man, whereupon the head steward, who had by then appeared, was so furious at the damage done to one cabin door, the property of the White Star line, that he threatened the destroyer with arrest when they got to New York.

There is going to be no coherent account of what happened in the last hour of the *Titanic*, because nothing coherent happened. The *Titanic* was a sixth of a mile long and had eleven decks. What happened in one place did not happen in another. What happened on the starboard side did not happen on the port. On

The *café parisien*: the other *Titanic* interiors illustrated are identical with those of the *Olympic*, her sister ship, but the *café parisien* appeared only on the *Titanic*

the port side, women and children only were allowed into the boats, which were even sent away half-empty when there were not women enough at that moment to fill them, although there were men. On the starboard side, men were allowed to enter the boats when there were not at any given moment enough women to fill them. There was even a difference of opinion as to what constituted a woman. Second Officer Lightoller took any women, except stewardesses. Fifth Officer Lowe accepted any women, 'whether first class, second class, third class, or sixty-seventh class . . . regardless of class or nationality or pedigree. Stewardesses just the same.' Lowe, however, said he fended off a lot of Italian men, Latin people, all along the ship's rails, 'more or less like wild beasts, ready to spring'. But the severe Lightoller saw none of this, and said that the men whom he refused to allow into his boats 'could not have

stood quieter if they had been in church'. Major Arthur Peuchen, who held his commission in the Canadian militia and got away into a boat because he was a yachtsman and could help to handle it, saw a hundred stokers with their bags crowd a whole deck in front of the boats until an officer he did not recognize, a very powerful man, drove them right off the deck like a lot of sheep. Others said not a soul emerged from the engine room. Certainly no single engineer survived. Lowe said they were never seen.

Everyone agrees that the band played until the last. There were eight of them, and none survived. They had played throughout dinner and then gone to their berths. About twenty to one, when the ship was foundering, the cellist ran down the deserted starboard deck, his cello trailing behind him with the spike dragging along the floor. Soon after that the band began

[73]

The *Titanic* foundering, sketched by Leo James Hyland, a steward who watched from a lifeboat

to play ragtime. They were still playing ragtime when the last boat was launched. That last lifeboat had to be lowered only ten feet into the sea: when the first boats had been launched they had had to descend seventy feet from the same deck to reach the sea. Until the decks sloped too much, McCawley, the gym instructor, remained in his gymnasium encouraging those who stayed with him to ride his electric horses and electric camels. There was electrical power until the end, and the lights stayed on. The two wireless operators at first transmitted CQD CQD, CQ being the call for all stations, and D meaning distress. Then they changed to the new distress call of SOS until the wireless deck was awash. This was the first time the new SOS signal was used at sea. The *Titanic*'s signals were heard by her sister ship the *Olympic*, bound outwards from New York and 300 miles west, by the White Star liner *Baltic*, 200 miles east, by one French and four German liners, and by the Cunarder *Carpathia*. If the *Titanic* was going to

founder within hours, the *Carpathia* was the only ship which could conceivably reach her, but by two o'clock, the time her last boat was launched, the *Titanic* was going to founder not within hours but within minutes.

Colonel Astor, having placed his young bride in one of the boats, lit a cigarette and looked over the rails. Benjamin Guggenheim changed into evening dress, saying that if he had to die he would die like a gentleman. Thomas Andrews leaned against a mantelpiece in the smoking room. A steward asked him, 'Aren't you going to try for it sir?' He did not reply. John Collins, aged seventeen, an assistant cook making his first sea voyage, saw the stewards with their white jackets steering some passengers along, making a joke of it. One steward was helping a woman with two children. The steward was carrying one child and the woman the other. Collins took the child the woman was carrying. 'Then,' he said, 'the sailors and the firemen that were forward seen the ship's bow in the water and seen that she was intending to sink her bow, and they shouted out for all they were worth we were to go aft, and we were just turning round and making for the stern when the wave washed us off the deck, washed us clear of it, and the child was washed out of my arms; and the wreckage, and the people that was around me, they kept me down for at least two or three minutes under the water.' The sea was calm as a board, but when the bow went under the water it created a wave that washed the decks clear, and there were hundreds on it.

At about this time, 2.15 am, Lawrence Beesley was a mile or two clear of the *Titanic* in a lifeboat. It seemed only a question of minutes until she sank. The sailors lay on their oars, and everyone watched the ship in silence, except those who did not want to watch and buried their heads in each other's shoulders. The surface of the sea was a lake. It was like a picnic on a lake, or on a quiet inland river like the Cam. Beesley remembered that at lunchtime the previous day a fellow passenger had said that when he got to New York he would take the first opportunity to stand some distance away from the *Titanic* as she lay at her berth, so as to get a proper view of her dimensions and proportions; and now he was having this view of her in mid Atlantic. It was very dark. The black outline of the *Titanic*'s profile against the sky was bordered all around by stars studded in the sky and all her funnels and masts were picked out in the same way: her bulk, in other words, was seen only where the stars were blotted out. The water had crept up almost to the captain's bridge. The stern was high out of the water. So far this had all happened so slowly that the ship had not been seen to move. But then she tilted slowly up, revolving about a centre of gravity just astern of amidships, until she stood almost vertically in the water, motionless. As she stood like this there came a noise which some people thought was an

The *Titanic's* last moments, a fanciful reconstruction from the *Illustrated London News*. No such view could have been seen. The night was pitch dark

Titanic survivors aboard the *Carpathia*. On the left are the only surviving honeymoon couple, Mr and Mrs George A. Harder, talking to Mrs Charles Hays, who lost her husband

explosion but which Beesley and most others came to believe was the engines and machinery coming loose from their bearings and falling the length of the ship, which was by then the height of the ship, smashing everything in their way. That noise lasted fifteen or twenty seconds. He supposed the machinery just fell down through the bows and down into the sea. He was perhaps two miles away but it was a stupefying noise, as if all the heavy things one could think of had been thrown downstairs from the top of a house, smashing each other and the stairs and

everything in the way all the way down. Still the *Titanic* stood upright like a column, and so she stood for four minutes. Then, first sinking back a little at the stern, she slid slowly forward through the water and dived slantingly down and the sea closed over her.

Second Officer Lightoller recalled that there was not a sign of lamentation. G. A. Hogg, an ordinary seaman, of Hull, said everybody had done their best, ladies, gentlemen, and sailor-men. Beesley said the stars were free from haze, and intense, as if they had seen that beautiful ship in distress below and had awakened all their energies to flash messages across the black dome of the sky to each other, telling of the calamity happening in the world beneath. And in the water he did hear cries of lamentation. The *Carpathia* took two hours to come up. By 4.30 am the first of the *Titanic*'s survivors were taken aboard her and by 8 am the last. It was as well the *Carpathia* took no longer, and that the sea was calm. Most boats had no compass and no light, no biscuit and no drinking water. The crewmen knew nothing about the position of the stars, and could hardly even pull together. Oars were lost overboard because men's hands were too cold to hold on. But in some ways it was all very orderly. In boat 13, one first-class passenger had had the foresight to bring with her all her coats. She offered a fur-lined one to a stoker who was clad only in a singlet but he refused and gave it to an Irish girl. The same woman gave other wraps to other passengers, a rug to one, a fur boa to another. When they came alongside the *Carpathia*, after two hours in a freezing sea, they all offered her back her clothes. The *Carpathia* picked up 711 passengers and crew. Thus 1,490 were missing.

The *Carpathia*, which had been bound eastwards for the Mediterranean, put back to New York, which took her four days to reach. To begin with she steamed slowly through icebergs, icefields, and bitter cold. Then there was brilliant warm sun, and thunder and lightning in the middle of one night. The peal followed the flash so closely that the women in the saloon leaped up in alarm, saying rockets were being let off again. Then there were fogs, then rain, and then a choppy sea. As the *Carpathia* came into New York bay, coroners and coffins assembled on the north river piers. She was still towing some of the *Titanic*'s lifeboats, and was carrying others hauled up into her own davits. The *Carpathia* stopped off her own Cunard pier. A tug took the lifeboats she was towing, the others were lowered from the davits, and all the lifeboats were then towed upstream to the White Star pier where the *Titanic* herself should have docked.

Harold Bride, the surviving wireless operator of the *Titanic*, huddled in a chair aboard the *Carpathia*

The news of the *Titanic* disaster had been known very soon after she had struck, but in many forms, and most very garbled. Eight ships had picked up the distress calls and relayed them to Cape Race. Thus different fragments of the truth were known from many sources, but became mixed in the transmission, and to this was added conjecture, and also pure invention. *The Times* of London said all passengers and crew had been lowered into lifeboats and were waiting the arrival of the *Olympic*. This was not surprising. On the other hand, White Star in New York were being alternately fearful and saying nothing, and optimistic and saying that the *Titanic*'s watertight compartments would hold. Then the steamer *Virginian* was reported to be towing the *Titanic*. Then the *Titanic* was reported to have foundered, but with no lives lost. All these conflicting versions, given as from conflicting sources, appeared in one day's *Times*. Newspapers throughout America also carried stories that vessels (sometimes two or three together) were trying to tow her to the shoals of Newfoundland. The *Titanic* was also, according to other sources, proceeding on her own steam to New York. Anything, of course, was more likely than the truth. It was not on the cards that she would have foundered with so great a loss of life. All the same, confusion

A paragraph in a London paper of Tuesday 16 April 1912 when there was still confusion and hope

TO-DAY'S STORY.

Tuesday Morning.

The weather forecast for to-day is:— Light, variable easterly breezes, becoming westerly to south-westerly later; fair or fine, local mist; temperature moderate to mild.

Lighting-up time, 7.55 p.m.

Mr. Balfour made a powerful attack on the Home Rule Bill in the House of Commons yesterday and Mr. Herbert Samuel made an important statement on the financial proposals of the Bill.—This page.

The White Star liner Titanic was wrecked by an iceberg off Cape Race on Sunday night All the passengers were transferred safely to other liners that responded to the Titanic's distress signal. The Titanic was taken in tow by the Virginian, and an attempt made to tow her to Halifax. Latest accounts state that she is sinking steadily, and efforts are being made to beach her off Cape Race.—This page.

alone could not have been the source of the circumstantial but false details which then began to appear. Dazed passengers had not rushed from their state-rooms amid the crash of splintering steel and rending plates, pinnacles of ice falling on the decks had not added to the horror, and the ship for one hundred feet back from the bow had not been a shapeless mass of broken steel. *The Times* of London, which had printed agency messages in good faith, later characterized some of them in a leading article as pure cruel inventions. In London, Liverpool, and New York all shipping companies flew their flags at half mast. In the House of Commons Mr Asquith, the Prime Minister, said he was afraid they had to confront one of those terrible events in the order of Providence which baffled foresight and appalled the imagination. The marine insurance market was depressed. The King of England and the President of the United States exchanged condolences. The widow of Captain Smith of the *Titanic* sent a message to all other widows made by the *Titanic*, saying, 'May God be with us.' Berlin said the Kaiser was in active telegraphic communication with authoritative personages concerned. At a great commemorative service in St Paul's cathedral, in the silence after the intoning of the lesson, there arose a vague, soft sound. 'It was as though great birds were fluttering their wings outside the windows of the cathedral. The noise increased. It was the sound of a mighty wind. Louder and louder it grew as the ruffle was played on the massed drums, until the vast cathedral was filled with a tempest of prodigious sound as though all the winds of heaven were rushing over the heads of the people, as though the sea were rising in fury.'

The greatest of all the *Titanic* heroes was the bandmaster, Wallace Hartley. It became rapidly established as a fact that as the ship went down the bandsmen played 'Nearer, My God, to Thee'. But as it happens, most people never heard the band play anything at all. This is not surprising, because they played outside the gymnasium on a first-class deck. Those who heard were most likely to be first-class passengers, and these agree that the band played ragtime. At the end,

The *Titanic*'s band. The leader, Wallace Hartley, is in the centre. The others are, left to right, top to bottom, F. Clarke, P. C. Taylor, G. Krins (sometime of the Ritz hotel orchestra), W. T. Brailey, J. Hume, and J. W. Woodward. There was also a French musician, R. Bricoux, who does not appear

as the ship was within a few minutes of going down, most of those first-class passengers who were going to survive, that is to say the women, were in lifeboats a mile or two away. Most of those first-class passengers who remained at the end, that is to say the men, were not going to survive to remember anything. But of those who did survive by chance, and had heard, some say the last tune was 'Nearer, My God, to Thee', and others that it was the episcopal hymn 'Autumn'. After the disaster it was the sheet music of 'Nearer, My God, to Thee', which suddenly began to sell in many thousands. Groups sang it at street corners after the manner of popular songs. In France, a version entitled 'Plus près de Toi, Mon Dieu', sold 50,000 in less than a week. More people attended Hartley's funeral in Colne, Lancashire, than had gone to St Paul's, and there marched in his funeral procession five brass bands, one orchestra, one choir, and a formation of bugler Scouts. Before he went to join the *Titanic*, Hartley had made his last appearance on land at the Leeds Savage Club, in a concert in aid of the Lifeboat Fund. After the disaster, and before his body was found, his mother said he was a good swimmer, and that she knew he would die clasping his violin, to which he was passionately attached. When Hartley was found, the body was identified largely because the violin case was still strapped to his chest. Colne town council resolved to erect a commemorative water fountain, 'for the rising generation to look up to in years to come'. Collections were made in churches, workshops, factories, and pubs. In London, a great concert to honour the memory of the *Titanic*'s musicians was held in the Albert Hall. Five hundred musicians played, and were conducted by Sir Henry Wood, Sir Edward Elgar, and Thomas Beecham. It was thought to be the greatest orchestra ever assembled in England. In Leeds, musicians from all the theatres, music halls, hotels, and cafés in the city organized a sacred concert in a Leeds music hall on a Sunday evening, which raised £107 7s. 9½d. towards the memorial fund. Hartley's funeral was on 18 May. From the chapel to the cemetery was a mile and a half, mostly uphill, and all the way was lined with spectators, many of whom wore in their lapels a large 'button' or card photograph of Hartley. On the green hills all around, for miles across the valley, people stood and watched. It was said that 30,000 people, three times the population of Colne, had gathered for the funeral. In the procession marched the brass bands of Colne, Mount Zion, Trowden, Nelson, and Brierfield, together with mounted police, mayors, and the musical director of the White Star company. The coffin appeared strange to the mourners. It had been made in America, where the body had first been taken, and was of an elaborate shape quite unlike that of an English coffin. The last post was sounded over the grave. Hartley was buried in the evening dress in which he was found.

There were inquiries both in America and England. The surviving officers of the *Titanic*, and the English marine world in general, seemed almost to think the American inquiry impertinent, although in everything but name the *Titanic*, though flying the British flag, was American owned, by I.M.M. The British also seemed put out by the questions asked by senators who were not seamen. 'What is an iceberg made of?' asked one member of the U.S. Senate committee. This is not so silly a question as it might seem, but the British were much amused when the British officer informed the American senator that icebergs were made of ice.

Senator Smith, chairman of the committee, wanted to know whether, when the ship was going down, the great number of people still on board her were huddled together.

SECOND OFFICER LIGHTOLLER: 'There was a great many of them, I know, but as to what condition they were in, huddled or not, I do not know.'

SMITH: 'Did they make any demonstration?'
LIGHTOLLER: 'No.'
SMITH: 'Was there any lamentation?'
LIGHTOLLER: 'No sir; not a sign of it.'
SMITH: 'There must have been about 2,000 people there on that part, the unsubmerged part of the boat?'

One of the many *Titanic* legends for which there is no evidence. Here in a sketch from the *Illustrated London News* Capt. Smith gives a baby he has rescued from the water to survivors balancing on an upturned lifeboat. Then, seeing there was no room for himself, he was said to have swum away to his death

LIGHTOLLER: 'All the engineers and other men and many of the firemen were down below and never came on deck at all.'

SMITH: 'They never came on deck?'

LIGHTOLLER: 'No sir; they were never seen.'

When Senator Smith asked Lightoller about 2,000 men still being left on the *Titanic* as she sank, he was forgetting to subtract the numbers of those who had already escaped in the lifeboats. There can have been no more than 1,500 still on board at the end. And this was the only mercy in the whole catastrophe, because it could have been many more. The *Titanic* was licensed to carry 3,547 souls, but she was nothing like full, and indeed carried only two-thirds of her permitted complement. She could have carried many hundreds more in the steerage, but emigrants at that season tended to travel in German ships from German ports.

There were only 2,201 passengers and crew on board. If there had been more in the steerage, their chances would not have been high. As it was, a much higher proportion of the first class was saved than of the second, and the second in turn did much better than the third. In all classes, a woman was at least three times as likely to survive; and a first-class woman passenger was eleven times more likely to escape than a second-class man. But it was never shown, in either inquiry, that steerage passengers had been kept away from the boats. The sad truth is more probably that they just could not find their way so easily to the decks. Open deck space was for first and second: you

[81]

could cross in the steerage on any liner and hardly ever get a glimpse of the sea.*

One thing that particularly concerned the American committee was that many lifeboats were very far from full. Each could take about seventy people, but some had only forty occupants, and one only twelve. This was principally because, at the time the first boats were launched, many women passengers preferred not to enter them, believing the *Titanic* in no danger. But then, when the *Titanic* was plainly sinking, these boats with only one exception failed to turn back to pick up more survivors, for fear of being swamped. Frank Evans, an able seaman in one boat, said, 'We heard these cries, but we took them to be the boats that went away on the starboard side of the ship; that they were cheering one another, sir.' Fourth Officer Joseph Boxhall had been in charge of one boat. He told the inquiry he had forty people aboard, and ordered his men to row back to pick up more. The passengers cried out that this was a bad idea. They might be swamped. Boxhall repeated that they could take more, but, as he put it, the whole crowd in the boat demurred to that. So

they stopped rowing and drifted, and did not go back.

SMITH: 'How many cries were there? Was it a chorus, or was it . . .?'

BOXHALL (*After twice saying that he would rather not answer that question*): 'There was a continual moan for about an hour.'

SMITH: 'And you lay in the vicinity of that scene for about an hour?'

BOXHALL: 'Oh, yes . . .'

SMITH: 'And drifted or lay on your oars during that time?'

BOXHALL: 'We drifted towards daylight . . . I would rather you would have left that out altogether.'

SMITH: 'I know you would; but I must know what efforts you made to save the lives of passengers and crew under your charge. If that is all the effort you made, say so —'

BOXHALL: 'That is all, sir.'

SMITH: 'And I will stop that branch of my examination.'

BOXHALL: 'That is all, sir; that is all the effort I made.'

The Senate committee, though mostly understanding nothing about ships and the sea, got to know far more than the later British inquiry. They asked more sharp questions about more particular things. It was they who drew out of Frederick Fleet, the look-out who had spotted the iceberg, that he had had no binoculars. He just had to keep a sharp look-out with his own eyes. He had been given binoculars for the short passage from Belfast down to Southampton, but they had been taken away. He had asked again before they left Southampton for the Atlantic crossing, but had been told there were none for him. He had been given binoculars before, on previous White Star ships, but they had been of poor quality. He had had such a pair once on the *Oceanic*, but, he said, gesturing towards a mirror in the committee room, they had been very poor, and had enabled him to see 'only from about here to that looking glass'. It is from the American committee too that the sense of bewilderment emerges more strongly. Of course there had not been enough lifeboats. But, as Philip Franklin, vice-chairman of I.M.M.,

* These are the detailed figures for survivors given in the report of the British Board of Trade Inquiry:

	Number on board	Number saved	Percentage saved
First-class passengers			
Men	173	58	34
Women	144	139	97
Children	5	5	100
Second-class passengers			
Men	160	13	8
Women	93	78	84
Children	24	24	100
Third-class passengers			
Men	454	55	12
Women	179	98	55
Children	76	23	30
Total passengers	1308	493	38
Crew	898	210	23
Total	2206	703	32

Taking each class of passenger as a whole, of the first class 63 per cent were saved, of the second class 42 per cent, and of the third class 23 per cent.

said, 'These steamers were considered tremendous lifeboats in themselves.'

The British Board of Trade inquiry was more formal, was presided over by Lord Mersey, a judge, lasted thirty-six days, and was very grave, and yet at times it was weird. There was a lot about unsinkability.

MERSEY: 'I suppose it is impossible to make a ship unsinkable and at the same time a commercial success? You can, of course, conceive an iron box riveted so that nobody can get into it, but that would not do as a ship . . . I suppose that some people would say you should carry the double bottom up to the upper deck?' [Laughter.] 'Has an unsinkable ship ever been constructed?'

THE ATTORNEY GENERAL: 'They are sometimes called unsinkable, but that means under conditions which comprise every form of disaster so far known. I do know a patentee who is anxious that I should interest myself in an invention which will save every passenger within five minutes.' [Laughter.]

MERSEY: 'And make you a fortune as well.' [Laughter.]

The court was much concerned with the allegations against J. Bruce Ismay, managing director of I.M.M., who had been travelling as a passenger and was one of the few men to escape. For this he had been derided, and called J. Brute Ismay. He was accused of having gone over the captain's head and interfered with the navigation of the ship, and, above all, of having escaped with his life while others died. He said in reply that he had helped to load passengers into the boats and had himself taken a place in one only when, at that moment, there were no other passengers about. Counsel for the dockworkers' union cross-examined him in so hostile a manner that Lord Mersey intervened to ask counsel whether he was saying that it had been Ismay's duty, as managing director, to remain on the ship until she went to the bottom. Counsel replied, 'Frankly, that is so, and I do not flinch from it.' Counsel for White Star replied that there was not the slightest ground for suggesting that another life would have been saved if Ismay had not got into the boat.

Was it Ismay's duty to have remained? He had violated no point of honour, and if he had committed suicide by remaining, and thrown his life away, it would have been said that he had done it because he dared not face the inevitable inquiry into the sinking. Lord Mersey concurred: 'The attack upon Mr Ismay resolved itself,' he said, 'into a suggestion that some moral duty was imposed upon him to wait on board until the vessel foundered. I do not agree. Mr Ismay, after rendering assistance to many passengers, found 'C' collapsible, the last boat on the starboard side, actually being lowered. No other people were there at the time. There was room for him and he jumped in. Had he not jumped in, he would merely have added one more life, namely his own, to the number of those lost.' Mersey also half-exonerated Sir Cosmo Duff Gordon, who with his wife got himself into the boat which only carried twelve passengers. One of the crew wanted to go back to pick up survivors, but Lady Duff Gordon objected and Sir Duff took her part. The boat did not return to try to save others, and Sir Cosmo later gave each of the crew members in it five pounds. Mersey said, 'The very gross charge against Sir Cosmo Duff Gordon that, having got into No. 1 boat, he bribed the men in it to row away from drowning people, is unfounded . . . At the same time I think that if he had encouraged the men to return they would probably have made some effort to do so and could have saved some lives.'

Then there was the matter of the ship lying close by the *Titanic*, perhaps five or ten miles off. Lord Mersey established to his own satisfaction that she was the Leyland liner *Californian*, and her commander, Captain Lord, was censured by the court. Lord himself always denied it was his ship which was seen that close. He calculated that he had been lying stopped in an icefield seventeen to nineteen miles from the *Titanic*, that he had seen rockets but did not know they were distress signals, and had not received her SOS because her wireless was closed down for the night. But the stigma of Lord Mersey's judgment remained with him for the rest of his life.

As to the sinking of the *Titanic* herself, the

court's findings were brief: 'The loss of the said ship was due to collision with an iceberg, brought about by the excessive speed at which the ship was being navigated.' That was plainly it. There had been a lot of bad luck. Ice was unusually far south that year. If it had not been pitch dark, the look-out might have seen the iceberg itself in time. If the sea had not been so calm, they might still have spotted the iceberg by the white water breaking at its foot. But all this said, it was the *Titanic*'s speed which did it. Yet Captain Smith had done nothing unusual in running full speed through a region where there might have been icebergs. Liner captains had done this as a matter of course for years. Icebergs inhabited parts of that sea, but Smith was being no more reckless than a thousand careful captains before him, who had taken the familiar but tiny risk, and pushed on. The insurance companies for years had accepted a liner's chance of striking an iceberg as one in a million. But immediately the *Titanic* struck, what had been ordinary then became reckless. The cries of human self-condemnation were very great. Man had exceeded himself and presumed too much. The *Titanic* had been too big, too fast, and too presumptuous, and a merciful God had taken the opportunity to demonstrate, as it was put in one piece of sacred doggerel published on the occasion, that Christ was the only unsinkable ship who could ne'er run adrift and no icebergs or storms could assail. There was quite a lot of such stuff. In Washington DC, a Presbyterian minister, the Rev. Wallace Radcliffe, preached a sermon asking why God had permitted the disaster, and supplied the answer that when God made a law he stood by it. God had loved Paul but had not stopped the headsman's axe. He loved the martyrs but had not quenched the flames. 'Most reverently be it said, if the incarnate Jesus had been on that sinking ship, He [Jesus] would have gone down with the rest . . . He [God] would not divert an iceberg one hairsbreadth from its reproof to human folly else more and wider disaster might follow.' Mr Radcliffe was being illogical. Having in his first paragraph quoted Matthew 14:25 about Jesus always walking on the sea, he

[84]

failed to see that, the *Titanic* having foundered, that is what the passenger Jesus might have done, and saved Himself. But the idea of a 'reproof to human folly' was general. *The Times* of London, in a leading article, wanted to know if competition in mere magnitude had not gone far enough. Was it not time to call a halt? The lavish and unbridled luxury, the wild indulgence in what was the very superfluity of luxury, were these things that could of themselves be contemplated with satisfaction? (Premonitions were afterwards remembered, all adding some colour to the pervading idea that all this had been God-devised, and that the premonitions were a warning, as it were, to desist in time.) Even Captain Smith was said to have been depressed, weeks before he ever saw her bridge, at the prospect of commanding the *Titanic* and to have felt that naval architecture had gone mad in its efforts for bulk, luxury, and speed. But then Captain Smith was the subject of many stories. He was said to have remained throughout on his bridge: and if that were true he would, since the *Titanic* sank by the head, have drowned some time before his ship in fact foundered. He was said to have shot himself. He was said to have stayed on board until the very end, and to have shouted his last order through a megaphone, in these words, 'Be British.' This was widely reported, and made much of, and there were equally those who discounted such a report as altogether too melodramatic and unlikely; but there was very little about the *Titanic*'s last hours that was likely. Captain Smith was also reported to have gone down with his ship but risen again and swum alongside a lifeboat, but then, seeing there was no room for him, to have said, 'God bless you,' and gone off into the dark. There were also reports that, before thus sacrificing himself, he had handed into the lifeboat a baby he had saved from the sea.

W. T. Stead was another who died but whose premonitions survived him. There were two of his. The first was not so much a premonition as a nightmare which he had on board the *Titanic* and which he related to his companions at table. He had dreamed about someone persistently throwing cats out of a top-storey window. The second was more real. It had come to him nineteen years before. He had at the time been unconscious of it as a premonition at all, though after his death it was much noticed. In the Christmas number of the magazine *Review of Reviews* for 1894 he had published a story called 'From the Old World to the New'. The story was set on another White Star liner, the *Majestic*, which was then commanded by the same Captain Smith who died on the *Titanic*. In the story the *Majestic* sailed into an icefloe. Every now and again an iceberg would capsize. On one iceberg a party of castaways were discovered, having made their presence known by telepathy. One sentence in the story reads, 'The ocean bed beneath the run of the liners is strewn with the whitening bones of thousands who have taken their passages as we have done, but who never saw their destination.'

The *Titanic* was the most resounding tragedy of the years before the First World War. Philip Gibbs, a writer for the London *Graphic*, after going through the usual stuff about human science almost seeming to defy God in such a ship, and how the passengers had gone to sea as they might enter a king's palace, forgetful of death, then said that those passengers had *not* been extraordinary people. Few men could go smiling to death, and there were many cowards aboard, but in the crisis these cowards hid their fears and rose above their weakness, and 'played the game according to their blood and breed'. Many did. It was noticed that many men had died very gallantly, and that many of these had been Americans. Insofar as what Mr Gibbs wrote was true, it was a moving thing that men had died like that: and even if not wholly true, it is moving that Mr Gibbs should possess, as the tone of his piece shows he did, the confident expectation that many had conducted themselves 'according to their blood and breed'.

It was true that Miss Sylvia Pankhurst, the suffragette, was reported to have said that men deserved no credit for giving up the boats to the women because that was the rule of the sea, but this drew from G. K. Chesterton the following reply: 'Whether this was a graceful thing for a gay spinster to say to 800 widows in the very hour of doom is not worth inquiry. Like cannibalism, it is a matter of taste.'

When the *Titanic* sank, Theodore Dreiser, a great American novelist, was at sea, crossing the Atlantic on his return to America from Europe. He was on the *Kroonland*, a much smaller liner, having sailed on her, rather than the *Titanic* which he could have taken, in order to save money on the fare. When the *Kroonland* received the news over her wireless, Dreiser and his companions went to the rail and looked out into the black, and then he went to his cabin 'thinking of the pains and terrors of those doomed two thousand, a great rage in my heart against the fortuity of life'.

After the *Titanic* sank, Thomas Hardy, a great novelist and a great poet, wrote this:

THE CONVERGENCE OF THE TWAIN

(Lines on the loss of the *Titanic*)

I

In a solitude of the sea
Deep from human vanity,
And the Pride of Life that planned her, stilly
    couches she.

II

Steel chambers, late the pyres
Of her salamandrine fires,
Cold currents thrid, and turn to rhythmic tidal
    lyres.

III

Over the mirrors meant
To glass the opulent
The sea-worm crawls — grotesque, slimed, dumb,
    indifferent.

IV

Jewels in joy designed
To ravish the sensuous mind
Lie lightless, all their sparkles bleared and black
    and blind.

V

Dim moon-eyed fishes near
Gaze at the gilded gear
And query: 'What does this vaingloriousness down
    here?'

VI

Well: while was fashioning
This creature of cleaving wing,
The Immanent Will that stirs and urges
        everything

VII

Prepared a sinister mate
For her — so gaily great —
A Shape of Ice, for the time far and dissociate.

VIII

And as the smart ship grew
In stature, grace, and hue,
In shadowy silent distance grew the Iceberg too.

IX

Alien they seemed to be:
No mortal eye could see
The intimate welding of their later history,

X

Or sign that they were bent
By paths coincident
On being anon twin halves of one august event.

XI

Till the Spinner of the Years
Said 'Now!' And each one hears,
And consummation comes, and jars two
        hemispheres.

And Lawrence Beesley, who had heard the
cries of the dying, said, 'Whoever reads the
accounts of the cries that came to us afloat on
the sea from those sinking in the ice-cold
water must remember that they were addressed
to him just as much as to those who heard them.'

Over the years the *Titanic* legend grew. In 1913,
Captain Remnant of the British steamship
Luciline thought he might have seen part of her
hull standing on end in the Atlantic off the
Grand Banks of Newfoundland. At any rate, he
saw what appeared in the half-light to be the
hull of a liner, covered with marine growth,
and reported this when he reached Philadelphia. He said the wreck had the appearance
of being held down by anchors and held up by
watertight compartments, and was perhaps

standing on the ledge of an underwater rock.

In 1935 another of the strangest things
happened. William Reeves was one of the crew
of a tramp steamer which left the Tyne in
April with a cargo of coal bound for Canada.
She was nearing the other side of the Atlantic
when she ran into a calm sea on a pitch black
night. Reeves took his turn as look-out. He
began to be afraid. He knew their position was
exactly that of the *Titanic* when she foundered.
He also remembered Morgan Robertson's story
of the *Titan*. He reflected that his own ship was
called the *Titanian*. He felt sure that she was in
danger and that he could save her by ringing
the alarm bell, but he hesitated, deep in worry.
Then he remembered that he was born on the
day in 1912 that the *Titanic* sank, and he hesitated no more, and sang out, 'Danger ahead.'
The *Titanian* stopped just in time. A huge iceberg towered in the darkness ahead, and the
ship was enveloped in the wilderness of an icefield. Icebreakers from St John's, Newfoundland,
had to come and rescue her.

The *Titanic* was always news. As the survivors died over the years, their obituaries were
made the occasion for a partial retelling of the
story. When Lady Duff Gordon died in 1935,
her obituary disclosed that she had been the
sister of the novelist Elinor Glyn. Under the
name of Lucile she had become one of the
world's most famous couturiers. She had
always said that her husband's life had been
ruined by the charges of bribery, which had
broken his heart. In 1939 the Rev. Charles
Richard Vallance Cook, who had been saved
from the *Titanic* as a boy of fourteen, killed himself a week after announcing his own marriage
banns. He believed himself to be haunted. In
1953 Commander Lightoller died, the man who
as second officer had done so much to save
the women but had steadfastly refused the men,
and who had himself been rescued from the
water after the *Titanic* foundered. In 1940 he
was one of the many old sailors who helped
to save the British army from Dunkirk in a
fleet of little boats. In 1958 Mrs Russell-Cooke
the daughter of Captain Smith, who was five
when her father went down with his ship, was

herself in the news. Her husband had shot himself. Shortly before that her mother had been killed by a bus. Mrs Russell-Cooke had married a stockbroker in 1925 and they had twin boys but one died of polio and the other was killed in the war.

J. Bruce Ismay died in 1937 at the age of seventy-four, having retired from public life soon after the disaster, but his wife lived to be ninety-six, dying only in 1963. Up to a year before her death, Ayrton and Alderson Smith, solicitors of Liverpool, were writing to the Press Association in London saying that certain newspaper articles had appeared which were in their view offensive to the memory of Mr Ismay and had caused distress to Mrs Ismay, and asking that future articles should be referred to them first. The Press Association replied politely but declined to do this. In 1964 George Rowe, the *Titanic*'s quartermaster, was remembering vividly in a newspaper article how he had been one of the few men to see the iceberg that sank her. He said a shiver went through the vessel as she struck. 'It became icy cold and my breath froze in the air. Then I saw the iceberg and I shall never forget it. At first I thought we'd hit a windjammer, as I caught a glimpse of something sliding past the ship on the starboard side.' In the light from a thousand portholes the ice looked like wet canvas. It was just a few feet away and he could have touched it. This is more circumstantial than any description at the time of the disaster, and Rowe's mention of the windjammer is a curious echo of the running down of the sailing ship in *Futility*. Perhaps he had read that book. The next year, 1965, Frederick Fleet, the look-out who had been the very first to see the iceberg, hanged himself at his home in Southampton.

At least four films have been made about the catastrophe. The first, called *Atlantic*, was made in England in the 1920s, and starred Madeleine Carroll and Adolphe Menjou. The second was a German propaganda film, *Titanic*, made in 1943 on the orders of Goebbels, who wanted it to portray Englishmen as cowards. It never served its purpose in Germany because by the time it was finished the allied bombing of German cities was so heavy that it was thought unwise to show scenes of panic and death to people already living on their nerves. But it was shown in Stockholm in 1944, and after the war in East Germany. Colonel J. J. Astor was shown engaging in an underhand deal with Ismay, who was having an affair with a Baltic woman passenger. At the moment of sinking, stewards were shown shooting German steerage passengers. Everything was represented to be the fault of English and American financiers who ordered the captain to go full speed ahead through icebergs to win the blue riband and thus send up the value of White Star shares. In 1953 Hollywood made its own *Titanic*, but the disaster was used mainly as a background to the main story, which was the disintegrating marriage of a couple played by Barbara Stanwyck and Clifton Webb. Far and away the best-known film is *A Night to Remember*, made in England in 1958, with Kenneth More playing Lightoller. It is a very circumstantial version of the *Titanic* story, but hard on Captain Lord of the *Californian*, who is shown negligently lying a few miles off and taking no notice of the *Titanic* distress rockets.

Captain Lord was by then near the end of his life, and had never stopped trying to clear himself. After his death in 1962 the Mercantile Marine Service Association twice petitioned the British government to reopen the inquiry to give them an opportunity to clear Lord's memory, but these requests were refused, even though evidence had come up which, had it been heard at the original inquiry, would almost certainly have exonerated Lord. First there was the matter of rockets generally. It had not been established at the inquiry that shipping lines often identified themselves to passing ships by firing rockets, and that the mother ships of fishing flotillas often used rockets to recall their rowing boats. The *Titanic* when she sank was near fishing grounds. So the mere fact of Lord's having seen rockets did not mean that he had ignored distress signals. But a much more important piece of evidence had emerged.

[87]

In April 1912 Henrik Naess was first officer of the Norwegian sealer *Samson*, 506 tons, which, with eight small boats, had been illegally working the Newfoundland icefloes. When Naess reached Iceland after this voyage, he heard for the first time about the *Titanic*, and went to the Norwegian consul saying that on the night of 14 April he had seen 'big stars' and lanterns and lots of lights which suddenly went out. Because the *Samson* was sealing illegally, and had thought the lights were from United States naval vessels, she had made off. She had no radio and so could not have heard any sos signals. 'If we had known,' he said, 'what might not we have done?' Why this took so long to come out is not known, but by the time the Mercantile Marine Service Association was petitioning the government to reopen the inquiry not only was Captain

The *Titanic* continues to be an image of disaster. In this cartoon from the *Honolulu Post* of December 1973, President Nixon, coming ever closer to the threat of impeachment for his part in the Watergate affair, is seen as the captain of the *Titanic* vainly throwing overboard first of all his principal advisers (Haldeman and Ehrlichman), then the tapes of his White House conversations, and then the financial details which he had omitted from his tax returns

[88]

Lord dead, but so was the Norwegian Henrik Naess.

Throughout the years, the *Titanic* has remained a symbol of disaster. When South Vietnam fell to the Communists in the spring of 1975 *The Times* of London said in a leading article that Saigon was sinking like the *Titanic*. When, at about the same time, General Motors was in a bad way and stocks of unsold new cars were piling up, a joke went the rounds in Detroit which asked, 'What is the difference between General Motors and the *Titanic*?' to which the answer was that on the *Titanic* at least they had a band. When in the Autumn election of 1974 Harold Wilson, leader of the Labour Party, was busy making it known that there was not going to be any economic crisis, at least not a big one, the London *Daily Telegraph* said he was a man, who, if he had been captain of the *Titanic* when she struck, would have assured the passengers that she had only stopped to take on ice.

And throughout the years that the *Titanic* has lain on the bottom of the Atlantic, three miles down, there have been those who have speculated about salvaging her. White Star considered it themselves, but gave up as she was far too deep down. The latest speculator is Douglas Woolley who in 1966, when he was aged thirty and working as a dye-machine operator in a stocking factory in Hertfordshire, registered the Titanic Salvage Co. He asserted that he owned the *Titanic*, and that Cunard, who would have inherited her along with White Star's other assets at the merger of the two shipping companies in 1934, no longer had any interest in her. The insurers, who had paid out £4 million after she sank, had no interest in her either. Mr Woolley *was* interested because of the £80 million of bullion and jewellery he believed to be on board. Furthermore he considered the ship was likely to be in good condition even after all that time. She was on her maiden voyage and therefore newly painted, and at that depth there would be little oxygen to corrode her. He planned to raise her by means of a scheme devised by two Hungarians. From a bathysphere, they would

The arrival that never was – the *Titanic* entering New York harbour on 17 April 1912. It is called 'The First Crossing', and is one of many Titanic paintings by Mr Ken Marschall, a member of the Titanic Enthusiasts of America. His research into detail is minute, and the lower Manhattan skyline appears as it would at that date

'The *Titanic* as she did founder. Painting by Henry Reuterdahl from a description by Frederick M. Hoyt, a survivor'

The Pompeian swimming pool of the *Imperator*, probably the most splendid ever built aboard ship. Here it is seen, after the *Imperator* became the *Berengaria*, in a Cunard advertisement

Below: First class music room and the lounge of the *Mauretania*

attach hundreds of plastic bags to her hull, fill these bags with water, and pass electricity through this water to break it down into its constituent elements of hydrogen and oxygen. The *Titanic* would be buoyed up by the gases and rise to the surface. She would then be towed to Cape Race, exhibited in America, and return to Liverpool as a floating museum, the bullion having been first removed. It remained only to raise £2 million for the salvage work, and to find the wreck. Mr Woolley was unable to do either.

The Titanic Enthusiasts of America wish he had. There are 300 members of this organization, all devoted to the *Titanic*'s memory, and in 1972, on the sixtieth anniversary of her sinking, they commemorated her in various ways. They supplied a wreath of 'genuine multi-colored flowers', carnations, daffodils, irises, and laurel greens, which was laid on the sea at the point where she foundered by the U.S. Coastguard cutter *Evergreen*. Attached to the wreath were two laminated packets, one containing a picture postcard of the *Titanic*, and the other a list of the names of every T.E.A. member and also a passenger list of the *Titanic*. On land other members constructed a four-and-a-half-foot-long model of the *Titanic* and a papier-maché iceberg, and floated both on a pond. The idea was that the model, which was radio-controlled, should strike the iceberg and sink, and the makers hoped that the follies of technology would thus be made evident. They were. *Titanic II* on her pond ran into gusty winds and was unable to reach the iceberg. Since the waves then threatened to swamp her, the Enthusiasts had to scuttle her by blowing a hole in her side by remote control. At 6262 Del Rosa Drive, San Bernardino, California, other Enthusiasts gave a fun party. In the garden they placed two lifeboats, and painted the name *Titanic* on them. 'Boat drill scheduled to start at eight o'clock,' said the invitation. '1912 attire required.'

But the Enthusiasts do cherish the *Titanic*'s survivors, printing news of them in their quarterly magazine the *Titanic Commutator*, for instance recording the seventieth wedding anniversary, in 1972, of Mr and Mrs Arthur Lewis of Alma Road, Southampton. He was a steward on the liner, and in 1972 had eleven grandchildren, twenty-three great-grandchildren, and twelve great-great-grandchildren. And at their 1973 convention at the Sheraton motel at Greenwich, Connecticut, the Enthusiasts managed to bring together seven of the perhaps thirty still-living survivors. 'Remember the Titanic,' said the bumper stickers on the cars in the parking lot outside. It was a weird occasion but full of unmistakable love and devotion. The enthusiasts sat and even knelt at the feet of the aged survivors of the *Titanic* they had brought to Greenwich — 'these living, fine, historical people'.

At a banquet they ate the same menu served to first-class passengers on the night of the disaster. They handled with awe the holy relics of that night — a fragment of a lifeboat and the sea-stained ticket recovered from the body of a victim. They prayed. They invoked God and the angels. And when they departed, some of them carried with them souvenir *Titanic* mugs, specially manufactured, price $2.

Apart from their enthusiasm, the Enthusiasts *know* more about the ship than anyone else. When, on the first morning of the two-day convention, a few ancient newsreel clips were shown, the sort that were projected on the nickleodeon screens of 1912, it was immediately pointed out that they were mostly faked and that the ship appearing in them was not the *Titanic* but her almost identical sister ship *Olympic*. In Suite 321 of the motel the relics were displayed. The discharge book of Frederick Fleet the look-out. He signed on the *Titanic* on 10 April 1912, at Southampton. Port of destination: 'Intended New York'. Date and place of discharge: '15 April, 1912, at sea'. His pay stopped at sea, the moment she sank. There was a cork from a bottle of champagne drunk by Selena Cook, a survivor. There was a piece of *Titanic* carpet, a rich green, taken from her by a steward as a souvenir before she sailed. There was a mounted rivet-head together with a certificate of authenticity from Harland

and Wolff saying this was indeed a rivet from the gantry under which the *Titanic* was constructed. Relics of the only true carpet and the only true rivet, and touched as reverently as bits of the only true cross. Then there were lesser mementoes. *Titanic* books of matches, made in quantity for the Enthusiasts. A *Titanic* jig-saw puzzle, rare, and framed. A pottery whisky bottle in the shape of the *Titanic*, four funnels and all, containing four-fifths of a quart of Kentucky Straight Bourbon.

One group of Enthusiasts, discussing possible salvage, agreed that in that depth and coldness of water the bodies too would have been preserved. Others went through passenger lists, checking off the names of those who were at the Greenwich Sheraton that day. These were treated with such awe that they were hardly approached except with shy requests for autographs, but when they were asked they told their stories readily. Mrs Madeleine Mann, *née* Mellenger, of Toronto, was thirteen at the time and travelling in the second class with her mother who had previously worked as a lady's companion with the Rothschilds and was going to America to be manageress of a Colgate millionaire's mansion in Vermont. She still had a postcard posted by her mother at Southampton to a relative, just before the ship sailed. It said: 'Safe and sound. This is the boat.' After the crash, she did not remember hearing the band play 'Nearer, My God, to Thee' or anything else.

In lifeboat 14, when they were rowing away from the ship, they heard the moans of people in the water. The lifeboat wasn't full but the people in it were afraid of being swamped and said, 'Leave them alone. They're only singing.' But she knew they weren't singing. At New York, Mr Colgate's chauffeur met them. Mrs Colgate took her shopping the next day and brought her new clothes and the first lacy underwear she ever had.

Mrs Margaret O'Neill, *née* Devaney, aged 80 and living in New Jersey, was nineteen in 1912 and coming over from Ireland. Her lifeboat could not free itself from the side of the ship. She had a little knife, which her brother had given her as a going-away present. That night, as it happened, they had had fruit for dinner. She had used her knife to peel it, and still had it on her, and with it they cut the boat free from the davits. A sailor said she had saved their lives, and in New York gave her a fragment of the lifeboat. She brought this with her to the convention. Mrs Edwina MacKenzie, aged eighty-nine and living in California, was the liveliest of the survivors present. She was an English girl, from Bath. They put her in lifeboat 13. She had since married two husbands whose birthdays were on the 13th. At the motel her room was 213. She had made 13 crossings of the Atlantic. 'My maiden name was Troutt,' she said. 'How could I drown?'

Mrs Frances James, formerly of Wales and later of Connecticut, was seventeen in 1912. At the convention she was perhaps in the process of adding a footnote to the *Titanic* mythology. Early on the first afternoon, she said that when, some time after the *Titanic* wreck, she had to make another crossing, she did so in the *Lusitania* and was so scared that she kept to her cabin the whole five days. Later on in the convention, she was saying that during that passage in the *Lusitania* she had seen the hulk of the *Titanic* sticking out of the water. As for compensation, Mrs James said she recovered £12,000 in damages from the White Star company, though her lawyer kept £7,000 of this. Mr Frank Goldsmith from Strood, Kent, was nine at the time. All he and his mother got from White Star was $15 and two tickets to Chicago. When they were in the lifeboat, and could see the *Titanic* sinking, his mother took his head in her hands and forced it down on to her breast so that he should not see. Then some people shouted that it was going to float after all, so she let him look up. Then it did sink. 'In the water,' he said, 'people were crying and carrying on, as they would. It sounded almost like people cheering when a baseball player hits a home run and you're a mile away from the stadium.'

The banquet in the evening had given a little worry to the Titanic Enthusiasts. They did not want to offend, and had feared that the survivors might think it not tasteful to repeat the *Titanic*'s last menu. But the survivors said they did not mind. A memorial service was held, at the breakfast table, the next day. A clergyman, giving the invocation, demanded that the *Titanic*'s dead should be received by the angels. An eloquent Titanic Enthusiast spoke an elegy to passenger liners and mentioned that in the case of the *Titanic* perhaps God had intervened and sunk the ship to give a glimpse of his infinite goodness. 'Nearer, My God, to Thee' was then sung. Then a painting of the *Titanic* was raffled at $3 a ticket. This was the work of Mr Ken Marschall, who has practically been adopted as the official *Titanic* artist, and whose paintings are much in demand. This is not surprising. They are unmistakably the result of the same devotion to the *Titanic* which shines in the eyes of all the members. When Mr Ed Kamuda, editor of the very good *Titanic*

Commutator, was presented with a certificate of appreciation for his work, he was very moved and said the *Titanic* was his only hobby and he put everything he had got into it. But this devotion, apart from ensuring that the Titanic Enthusiasts really do know more than anyone else about the ship, also cannot help sustaining and to some degree enlarging the *Titanic* myth. Mr Marschall has painted the *Titanic* in every conceivable way. One of his pictures shows her cutting through a swell such as she never encountered, since for all four days of her first and only voyage she sailed through that flat calm which is implausible for the North Atlantic at any season. He has also done a painting — and this is pure surrealism — which shows the *Titanic* approaching the Statue of Liberty.

CHAPTER FOUR

How the Eagle
Lost Its Wings

In April 1912 the Christian world and the London *Graphic* may have been anxiously inquiring if it had not been almost a defiance of God to build so great a ship as the *Titanic*, and an act inviting divine retribution; but within a month the Germans were preparing to launch an even vaster ship, though with extra lifeboats put on at the last moment. On 25 May, the day the Kaiser launched this ship at Hamburg, naming her *Imperator* after himself, fashionable

audiences were still crowding the drill hall in London where the Titanic inquiry was being held. The *Imperator* was of 52,000 tons and 900 feet long. If the *Titanic* had survived she would have remained the world's largest liner for only a month. The *Imperator* was the first of three great liners to be built just before the war by the Hamburg-Amerika line to restore the German ascendancy lost to the new Cunard and White Star liners.

Imperator, Vaterland, and *Bismarck* were all launched within two years. Each was slightly larger than its predecessor. All were to have long lives, but the war was to make theirs the saddest story, and indeed to bring the ruin of the entire German merchant marine. At the *Imperator*'s launching a steel hawser snapped and only just missed the Kaiser.

In New York, Hamburg-Amerika ran a publicity campaign. They distributed huge oil paintings of the *Imperator* showing a British liner small and insignificant in the shadow of her bows, with the German captain standing on his lofty bridge flicking cigar ash on to the British deck. Hamburg-Amerika's American publicity man in those days was Mathew B. Claussen, and it was, said Jack Lawrence, shipping news reporter for the New York *Evening Mail*, a bitter day for Claussen when Cunard announced, at just this time, that their forthcoming *Aquitania*, though of lesser tonnage, would be the longer — 901 feet to the *Imperator*'s 900. After a week Claussen called a press

Kaiser Wilhelm II, left, at the launching at Hamburg on 25 May 1912 of the *Imperator*

The *Imperator*, 52,000 tons, and Hamburg–Amerika's previously largest liner, the *Kaiserin Auguste Victoria*, 24,600 tons. After the war Germany lost both ships. The *Imperator* became Cunard's *Berengaria* and the *Kaiserin Auguste Victoria* went to Canadian Pacific as the *Empress of Scotland*

conference to admit that he had made a mistake, and that he ought to have said the *Imperator* would be 917 feet. The difference, as the reporters were to discover, was accounted for by the sudden addition to the German ship of a huge bronze figurehead in the form of an eagle, which leaned forward over the bows, clutching in its gilt talons a globe of the world bearing the company motto 'Mein Feld ist die Welt'. This bird had an open beak and a crown on top of its head. Later, American reporters were invited to cross to Germany on the company's *Kaiserin Auguste Victoria*, spend three weeks in Europe at the company's expense, and then return on the *Imperator*'s maiden voyage. They were lavishly entertained. It must have been one of the first public relations binges of modern times. The *Imperator* could do 24 knots. Her interior was designed by the man who built the London and Paris Ritzes. Her passenger lists carried advertisements offering those who returned to Germany airship excursions by Zeppelins from Frankfurt to Baden Baden. She

came into New York harbour with her band playing 'The Watch on the Rhine', and listing badly. She always listed one way or the other, not because anything particular was wrong but just because she was top heavy. To help remedy this, nine feet was chopped off each of her three funnels and concrete poured into her bottom. One day she ran into a gale which tore both wings off her eagle, and the remains of the figurehead were then removed.

The second of the Hamburg–Amerika three was the *Vaterland*, of 54,000 tons, launched by Prince Ludwig of Bavaria, and the third the *Bismarck*, 56,000 tons, which remained the world's largest ship for nineteen years. She was to have been launched by Bismarck's grand daughter, but Miss Bismarck swung the bottle and missed, and the ceremony was properly completed by the Kaiser, standing by her side, who caught the bottle and aimed better. Few remembered that one of the Kaiser's first acts on coming to the imperial throne in 1888 had been to dismiss Bismarck as

[95]

Chancellor. The *Bismarck* was never finished before the war; of her two sister ships that were completed, it is a toss-up which was the more gloriously appointed. Probably the *Vaterland* had the more lavish original paintings, including one by Gerard de Lairesse, a seventeenth-century artist from Liège, depicting Pandora and her opened box. Pandora stands naked, but with a veil over her loins, and to her left, in proud and lustful stance, are two man-god creatures. This was given to the *Vaterland* by the Kaiser, who had it himself from the Tsar of Russia.

The virtual creator of these three ships was Albert Ballin, who was Hamburg–Amerika's managing director and impresario, and a friend of the mighty. He knew the Kaiser well. In London too, he was received by Edward VII at Marlborough House and Buckingham Palace. He was born in Hamburg of a Jewish family, and

Kaiser Wilhelm II and his friend Albert Ballin

in 1874, when he was seventeen, joined his father's agency which was engaged in shipping emigrants from Europe to America. In 1886, when he was twenty-nine, he joined Hamburg-Amerika whose managing director he became only three years later. In 1903, when J. P. Morgan had taken over White Star, and when only Cunard among the other British shipping lines was holding out, and feebly at that, Ballin negotiated with Morgan an agreement which was certainly no American takeover of Hamburg–Amerika, but something like a 'community of interest' agreement. This he showed to the Kaiser, pointing out that whereas the British companies were as good as absorbed, the German lines remained independent. The Kaiser and Ballin met in a hunting lodge, where the Emperor himself read aloud every clause of the agreement, concurred, and then bestowed upon Ballin the Order of the Red Eagle with Crown, second class. Ballin was himself a frequent transatlantic passenger, and was apt, after a crossing, to send memoranda to the purser saying the linen cupboards were too small, and so were the bathroom towels, that the stewards should wear white jackets, that toast should be served in warm napkins, and that celery glasses were needed. By 1908 he had also noted that Hamburg–Amerika badly needed new and much bigger steamers, and these he built. His enemies talked about *ballinismus*, by which they meant his ruthless pursuit of whatever he wanted. In 1914 Walter Freyer, a former president of the Hamburg ships officers' union, wrote a novel called *The Struggle for the Ocean*. It is about destruction and death, and ends with Britain and Germany on the verge of war because of the machinations of one Moritz Bebacher, a giant among German shipping magnates, a Napoleon of the Sea. Bebacher was taken to be Ballin.

By 1914 Ballin was being more than a giant among shipping magnates. He was also acting as the Kaiser's representative in negotiations with the British government. In July he slipped across the North Sea to tell Lord Haldane, a former Minister of War, that the German Foreign Office was getting apprehensive about the Anglo-Russian talks on the strengthening of the triple entente between England, France, and Russia, and to hint that such talks could have dangerous consequences. Later Ballin saw Winston Churchill, then First Lord of the Admiralty. 'Suppose,' said Ballin — and this is Churchill's account — 'suppose that Germany had to go to war with Russia and France, and suppose we defeated France but took nothing from her in Europe, not an inch of her territory, only some colonies to indemnify us. Would that make any difference to England's attitude? Suppose Germany gave a guarantee beforehand?' Churchill replied that England would judge events as they arose, and that it would be a mistake for Germany to assume that England would stay out. This was in July 1914. Ballin was not anti-British. He has frequently been to England, spoke English fluently, and admired her naval power, even if not the way she ran her mercantile marine. As late as the beginning of August he still hoped that in a European war England would maintain a friendly neutrality. Even when German troops crossed the Belgian frontier on 3 August he hoped for this neutrality, and was surprised when England declared war the next day.

And here, in the competing history of the British and German merchant marines, there is a strange sidelight. On 21 June, at the Kiel regatta, Ballin and the Kaiser reviewed the newly-launched *Bismarck*. On 28 June Ballin was on holiday when he received a telegram, saying that the Archduke Francis Ferdinand, heir-apparent of Austria, had been murdered at Sarajevo. This was one of the events that precipitated the war. He ordered flags to be flown at half mast on all Hamburg–Amerika ships. And as it happened, the assassins had been unwittingly helped by the Cunard line. In June 1914 Harry Grattidge was fourth officer on board the *Carpathia*, the same ship that had picked up the *Titanic* survivors. In 1914 she was doing the leisurely southern Atlantic crossing from New York to Madeira and sometimes the Azores, and then on to Gibraltar, Valona, Genoa, Naples, and finally Trieste and Fiume. One afternoon towards the end of that

June she was anchored at Trieste, taking on passengers for the last leg of the crossing. From the sun deck, Grattidge noticed five men in dirty trench coats who kept together in a tight group. That night they reached Fiume, and anchored until morning, when they would land their passengers. Late at night Grattidge was summoned to the captain's cabin. Outside it, huddled apathetically together, were the five men in trench coats. 'Look,' said the captain, 'outside are five fellows who have spent the last three hours badgering me to land them now, this minute. I've had about enough. Take them ashore, will you, and let's have done with it?' Grattidge got together a boat crew and took the men ashore. Above the creak of the rowlocks he could not even make out what language they were speaking. The boat beached, Grattidge put them ashore and said good night, but they did not reply. The last thing he remembered as he pulled away back to the ship was the five of them standing there still whispering excitedly among themselves 'as if they had found themselves in a predicament from which they could now see no way out'. A few days later, their photographs were in all the papers, and among them were Gabrinovitch and Prinzip. They were the assassins, and they were the men he had landed. Grattidge said later that he felt he had served as the blind instrument of fate.

When, much to Ballin's surprise, war was declared, the British navy dominated the Atlantic, and everywhere German merchant ships were running for home, or putting into neutral ports. One of these was the *Kronprinzessin Cecilie*, 19,400 tons, one of North German Lloyd's élite liners that before the coming of the *Lusitania* had shared the honour of being the fastest on the Atlantic. On the night of 31 July she was four days out of New York bound for Plymouth and Bremerhaven when she received a wireless message ordering her to put back to an American port to avoid French cruisers thought to be in her vicinity. She had on board $10 million in gold bullion, and another million in silver, and would have made a fine prize. At the time the message was received, the first-class passengers were dancing after dinner. The ship's band was playing the new Castle Walk and the Hesitation. The sea was getting up, and several couples, finding dancing too difficult, went on deck for some air. There they noticed that the moonlight, which had been flooding the starboard decks, was now shining on the port side.

In the smoking room, Captain Polack assembled the first-class male passengers — no woman and no persons from any but the first class — and told them what had happened. The moon was on the wrong side because he had already turned back. Electric lights were extinguished and replaced by a few oil lamps, all portholes were blackened with canvas, and the ship steamed full speed, 23 knots, through a dense fog. In the smoking room there was nervous laughter, and some applause. A few passengers swore at the captain. The members of a shooting party were particularly displeased, because they would now have difficulty in reaching Scotland in time for the opening of the grouse season. Also on board were three American congressmen and one State governor, a Utah copper-mine owner, and a few other rich men who wanted to continue towards Europe and decided that one way of achieving this would be to buy the ship. They made the captain a fair offer of $5 million for her, intending, if he accepted, to run up the Stars and Stripes and make for Plymouth after all. Captain Polack politely declined. The passengers asked to send wireless messages, but this request he declined too, saying it might give away the ship's position. The ladies became frightened at the speed with which the ship was being driven through fog, and one was restrained from jumping overboard. Captain Polack then made his only concession, which was to blow his ship's horn occasionally. He assured everyone that there was little danger because he was not in a much-used shipping lane. Colonel G. F. B. Cobbett, an Englishman, made clear to all aboard his disappointment at being unable to rejoin the British army immediately, there and then. German officers on board smoked and laid bets on the American port they would eventually make. The captain

had black bands painted on the tops of the four funnels so as to make his ship resemble the *Olympic*, though whether she could ever have done so except at ten miles distance and in a fog is difficult to say, since she was half the *Olympic*'s size and had her funnels arranged, like those of all the German four-stackers, in two pairs of two, and not equally spaced like the British liners. She had not the fuel to make New York, and arrived one morning at the holiday resort of Bar Harbor, Maine. The U.S. Coastguard took off the gold and silver. A firm of bankers sued North German Lloyd for failing to deliver the bullion, and a U.S. Federal Marshal duly seized the ship. She was later escorted to Boston and there interned, just as other German liners had been interned at Norfolk, Virginia, and as Ballin's *Vaterland* was at New York. The *Imperator* was safe in Germany. So was the *Bismarck*, which had not yet been fitted out. Ballin could not have known that none of his three great liners would ever again sail under the German flag. If this was assured by one event more than by any other, that event was the sinking of the *Lusitania*, because as much as anything else that brought the United States into the war.

Now Ballin had advocated the use of U-boats, and he said at the time of the sinking: 'There is at least one good thing about the *Lusitania* — up to now the hides of the English had not been scratched and our U-boat campaign was beginning to become a little comical . . .' And later: 'Whether it was right to torpedo a *Lusitania* with 1,600 passengers, most of them neutrals, is a question which I will leave aside for the moment. But every intelligent man must admit that our entire U-boat action has contributed to reducing the arrogance of the English . . . In the next war — which we will certainly not be spared — we will obtain with two hundred submarines that which strange visionaries already forsee: we will bring England to its knees and destroy its world power.'

It now seems astonishing that in time of war the *Lusitania* was there at all to be torpedoed, but she was. She and the *Mauretania* had been built with the express idea that they should be convertible in wartime to armed cruisers. This was an archaic idea. The very first Cunarders had been so conceived. The Collins liners of the 1850s had been provided with an American government subsidy on the same understanding. Of course, by the time *Lusitania* and *Mauretania* were being planned, the armed cruiser idea may have been nothing but a pretext to allow the government to subsidize their building, but convertible to cruisers they were supposed to be, and to this end they were much more elaborately subdivided into watertight compartments than the *Titanic* had been, and moreover the coal carried in bunkers along their sides was supposed to give additional protection against enemy shells.

In fact it was mostly the Germans, because of their much smaller navy, who commissioned merchant cruisers. The *Kaiser Wilhelm der Grosse*, the famous liner which had been the first German ship to take the blue riband, was immediately fitted out as a commerce raider and sank two freighters but allowed two passenger ships to go. Then, on 26 August 1914, as she was coaling at Rio de Oro on the Spanish Sahara coast, she was found by a British cruiser and scuttled by her own crew. The only first-rate liner ever to succeed as an armed cruiser, which by then meant nothing more than a picker-off of small merchantmen, was the *Kronprinz Wilhelm*, which picked off twenty-six in eight months, mostly in the south Atlantic, and then limped to the neutral United States where she too was interned but was so badly shaken that she was broken up after the war. The old Cunarder *Campania* was converted to an aircraft carrier, and foundered after a collision with a British battleship. The *Carmania* did actually sink a German liner of the Hamburg-South America line, in the only fight between two such equals, but very few liners ever justified the 'armed cruiser' theory unless the performance of the *St Louis* and *St Paul* in the Spanish-American war of 1898 can be counted, but all they demonstrated was that any ship with a gun can outmaster a defenceless opponent.

But a ship like the *Mauretania* was much too

The *Mauretania* dazzle-painted as an armed cruiser during the First World War

big. At the outbreak of war the navy did commandeer her but rapidly found that she was next to useless because she consumed enormous quantities of coal. She could be only lightly armed and not armoured at all, and her only virtue was likely to be her great speed. The navy therefore left H M S *Mauretania* tied up at Liverpool, and left the *Lusitania* with Cunard, who continued to run a transatlantic service with her. She could outrun most warships, and was twice as fast as any U-boat that existed, but her one priceless asset, her speed, was reduced when Cunard decided to economize on coal and

[99]

run her on only three-quarters of her boilers. They did however, as a precaution, paint out the name *Lusitania* on her bows and stern. In this condition she sailed from New York on 1 May 1915 with 1,600 passengers, 1,198 of whom were going to die. Few prospective passengers had been alarmed enough to change to another ship by the German Embassy's advertisement in the New York newspapers warning them they travelled on the *Lusitania* at their own risk. Few thought that the *Lusitania* could be caught, and even fewer that the *Germans*, in their right senses, would sink a vessel carrying so many neutral, American, passengers.

The advertisement published by the German Embassy in New York papers on 23 April; the *Lusitania* sailed on 1 May

NOTICE!

.TRAVELLERS intending to embark on the Atlantic voyage are reminded that a state of war exists between Germany and her allies and Great Britain and her allies; that the zone of war includes the waters adjacent to the British Isles; that, in accordance with formal notice given by the Imperial German Government, vessels flying the flag of Great Britain, or of any of her allies, are liable to destruction in those waters and that travellers sailing in the war zone on ships of Great Britain or her allies do so at their own risk.

IMPERIAL GERMAN EMBASSY
WASHINGTON, D. C., APRIL 22, 1915.

At 3.10 on the afternoon of 7 May, off the Irish coast, in warm water, the *Lusitania* was sunk by one torpedo fired by the U-20, commanded by Kapitanleutnant Walther Schweiger, who was a witty officer and kind towards the men under his command. He had already sunk three freighters in a week. There is some controversy whether he really knew what he was sinking on 7 May.

At first he believed he had seen two steamers, one towing the other. But as his log makes clear, he fired his torpedo at a range of 700 yards under a blue sky at what he had by then realized to be one enormous four-funnelled ship. Only fourteen four-funnelled liners were ever built in the whole history of the north Atlantic. Some of these were German, but no German liner was going to be sailing along off the coast of Ireland. This left him with five British ships to choose from — *Olympic*, *Britannic*, *Aquitania*, *Mauretania*, or *Lusitania*. If he did not know exactly what ship she was, he knew the nature and magnitude of what he was doing.

He knew he was going to torpedo and probably sink a large liner, and quite likely drown many people, and he did torpedo her. But he was then amazed how rapidly she sank. Other vessels torpedoed by him had floated until he had finished them off with gunfire, but the *Lusitania* went with an almighty explosion and settled fast. The morality of torpedoing passenger ships without warning is one thing. But that aside, the fact is that the *Lusitania* sank so quickly not from the force of one torpedo but because she was ripped apart from inside by the contraband munitions she was carrying. One reason Cunard were still running her was that the British government wanted the company to because, with the connivance of both British and American governments, and helped by the laxity of the New York customs, she was carrying vast quantities of explosives which never appeared on her manifests. It seems now proved beyond doubt that the *Lusitania* was carrying, apart from 1,600 passengers, fifty-one tons of three inch shells, six million rounds of rifle ammunition, and, dressed up as parcels of cheese or furs, 3,813 forty-pound parcels of an explosive called pyroxylin. The suggestion that she was deliberately sacrificed to the Germans, and indeed was set up for them in order that American opinion should be outraged, is, on the other hand, far-fetched and far from proved. The Irish coroner's jury brought in a verdict of murder. Lord Mersey, who conducted the English inquiry into the disaster, as he had conducted that into the *Titanic*, said privately that it was a damned dirty business, and by that he meant that the truth had been concealed; but he almost certainly meant the truth about the contraband cargo, not that the Admiralty had infamously sacrificed her. He refused his judge's fee.

Seeing the *Lusitania* sink so quickly, knowing he could save very few of her passengers, fearing that a British warship might come up at any moment, and finding the scene too horrible to watch, the commander of the U-20 dived and sailed away. In Germany, the Kaiser declared a national holiday and commemorative medals were struck. In Cologne, braid for women's skirt bands was sold depicting the sinking: in England it was thought appalling that women should encircle themselves with such infamy. And yet, where is the truth here? Inquiries suggest that though a medal was struck, fewer than fifty copies were made in Germany, but that another 30,000 were made and distributed as propaganda by British Naval Intelligence. What credit, then, should be given to the skirt braid? It was indeed a dirty business all round.

What is plainly known is that on the Irish coast the *Lusitania*'s bodies were washed up. Among them was not that of her famous Purser McCubbin, who had been such a gift to the New York shipping reporters. On the *Lusitania*'s last call in New York he had produced not the usual two bottles of Scotch but four, and told the reporters that he was being obliged to retire because he had reached the regulation age and that the passage home would be his last. He was last seen in his cabin.

Cables flooded in from relatives in America demanding news of who had survived and who

The Lusitania medal, struck in Germany but mainly manufactured and distributed by British Intelligence as anti-German propaganda

died, and giving descriptions. Cunard kept a ledger. One entry says:

Anderson, George A. Mrs. 'New York cable. Wore wedding ring inscribed George to Margaret September 19, 1912. Diamond ring inscribed Whatever betide let love abide . . . Cable when recovered.'

There is an endorsement saying the body was found and sent to Tenby on the instructions of the relatives on 24 May.

Bodies drifted some way off. There is a telegram from the Ballyhaigue police to Queenstown police saying they had found a man about six feet tall with the flesh gone off his head, right leg complete, wore blue serge trousers over striped flannelette pyjamas, letter к worked with red wool on sock.

Cunard's Liverpool office cabled to Queenstown about the 'Docherty infant', and received the reply that as already stated there had been no unclaimed children or infants after the first day or two. Later William Thomas Docherty, infant, was found alive. Queenstown, explaining to Liverpool, said it was a pity they had already told New York he was dead, but had now immediately cabled saying he had survived. It appeared that Mrs Docherty, with

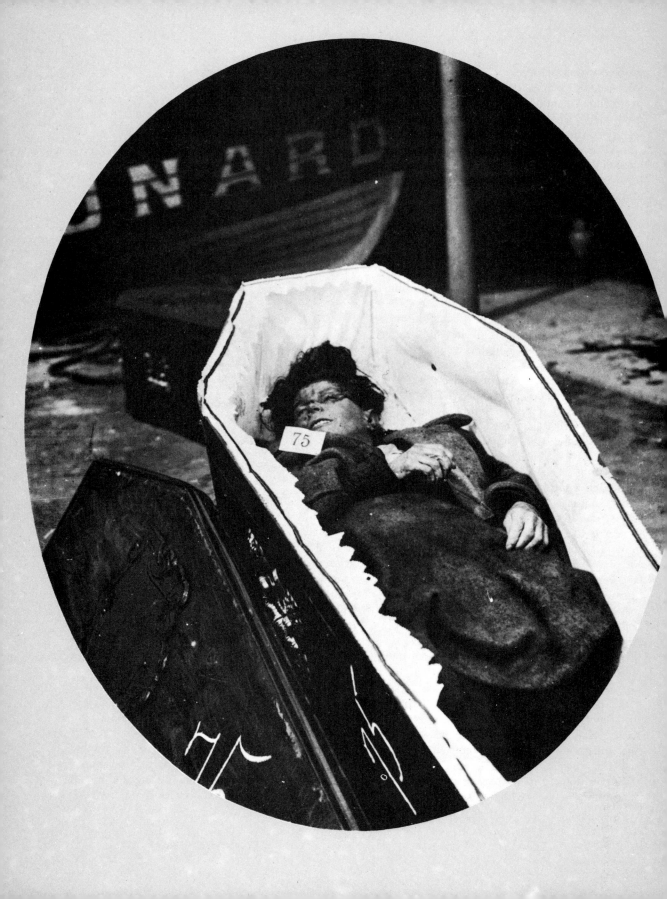

the child, had stayed at Maddox's Boarding Establishment for two or three days.

Cunard received many claims for help from the relatives of the victims. Mrs William Howard wrote from 24 Southampton Road, Kentish Town, London NW, and her claim, number 112, was entered as follows: 'Husband (3) lost; appeals for assistance'. Claim 114 was from Mr T. Hubbard of 73 Rosslyn Road, Tottenham, London, and is recorded thus: 'Ron F. Hubbard (2) lost. Father states son allowed him 30/- weekly'. The figures (3) and (2) in the company records indicate the class the victim had been travelling.

Cunard also photographed the bodies of the unidentified victims, and these photographs, taken by 'M. O'Keeffe, Photographer, Cycle and Antique Dealer, Queenstown', still exist in the Cunard archives in a cardboard box numbered LU/S 11. Here is also preserved, in a small envelope, a fragment of brown-and-white cloth, labelled, 'Pattern of trousers found on body No. 22'. Kapitanleutnant Schweiger was himself drowned two years later, in another U-boat.

After the *Lusitania*, Cunard suspended their Atlantic passenger services. The armed cruiser nonsense having also been suspended, British liners were then used for what they were best at, carrying troops or wounded. *Aquitania*, *Mauretania*, *Olympic*, and *Britannic* were all used in this way. The *Britannic* was lost. When war came she was not completed. She never worked as a passenger liner. As soon as she was completed, she sailed to the Mediterranean to bring home wounded from Gallipoli. She was unmistakably a hospital ship, painted white, as Mediterranean and Caribbean cruise ships were later to be painted, and bearing red crosses all over her. She was not sunk by a U-boat, but on her sixth voyage she struck a mine in the Aegean. It was God's luck that at the time she was on her way to Gallipoli and not on her way back home, and there were no wounded on board. There was a crew of 1,100, including many nurses and doctors, but only twenty-eight lost their lives. The last to leave was the captain, who stepped from his bridge into the calm sea. Another survivor was Violet Jessop, a nurse,

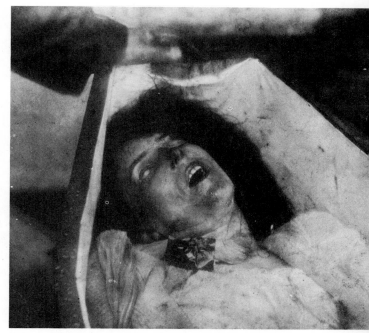

Left and above. Unidentified victims of the *Lusitania*, photographed by M. O'Keefe, Photographer, Cycle and Antique Dealer, Queenstown

who as a stewardess had four years before survived the foundering of the *Titanic*. The *Britannic* took an hour to sink, and with her, for good and all, went whatever was left of the idea of the unsinkable ship, or even of the ship that could stay afloat for any decent length of time after sustaining great damage. The *Titanic*'s watertight bulkheads had stood no chance of saving her. The *Lusitania*, which was partly built, after all, to withstand enemy attack, and equipped with watertight bulkheads running the length of her as well as across, had stood no chance either. And now the *Britannic*, which after the *Titanic* disaster had been fitted with what amounted to a double skin, had gone down fast too.

The *Olympic* and others continued in service, transporting troops to Mudros, which is a hundred or so miles from Gallipoli, which is in its turn about one hundred and fifty from Constantinople. It is a mystery now, as it was to many then, how the fall of the Asian city of

The *Britannic* at Mudros as a hospital ship, loading wounded from the Gallipoli campaign

Constantinople to the allies could in any way have helped to win a European war, but such was Winston Churchill's belief. Atlantic liners were suitable as transports because they were very big and very fast, and it happens that the passage from England to the eastern Mediterranean is almost exactly the same distance as that from England to New York. Atlantic liners had not, however, been constructed to carry passengers in hot climates. This was particularly hard on the wounded. Those who died on the passage were buried at sea. On the *Mauretania* the boatswain and the lamp-trimmer, old Cape Horners, sewed up the bodies in canvas with furnace bars at the feet to make them sink. They smoked and chewed tobacco as they sewed, and were discovered by an officer, who inquired if this was not disrespectful. 'Well, sir,' said the boatswain, 'it's

like this. We ain't disrespectful by no manner of means, but these here sojers might have died of some catching disease. You know yourself, sir, that tobacco smoke kills germs. What's more, if we pricks our fingers with the needle, a quid of chewed tobacco stops the bleeding, and also stops germs from getting in. So we hopes, Mister, as how you won't mind if we smokes and chews at this job what has to be done by somebody. And we knows, Mister, that the dead sojers won't mind if we smokes and chews while we sews 'em up. It will be the last kind thing that we can do for them.'

And in those Mediterranean temperatures, even passengers who were alive and fit discovered what Mediterranean cruise passengers were to discover afresh in the 1930s, that there were times when the deck was the only possible place to sleep. Unfortunately the liners

The *Olympic* at sea as a troop carrier

were packed more tightly by the British government than they later were by Cunard or American Express, and so there was not enough deck space to sleep on. The *Olympic* regularly carried 6,000 troops. Some of them had fun. On one voyage, large detachments of Southern Counties Yeomanry were aboard. Bertram Hayes, the *Olympic*'s captain, said he was not quite certain of the exact figures, but thought he had got the proportion fairly accurate when he said that if there were sixty-four Masters of Hounds in the whole of England, then on one crossing forty-two of them were on board, and they held a Hunt Dinner at which each Master sounded on the horn the call of his own hunt.

Of the three White Star liners, *Olympic*, *Titanic*, and *Britannic*, only the *Olympic* survived by 1916, and indeed she was the only one of the three ever to see New York. Even she was lucky. On one occasion she was attacked by a U-boat but rammed and sank it. On another she was hit by a torpedo, but it did not explode.

In 1917 the United States came into the war, and that ensured that for the next ten years the German marine had no future. All German ships in what had previously been neutral American ports were seized. The biggest prize of all was Ballin's *Vaterland*, which was refitted and officially renamed *Leviathan*, but called the *Levi Nathan* by the American troops she carried to Europe.

By late 1918 Germany was in chaos. On 3 November, German seamen mutinied at Kiel, on 5 November a Soldiers' and Workers' Council was established in Hamburg, and on 8 November this council took over the Hamburg—Amerika buildings. Ballin swallowed a handful of sleeping tablets, and on 9 November he was dead. His friends disagreed whether it was an accident or suicide, but Ballin himself had said he had no wish to survive to see the Hamburg–Amerika line destroyed, and Germany vanquished. The armistice was signed on 11 November. At the Cunard office in London the general manager said this was probably the greatest day in the history of the world, so they sang 'God Save the King' and 'Rule Britannia' and said the Ten Commandments, and then played some ragtime.

There then followed a severe peace. By the terms of the Treaty of Versailles, Germany was to lose all ships of more than 1,600 tons, and all ships whose keels had been laid down before the peace was signed. North German Lloyd, which had possessed 494 vessels in 1914, and had lost only five sunk in the war, then forfeited the rest to Italy, Portugal, China, Siam, Peru, Brazil, and the United States. Brazil, as the company bitterly remarked, contented herself with fourteen steamers. The United States took the largest and most beautiful, among them the *Kronprinzessin Cecilie* and *George Washington*. The last had been a German ship in spite of her name. The result was that North German Lloyd was left with no passenger steamers. The miserable remainder left to her consisted of tugs, launches, and lighters. Her largest vessel after Versailles was the *Gröss Gott*, a seaside resort steamer of 781 tons.

This, alas, was unjust, and not forgotten.

Hamburg–Amerika of course, lost her ships too, and since Ballin's three were the three largest ships in the world and the largest prizes of war, they were the most squabbled over. The Americans kept the *Vaterland*, now the *Leviathan*. She had been renamed by the Woodrow Wilsons. When she was seized, the U.S. Shipping Board invited Mrs Woodrow Wilson to rename her. She considered for weeks and then asked her husband the president who said, 'Leviathan, master of the deep. It's in the Bible.' Later President Harding, who took office in 1921, agreed to have the ship renamed after himself, but changed his mind just before the Teapot Dome scandal of oil, bribes, and

federal graft broke in the newspapers. She remained *Leviathan* for the rest of her unsuccessful life. She was probably the best of the Hamburg–Amerika three, but what with the way she was managed by the United States Lines, and what with prohibition, she never had a chance.

Both *Imperator* and *Bismarck* went to Great Britain, obviously in reparation for the sunken *Lusitania* and *Britannic*, though this was never openly stated. Cunard and White Star bought them jointly, but they were separately run, the *Imperator* going to Cunard and the *Bismarck* to White Star.

Cunard took the *Imperator* as she was, changing very little except to remove the number 13 from cabin doors. Ashtrays were still marked 'Zigarren'. Cunard held their annual dinner of 1920 on board her at Liverpool and then put her into service. There was dancing in the vast lounge every night from nine o'clock. The famous Pompeian swimming pool, modelled after one which was not at Pompeii but in the Royal Automobile Club in London, was open to both ladies and gentlemen, but at separate times. The *Imperator* listed as she always had done. In one storm, rats were observed to be leaving at least parts of the ship. In any heavy sea she rolled horribly. Cunard were very discreet about this. Here is an item from *The Cunard Daily Bulletin* published on board her at sea on 31 August, 1920.

THE IMPERATOR JOINS THE DANCE

Last evening's pretty dance in the lounge was a great success. There was an excellent attendance, and light-hearted men and daintily gowned women made a wonderful picture of gaiety as they two-stepped to the music so well provided by the ship's orchestra. The *Imperator* herself caught the spirit of the evening and indulged in a little affair of her own, but she did it with the same gentleness and grace as the happy throng in the lounge, and so no one seemed to mind her little burst of Atlantic merriment. She was still keeping it up at an early hour this morning.

What Cunard could do with her, they did. All the marble bathtubs were thrown out from

The magnificent *Imperator*, the world's largest, and, if you counted the eagle at her prow, the world's longest ship. From a Hamburg–Amerika advertising pamphlet of 1913. ▶

The White Star *Olympic*

The bedroom of the Empire Suite
of the *Olympic*, with beds in satin
brass and Silvex silver

[108]

the first-class cabins and replaced with metal tubs, to make her less top heavy. A ballast of pig iron was added to the concrete the Germans had poured into her bottom in prewar days for the same purpose. Her name was changed to *Berengaria*, in line with company policy of ending its ships' names in *-ia*, and she was in fact the first Cunarder to be named after a queen and not after a country or province, Berengaria having been the wife of Richard the Lion Heart. Until the *Queen Mary*, the *Berengaria* was flagship of the Cunard line.

The *Bismarck* had been launched before the war but never fitted out. After Versailles, she was surrounded by rumours. The first was that she might be the one ship the Germans would be allowed to keep. This was not so. The second, widely held among British naval officers, was that though she might leave Germany for Britain she would never get there, and would somehow be scuttled as the Germans scuttled their battle fleet at Scapa Flow. This did not happen. The third was that she had been awarded to the French, and the Germans at this news were determined never to let her go, but to finish her off somehow. This has the ring of truth; but she was awarded to the English, and in March 1922 White Star went to the Blohm and Voss yard at Hamburg to take her over. There they found that she was not completed. Many of her brass fittings had been stripped to make ammunition during the war. Work had, however, continued on her until the German cause had appeared hopeless, it having been intended that she should take the Kaiser and Crown Prince on a triumphal victory cruise round the world. The two big suites on C deck were the Kaiser and Crown Prince suites. After the war there was no cruise. She was taken on her sea trials by Captain Ruser, who had commanded German liners before the war but who, on completion of this last job, left the sea to become a partner in a firm of wine-merchants. Commodore Bertram Hayes who arrived to take possession of her for White Star was not welcome. He found the captain's cabin full of spare wash basins.

On 28 March she left Hamburg with the name *Bismarck* on her bows and across her stern, and her funnels painted in the Hamburg–Amerika colours, but with no flag flying. English sailors painted out *Bismarck* and painted in her English name of *Majestic*. Others painted the funnels in White Star colours. Commodore Hayes said he felt he had a good ship even if she was made in Germany, but he had to say he continued to look for the nigger in the wood-pile for many a long day, though he never found one. Hayes said: 'The principal people from Blohm and Voss's yard implored us, with halting voices and tears in their eyes, to do the best we could with the ship.' As she moved from her fitting-out berth, workmen from all over the yard came to watch her go, but not a sound came from them, or from the thousands who lined the banks of the Elbe, and the ship passed down in silence except for some young men in a launch under her stern, who sang a lament.

CHAPTER FIVE

'Deck—Ship—At Sea!'

Just after the war, the *Olympic* was approaching the American coast when a United States destroyer took station next to her and accompanied her. The captain wondered what dignitary he might have on board. Then the destroyer signalled asking if a certain lady was on the passenger list of the *Olympic*. He replied that she was. An exchange of messages followed, ending in a loving one from the young woman to the captain of the destroyer, which then followed the liner all the way up New York bay and anchored near her at quarantine. There the young officer bounded up the gangplank and the young woman, running towards him, took a flying leap into his arms from half-way down the last flight of stairs. It made columns in the New York papers. The United States Navy, after consideration, decided there was no call to reprimand the young officer. White Star were delighted with the publicity. It is strange that of all those columns in the New York papers I have been unable to find an inch, particularly since the anecdote so stuck in the memory of the *Olympic*'s captain that he related it in his memoirs, and it is he who said it made columns. Captains of White Star liners did not, surely, even to delight their publicity people, imagine such events, so it must have happened. It catches exactly the tone which the steamship companies liked to think of as the tone of their times, which were the Great Gatsby 1920s.

Here is a bit of another story. In the boudoir of her suite the senator's daughter awakes and opens her eyes. The draperies are pale blue, graciously appropriate for such as she. Slowly her soft arm stirs and, one soft finger having touched the bell, a white-capped stewardess enters immediately. Across the corridor, the princess awakes in a bower of rose and grey, and then, being European and not go-ahead American, turns over and decides to fall asleep again. This is company brochure fiction, even if it is French Line fiction, which was always the best. It may have tone, but it does not even sound real. The French Line could do much better than that when it turned its attention to realities. It is *true*, for instance, that when Mme Mathis, the wife of a car-manufacturer, mentioned one night at the captain's table that she liked music in her bath, the next morning she was, in her bath, serenaded for an hour by the ship's orchestra which had been assembled outside her state-room for that purpose by the captain of the *Ile de France*.

The best extravagances were always true. Some women did find themselves unable to travel with fewer than a hundred trunks, valises, and jewel-cases; and the Prince of Wales, though a little later, went several better than this by making the business of travelling with 135 pieces of luggage seem reticent and effortlessly British. A woman impresario, American of course, was one day being driven down Fifth Avenue when she remembered she should be in Paris buying a certain play, and so she picked up the speaking-

Publicity photograph of a night scene aboard the *Berengaria*, which Cunard entitled 'Hollywood afloat' ▶

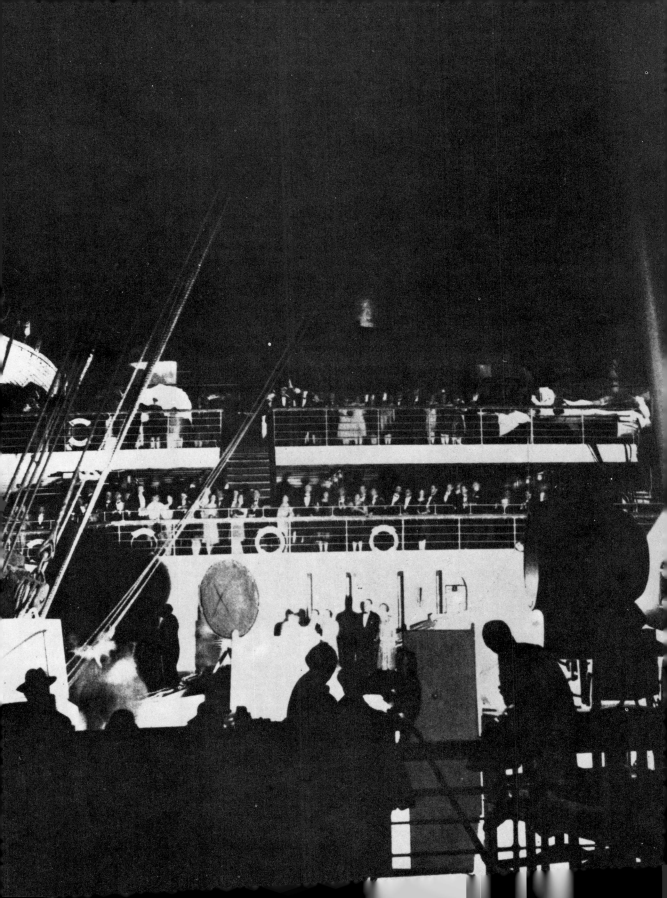

tube and asked, 'What boat's going today?' It was the *Olympic* and she took the royal suite. Another determined woman, Señora Zelmira Paz de Gainza really did habitually cross with ten maids, four cars, and a chamberlain. The baron of beef in the first-class dining-room of the *Majestic* one Christmas Day really did weigh 334 lb. Montagu Norman, governor of the Bank of England when the Bank of England was as steady as the Bank of England, insisted on travelling under his mother's maiden name of Collette because the markets would have gone wild with speculation had it been known he was travelling at all; but then he made himself noticed by playing the hardest, most relentless game of deck tennis the crew had ever seen. And as for card-sharpers, on the Atlantic they were the sharpest, and so said Edgar Wallace. There was even skulduggery. 'Confidential,' said the typewritten note handed to the captain of the Cunarder *Ascania*. 'See that passenger H. Dubois in room C61 is buried at sea. Important documents. On return trip you will be rich.' No Cunard captain was ever known to have got rich. They observed the rich. Captain Harry Grattidge described the *Berengaria* as the place where the rich were always with us. 'She was principally a gleaming and bejewelled ferryboat for the rich and titled – the Sultan of Johore, the Earl of Warwick, the Cortlanders, Vanderbilts, and Swopes.' The aura of money, he said, was as blatant and inescapable as a price tag. Everybody on board the *Berengaria* was socially prominent, even the dogs. One of the dogs was Rin-Tin-Tin, whose keeper had a first-class ticket but lived night and day with his dog on the third-class deck. On the *Aquitania*, Choonam Brilliantine, a chow bought in England for £2,000 by Mr Earl Hoover of Chicago, crossed the Atlantic in 1925 in a special kennel with raw eggs for lunch. The most celebrated animal passenger on board the *Aquitania* was a racehorse, and what is evident from the accounts of the crossing and the later events is the way famous animal and famous ship reflected glory on each other. Papyrus, the winner of the 1923 Derby, was taken over to America by Colonel Fitzgerald,

who ran Belmont Park racecourse, New York. A clause in the Merchant Shipping Act made it illegal to house cattle, horses, mules, donkeys, sheep, or goats over any accommodation occupied by passengers or crew, so a special stable had to be built midships. It was padded with air cushions to prevent Papyrus, who was worth his weight in gold, being injured by the movement of the ship, and the floor was corrugated with wooden battens to enable him to keep his feet when the ship rolled. Papyrus was accompanied by a vet, stable boys, and his own blacksmith. For encouragement, he was also given a travelling mate, another horse called Bar Gold, but while Papyrus was a good sailor, swaying round on his hoofs like an old salt, Bar Gold was seasick all the way. The nearest Papyrus came to a mishap was when he was being taken out at the New York pier. The passengers of the nearby *Caronia* cheered, at which Papyrus reared and nearly fell off the gangplank into the river. But he recovered his balance, and Papyrus and the *Aquitania* had safely arrived. At Belmont Park, for the race, the *Aquitania*'s band was specially asked out to play. For the captain of the *Aquitania*, Sir James Charles, a box was reserved. It was not Cunard's fault that Papyrus lost by six lengths. It was muddy. He was robbed.

But who were the passengers who crossed first class in these jewelled ferryboats? There were the celebrities, who were often just famous for being famous, but who, being famous, are well recorded. Then there were the very rich, who must be carefully distinguished from the ordinarily rich; and then there were those who were just on business.

'Very few celebrities are shy of reporters,' said Commodore Sir James Bisset, who in his time saw thousands. 'That is one reason they are celebrities.' There was Douglas Fairbanks, junior, becoming a celebrity very early by telling reporters at Liverpool in 1924, when he was only, by his own account, aged between fourteen and seventeen, that he had already made his first film and had his eye on the Olympic Games of 1928. He did not say in which events he had decided to represent the

[112]

United States. His parents, Douglas Fairbanks, senior, and Mary Pickford, were surely the most photographed of all Atlantic passengers. Then there was Jack Dempsey, world heavyweight champion, denying on board the *Aquitania* that he was engaged to one of the Dolly Sisters and cracking that this was a thing he dared not do because he could not tell one from the other. The Dolly Sisters gave the *Aquitania* two white Persian cats as a consolation prize. Bud Fisher did not mind marrying. He was the creator of the Mutt and Jeff cartoons, and possibly of the whole genre of coloured comic strips in newspapers. He met and courted Countess Adeita de Beaumont on one voyage, married her on a second, and separated from her on a third. They were married by Captain Herbert Hartley of the *Leviathan*. It was the ninth wedding Captain Hartley conducted, and the last, since the United States Lines decided they could do without the publicity which surrounded the marriage, and particularly without that which followed the rather messy separation.

It was never quite true to say that celebrities were two a penny. The steamship companies had need of them, and encouraged them. When five Princes of the Church from France, Hungary, Austria, Spain, and Italy arrived in New York via the *Aquitania* for a Eucharistic Congress they sent a telegram to Cunard saying, 'VISITING CARDINALS ALL EXPRESS EXTREME SATISFACTION . . .', and it would be a reasonable assumption that Cunard, though they would not of course have solicited such a message, might have encouraged it. Rivalry between Cunard and White Star was fierce, and both fed the newspapers with lists. In a sample week in October 1923, White Star carried Dame Nellie Melba, Dame Clara Butt, Rudolf Valentino's wife, Mr David Lloyd George, Pavlova, the organist of Notre Dame, Paris, 'Mrs Rosita Forbes, the famous traveller', and the Prince of Wales travelling as the Duke of Renfrew. He did not remain undetected, but, because he was spirited away by launch at the end of the crossing, he went through less of an ordeal than the Prince and Princess of Japan. When they disembarked they were met with

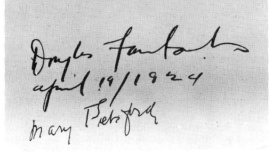

Douglas Fairbanks senior, and Mary Pickford, aboard a White Star liner, 1924

much bowing and respect by hissing Japanese wearing tall hats and frock coats, and also by Izzy Kaplan, photographer of the New York

[113]

Helen Wills, tennis champion, photographed as a celebrity on board an unidentified liner in the mid 1920s

Daily Mirror. 'Now,' said Izzy, 'stan' there, you! That's right. Now, prince, put your arm

around the li'l princess's waist, can't you . . . No – not like that, like this.'

A celebrity for a voyage could be created not even by a man's own fame, but by his connection with someone else's. Billy Leeds, the son of an American tin-plate magnate, who at the age of twenty-four was already famous for being a millionaire and a friend of the Prince of Wales, and also for having married Princess Xenia of Russia, conferred celebrity on Officer McIntyre, a traffic policeman on duty at the Cunard dock in New York, by taking a liking to him and sending him and his wife on a trip to Europe, first class. Even telegrams from celebrities had celebrity value. Katharine Hepburn once crossed to France for a month's holiday but returned after only five days. The London *Daily Mail* wirelessed asking if she would care to give the reasons for her sudden return. She wirelessed back, 'NO REASON AT ALL. REGARDS. HEPBURN,' and the *Mail* published it. A dead celebrity could have especial celebrity value. Edgar Wallace did when they brought his body home from Hollywood where he had been scripting *King Kong* at $3,000 a day. The *Berengaria*, carrying the coffin, steamed up Southampton water with her ensign at half-mast. Even unaccompanied luggage could be celebrated – like two suitcases sent freight on board the *Olympic* and addressed to Mr and Mrs Jim Mollinson, intrepid aviators, Plaza Hotel, New York. But the sad thing in going through these lists of the famous, is to discover how obscure by far the greater number of them have become, or perhaps always were. There is Miss Madge Bellamy, film star, waving a cheery good-bye; Mrs Corson, the first American mother to swim the English Channel; and Miss Leonore Ulrich, prominent star of stage and screen, taking the first bite from a sugar model of the *Aquitania*. The chefs of the principal liners made sugar-icing models to be thus bitten into and photographed. In August 1925 Cunard carried a celebrity called Bernard Johnson, whose name remained obscure but one of whose ideas did not. He was an American who claimed to have invented a death ray, and arrived in England to search Europe for the rare mineral bed which was needed to make his invention a commercial success. He also said that if one could split the atom the result would be such an explosion of energy that as little as half a pound of hydrogen and an atom-smashing machine could provide all the power needed for a single crossing of a liner. There was sufficient latent power in half a glass of water to run the *Mauretania* across the Atlantic.

So much for the celebrities. Then there were the very rich, who sometimes crossed two or three times a year, for the London season perhaps, or just because it was their custom to do so. They were, it went without saying, millionaires many times over. William Pfahl, in the 1920s a very old man, had emigrated to America with his parents when he was two, had served in his teens as a corporal in the Union Army, and said he was the last man alive who had heard Lincoln make his Gettysburg Address in 1863. He had become president of the Armstrong Cork Company. Charles Schwab, of Bethlehem Steel, was a frequent passenger on the *Olympic*. He once gave a lecture in the saloon saying he was taxed 92 per cent, at which even some of his first-class companions said they would like to try to live on the other eight. Mr E. H. Van Ingen celebrated his eighty-eighth birthday on board the *Olympic* and danced a jig in honour of it. He was known as the Commodore of the Atlantic. Once, back in the 1890s, he had failed to get the stateroom he wanted and so, in the great tradition of Vanderbilt and Morgan, had engaged rooms on the White Star liners *Germanic* and *Britannic* on the sailings nearest to 20 April and 20 October for the next ten years in advance.

Then there were the merely rich, in small part a riff-raff of émigrée princesses whose names looked good on a passenger list. One such princess, Russian inevitably, demanded to see the captain of the *Olympic* and informed him she would remain in her cabin throughout the voyage and not come to meals because she had had all the skin removed from her face and shoulders so that she might be more beautiful when the skin grew again. Also on board were the men who had done the operation. 'Charlatism

was written all over them,' said the captain. 'I wouldn't have trusted any one of them to shave a poodle.' But most of the rich were not skinned Russians but Americans who, having made their fortunes, wanted to see Europe. They may have been the merely rich, but they were the solid rich. They were the people who formed many of the 1,700 passengers of the *Majestic* when she sailed from New York in December 1923. Most of the first class went ashore at Cherbourg so as to arrive on the Riviera in time for Christmas. These were the customers White Star had in mind when they advertised that the daily life of an ocean voyage on board a super liner de-luxe went on in a social atmosphere reflecting in essence the polite manners of bright continental cities known to tourists, and the best among English and American clubs and houses. These were the people at whose daughters the following advertisement in a Cunarder's daily news-sheet was aimed:

The Ladies' League of 118 New Bond Street, W.1. introduces Titled and other Chaperons, and provides an Entree into the Highest Social Circles. Under Royal Patronage. Also Supplies Companions and Governesses.

Of all these solidly rich Americans, those that still most solidly exist are two created in the imagination of Sinclair Lewis and described in his novel *Dodsworth*. It is a novel, but it does not matter. They are now more living than the thousands of real rich Americans of that era, because those real rich are now very old or dead. The characters of the novel are Samuel Dodsworth and Fran Voelker, a girl whom he meets in 1903, a time he conceives to be the climax of civilization. 'Ah,' he thinks, 'if she desired Europe, he would master it, and give it to her on a platter of polished gold.' By 1908 they are married and have two children, and Dodsworth is manufacturing motor cars. By 1925 he is fifty and his wife is forty-one. He is a captain of industry, president of the Revelation Motor Company, and rich. He can at last give her Europe. She wants a year's holiday, and he wants to see over the Rolls Royce and Mercedes factories. They cross on the ss *Ultima*. Four hours out of New York he is walking round the ship reciting Kipling and muttering, 'Free!' to himself. It is a midwinter crossing. 'A sudden meaningless spatter of snow, out on that cold sea. How serene the lights in the music room. He began to feel the gallant security of the ship, his enduring home.' He explored the ship. She was the most impressive mechanism he had ever seen, more satisfying than a Rolls, which to him used to be the equivalent of a Velasquez. He wondered that in that ship, which was after all only a floating iron egg-shell, there could

A set of photographs, all taken on board the White Star *Majestic* by H. W. Scandlin and Bedford Lemere, who with their grainy pictures conveyed better than anyone else the lush life afloat that the steamship companies were selling. They are from a pamphlet, *c.* 1922, called *Majestic, the World's Largest Ship*. The company's captions read in part as follows, left to right;
'With dignity and proportions of a noble mansion'
'A grand piano of exceptional size and beauty'
'In the hours for women at the bath . . . the luxury of Imperial Rome lives again'
'Crusaders in chain mail flank the stone fireplace'

be a roseate music room, a smoking room with its Tudor fireplace — solid and terrestrial as a castle — and a swimming-pool where green-lighted water washed beneath Roman pillars. As he looked across the sweep of the gangways, past the ventilators like giant saxophones, past the lofty funnels serenely dribbling black woolly smoke, some never-realized desire for seafaring was satisfied in him. Standing outside the wireless-room he was pricked to imaginativeness by the crackle of messages springing across bleak air-roads to bright cities on distant plains. He thought, 'I'm at sea.' In his cabin, his wife stood in a litter of shaken-out frocks and the stores of conserves and fruit given them by

friends to help out the liner's scanty seven meals a day. He walked on deck with his wife, cumbersomely proud of her and of the glances which the other men snatched as they swung round the deck. Always before them were the long straight lines of the decking planks, rigid as bars of music, divided by seams of glistening tar. He thought, 'Deck — ship — at sea!' And what delightful companions they found. Lockert, English adventurer; a jolly Jewish millinery buyer from Denver, the cleverest man aboard; Lechintskey the pianist; the American military attaché at Constantinople; Sally O'Leary, satiny movie actress; Professor Deakins, the Assyriologist; a Norwegian aviator; and a

New York banker. At the captain's dinner, the last night out, the saloon was draped in scarlet, the stewards wore pink hunting coats, and the passengers were summoned to dine by a hunting horn. Champagne was free. At first Dodsworth was excited by the merriment everywhere, but then it seemed to him pitiful that all of them, and he himself, should so rarely range like this from their indignant assertion of the importance of their own little offices and homes and learnings, and let themselves rejoice in friendliness. He felt a little the *lacrimae rerum* of the whole world. He wanted to weep over the bedraggled small-town bride who for the moment forgot that she had not found honeymooning quite glorious, nor the sea so restful. He danced with the satiny film star: the steamer rolled, and they struggled to dance uphill.

The young female American rich, the sort the Ladies League of New Bond Street were looking

The cover of a White Star advertising pamphlet

to for customers, naturally hoped to meet the right man. White Star created a vacuous creature called Eve, and handed out a glossy pamphlet entitled 'Eve's Day', which is supposed to be the girl's diary for one Atlantic day. At 8 am she is awake and writing that the sheets are fine as cobwebs and the blankets warm as muffins. After a divine omelette for breakfast, she puts on silk stockings and a bewitching *crêpe de chine* frock, telephones daddy from mid ocean on the transatlantic phone, and by 11 o'clock is saying that everyone on deck is nice, especially one man. After a heavenly *à la carte* lunch, she goes to the pool and her new-found escort admires the green swimsuit she bought in the ship's shop and says she looks like Aphrodite. 'Memo,' writes Eve. 'Must look up Aphrodite in peerage and see who she is.' At 6.15 she has her hair done, and at 9 is at a dinner dance. 'My partner dances divinely! Who was it — Shakespeare or Darwin or somebody — who said: "What a piece of work is a man. How like an angel!" Well, it's true! He is! And the perfectly sprung floor, and the orchestra! Why, they just both make love to your toes.' After going on deck to look at the moon, Eve goes to bed, alone, to write the day's last lines in her diary: 'What a glorious night it was on deck. Wouldn't it make a perfect honeymoon trip?'

The passengers who crossed just on business were the most cherished by the steamship companies. They were not celebrities. They were not publicized. But they were money. They travelled often. The most cherished of all were the buyers, thousands of whom crossed from New York to Europe, to Germany and to England, but principally to France. About one-third of them were women looking for baby linen, dresses, millinery, fashions of any kind. Buyers made the trip perhaps twice a year, and of all the passengers, with the possible exception of Pfahl, Schwab, and Van Ingen, they were the most experienced and sophisticated. If you sat at a table with a man who was the dean of buyers, who had crossed 240 times, what would he be talking about? Of how he escaped from the *Titanic?* Of what adventure?

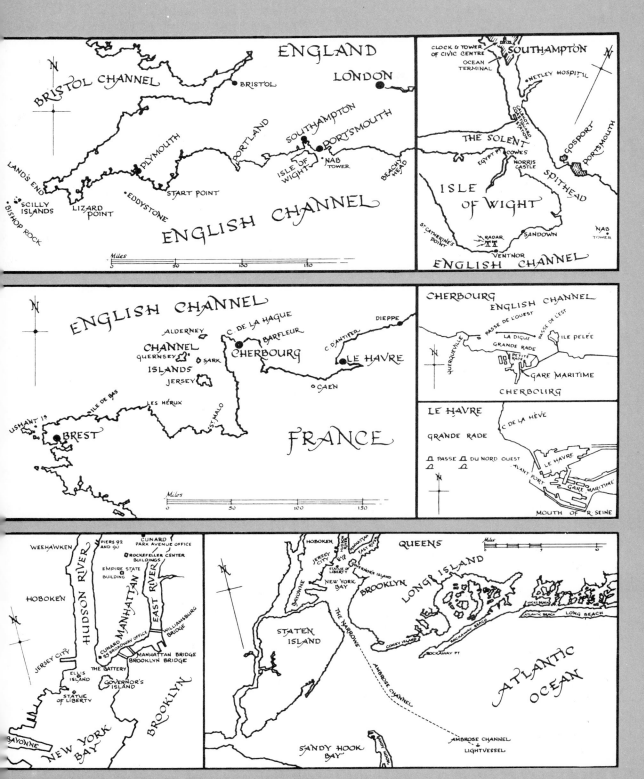

The approaches to Southampton, Cherbourg and New York

'They give you better caviar on the German liners,' he says.

Samuel Zucker, a buyer who made nearly one hundred round trips, was seasick on every one until his fiftieth, but was then never seasick again. Robert Lloyd, a silk-buyer, had travelled on every large liner running between France and America, and of all preferred the French Line's *De Grasse*. Charles C. Kurzman, of the dress-making house of Kurzman, preferred the *Leviathan*. Because they were the steadiest patrons, the buyers got the best cabins and best service. William Hargreaves, with 275, probably held the record for the greatest number of crossings. W. P. Willis, a wool-merchant, had 200. Few passengers approached the buyers in the number of crossings made. Miss Carolyn Cruikshank Timpson, aged eighty-five in 1934, had by then made 137 because she had promised her father she would not forget the old country. When in 1925 Mrs Thomas Winthrop of Boston crossed to Liverpool on the *Samaria* it was her seventy-fifth, the first having been in 1865 on the Cunard paddle steamer *Europa*. Most of these figures are likely to be more or less apocryphal, but those for two doctors employed by steamship lines will be more accurate. Dr A. W. Mackenzie of Cunard had made 650, and Dr Beamount of White Star 1,002.

There were other professionals than the buyers on board. There were the card-sharpers and the stowaways. As to the gamblers, Commodore Hayes said most of these gentlemen had the trade marks of their profession written all over their faces. But there was one who had the manners of a mild curate and dressed himself in a kind of clerical costume to assist in his business. For the first two days of the passage he played with the children on deck, and then, having made the acquaintance of their fathers, made a good haul in the last day or two. Another was a quiet little man who carried some such book as *The Life of Ibsen* under his arm, but could do anything with the dice. Most became known to the stewards and were greeted on board with, 'What name this time, sir?' On the *Berengaria*, a junior purser

[120]

would walk at intervals through the smoke room announcing, 'Ladies and gentlemen, we have reason to believe there are card-sharpers aboard,' but then the rest was left to fate. Captains of other ships were more active against evil. The master of the *Franconia* found in 1927 that a gang of card-sharpers had relieved one passenger of $2,400 and another of $600. He had the gamblers brought to his cabin, and gave them the option of being arrested and handed over to the police on arrival, or refunding the money. They refunded it. On the whole there was little a ship's captain could, or should do. The first, softening-up, games may have been conducted in the public rooms, but the real fleecing went on in smoke-filled private cabins. There was, besides, a sneaking regard for the gamblers' boldness. Charles Spedding, for many years purser of the *Aquitania*, said the most famous crook he ever knew made a fortune on board ship, but then retired and repented, and had always conducted himself like a gentleman. In any case, towards the end of his busy and prosperous career he became too well known to attempt to cheat, but many passengers would ask him to play just to say they had pitted their wits against his. Furthermore, said Spedding, 'I know two ex-British army officers who make a very good living at playing cards, chiefly bridge. They never cheat at all, relying entirely on their skill.'

There were also passengers who won, though more often on the pool than at cards. The pool was a gamble on the number of sea miles covered from noon one day to noon the next. The winner gave 10 per cent to the stewards. In April 1925 John McKeon, first-class passenger on the *Aquitania*, was described by the *New York Times* as a lucky bargee, a dilettante who drifted around with everything going his way, having on his last passage to New York won $2,000 on two pools and another $4,000 at baccarat, where the stakes were as high as $1,000 on the turn of a card. Two voyages previously, he had made $7,500 by winning three days' pools on the ship's run. This was more sporting than the conduct of Mrs Paul Dubonnet, who won by taking no risk at all,

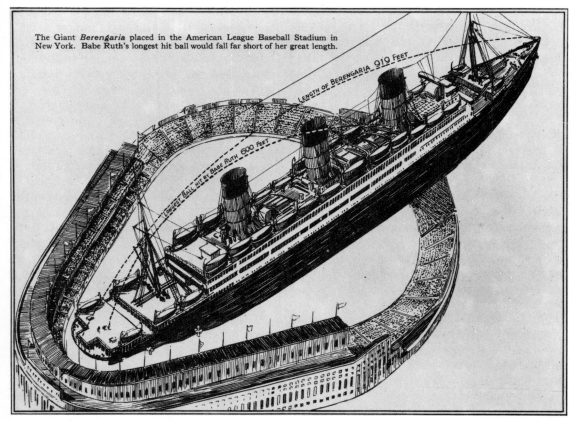

The Giant *Berengaria* placed in the American League Baseball Stadium in New York. Babe Ruth's longest hit ball would fall far short of her great length.

LENGTH OF BERENGARIA 919 FEET

LONGEST BALL HIT BY BABE RUTH 600 FEET

Babe Ruth no match for the *Berengaria*. An illustration, typical of many, from a Cunard pamphlet for the American market

by simply buying all the tickets in the pool. This would seem a way to win nothing except your stake money back, minus the stewards' 10 per cent, but she had previously placed a large bet that she would win the pool, and thus made her rather sharp profit. She was a woman who changed her gown every three hours.

Stowaways were not all that frequent, and were usually found in time to be evicted. That was all that could be done to stowaways who were then landed in America, because they could not be prosecuted under New York criminal law for stealing a ride. In English law it was a crime, and English or American stowaways landed in Britain usually got two weeks to a month in prison. At Southampton in 1926 two Americans, Albert Morris, aged twenty-one, and Thomas

McClarry, aged nineteen, were both given twenty-eight days. McClarry, after the first night out from New York, was found taking a dip in the swimming-pool at half past five in the morning, but got away with that by telling the steward he had been unable to get into his state-room the night before. He was successfully passing himself off as a first-class passenger when he had the ill fortune to be intruded upon, in the state-room in which he had installed himself, by Morris, another stowaway, with whom he had no connection. A world champion stowaway once boarded the *Aquitania* at Cherbourg, but rather let herself down by inhabiting the third-class decks. Stowaways of any style always travelled first. She was however selling postcards of herself at sixpence each, describing herself as world champion, and giving a list of ships stowed away on and punishments endured. She was taken to New York in the lock-up, and then all the way back to Southampton where she was sentenced to a month's hard labour. The smoothest stowaway was Harry Gerguson, who was probably born in New York in 1893 but preferred to be known as Prince Michael Romanoff. After one crossing the French Line kicked him off at New York, saying he had slept in a kennel. But he was not a Romanoff for nothing. On another crossing, having been seen with Andrew Mellon, U.S. Secretary of the Treasury, and taken for his friend, he was invited to the captain's table, the only stowaway known to have achieved this honour.

The greater efforts of purser and stewards were almost entirely directed towards the comfort of the first-class passengers. Dining stewards, deck-chair stewards, and bed-room stewards worked all hours, and the last were treated pretty well as personal servants. At the start of a voyage, said an American giving advice in 1927 to fellow democratic Americans, you should ring for the steward and tell him his programme for the voyage. 'You will find my dinner clothes in that valise. I shall require them pressed every night and laid out for me by eight pm.' And so on, down to the time for the bath to be prepared next morning, and the time for breakfast to be brought. Still, there was a chance for a steward, if he would use his contacts. Sydney Towlson, of the White Star *Homeric*, was given a film test at Elstree, was successful, and expected to be sent to Hollywood. If he was, he became one of the lesser-known celebrities.

The corps of stewards was ruled over by a purser. One of the best known pursers of the 1920s was Spedding of the *Aquitania*, the man who observed that, though British officers might win money at cards, they did not cheat. Spedding traced his ancestry back to that James Spedding who had been an officer on the *Mayflower*, and this made him at least the social equal of all his American passengers. He regarded Mayor Jimmy Walker of New York as a great friend. Now Spedding loved

bull-fighting, which he had seen once, at La Linea, near Gibraltar. One of these days, he said, he hoped to persuade his friend Walker to let him put on a week's real Spanish bull-fighting in New York, presumably with Walker financing the venture. The cheapest seats would be one hundred dollars, and at the end of the week Spedding said he would pack up, buy J. P. Morgan II's yacht, and sail for some beautiful island where life would be happy ever after. He had many friends. He remembered that on the *Mauretania* General French, First Earl of Ypres, used to come into his cabin every night, fight the Boer War over again, and have a whisky and soda before going to bed. Spedding loved his anecdotes of the great. He remembered that in the rush of Americans to get home from Europe in August 1914, young Mr Armour of the Chicago meat-packing firm, who had been on honeymoon and booked a return suite on the *Laconia*, gave up that suite to about a dozen American girls to sleep in. His bride retained a single bunk, and Mr Armour slept in the ship's hospital.

The captains of great liners were themselves great men, for a time; and one of them was Sir James Charles, master of the *Aquitania*. He was born in 1865 and at the age of fifteen was apprenticed in sail. He worked his way to his master's and extra master's certificates, and then joined Cunard. It was usual for young men to work themselves all the way up in sail and then join a steamship company as fourth officer. Charles's work with the *Aquitania* when she was a troopship in the war brought him to the notice of the British government, which gave him a knighthood, and his eminence as her peacetime commander recommended him to Lucius Beebe, a sort of minor Pepys who lived by writing gossip of the great and published a book called *The Big Spenders*. The *Aquitania* was full of big spenders, and over them presided Sir James. At his captain's table he demanded full dress with decorations, which was inclined to put Americans to a disadvantage unless they had been in the army. He was a huge man, and his tastes at table were rather like those of an actor playing Henry VIII. Beebe said stewards would wheel in carcasses of whole roasted oxen one night, and the next evening small herds of grilled antelope would surround a hilltop of Strasbourg *foie gras* surmounted by peacock fans. Electrically illuminated set-pieces, masterpieces of the ship's confectioner's art, represented the Battle of Waterloo, while the ship's orchestra played Elgar. Soufflés the size of chefs' hats blossomed towards the end of the dinner. Mumms and Perrier-Jouet circulated in jeroboams of ten or twelve quarts. In July 1928 Sir James was about to bring the *Aquitania* from New York to Southampton for the last time, and then retire. In New York he was presented with a silver plaque bearing a model of the *Aquitania*, and said in reply that he had become part of his ship and had not expected the break from it to be such a severe wrench. The homeward passage was in sunshine and calm seas. He said it was the most perfect he could recall in 728 crossings of the Atlantic during forty-nine years at sea. Having brought his ship back to Europe, he collapsed at Cherbourg. There are two versions of this. Lucius Beebe says Sir James died in the line of duty, at sea, almost literally leading an assault on a citadel of pastry moated with diamond-back turtle stew *au Madeira*, and that when they took him ashore at Southampton it was necessary to open both wings of the ship's half-ports to accommodate his going, which was that of a nobleman and a warrior. The newspapers, on the other hand, said he fell ill just after handing over to the Cherbourg pilot, and was brought unconscious to Southampton where he died quickly and peacefully. There were those who said the wrench had been too much, and had broken his heart. For his funeral at Netley cemetery, a special trainload of mourners came from head office at Liverpool. The crew of the *Aquitania* walked the six miles from Southampton docks to the church on a sweltering day. Eight seamen carried the coffin, which was covered by the Union Jack and the Cunard house-flag. Bert Mellor, pianist in the *Aquitania*'s orchestra, played Beethoven's funeral march on the church organ. At the open grave the Bishop of Winchester recited Tennyson's 'Crossing the Bar'. Princess Xenia of Russia, the woman who had married the millionaire who took a liking to the New York traffic cop and sent him on a trip to Europe first class, sent a wreath expressing the most sincere sympathy.

But captains like Henry VIII, and the extravagances of first class, were the glitter of the Atlantic trade. The big spenders may have set the tone, but in the twenties the steamship companies came to depend more and more on a new breed of passenger called tourist third. These were, again, mainly Americans, but this time Americans who were not rich but who were discovering that you did not need to be rich to see Europe. During the year or so that the United States had been in the war, two million American soldiers were shipped to Europe. They had seen it; they knew it was there; it was no longer so remote. It was possible. Ordinary Americans were also becoming, by European standards, rather well off. A dollar would buy a lot in Paris. All this was lucky for the steamship companies, who would otherwise have had very empty ships, because the old steerage traffic had collapsed. Before the war the United States really was still welcoming huddled masses yearning to breathe free, certainly as long as those masses were European. The federal policy was still to accept all who wished to come. The ideal was still that immigrants of all nationalities would subscribe their native gifts to a still-forming American character. This was the melting-pot theory. But by 1919 the United States had won a world war for the Allies, and the very different philosophy of an already formed, and superior, American national identity was beginning to assert itself. Having settled the affairs of the world, America could assert her splendid isolation. America had also taken enough people in anyway. The labour unions said so, loudly. In 1921 the United States restricted annual immigration to 3 per cent of the foreign born population of America according to the census of 1903. The Johnson-Reed Act of 1924 went even further, almost stopping immigration altogether, and at any rate cutting

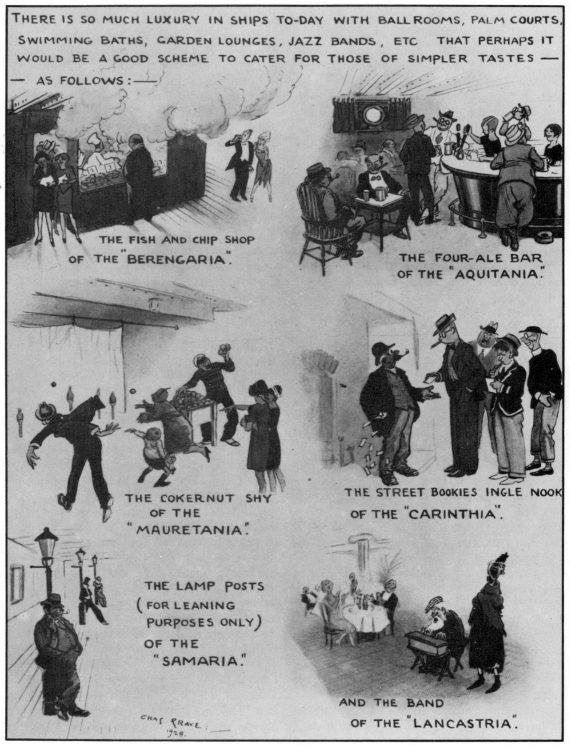

A Cunard cartoon of 1928, expected perhaps to attract tourist-third passengers

the quota to 2 per cent and basing it on the census of 1890. Before the war there had been a million steerage passengers a year. By 1924 there were 150,000. Nor had the pre-war annual millions come mostly in special immigrant ships. The most splendid liners carried their share. The *Mauretania* could carry 2,145 passengers when full, of whom 1,138 were in the third class. These people were already, before the war, beginning to demand a little more. In 1914 the chief third-class steward of the *Lusitania* reported to head office that on the last voyage 'quite a number of the third-class passengers, who were of a very superior type, inquired for sheets for the beds', and Cunard obtained an estimate of £358 for 20,000 sheets and 1,000 quilts. When the *Imperator* was built, Hamburg-Amerika gave her accommodation for 4,100 passengers, a number which in peacetime she never carried, and of these 1,000 were third class, and another 1,800 fourth — 2,800 in what could properly be called the steerage. When Cunard refitted her after the war they put only 1,000 tourist-third passengers in the space at first intended for those 2,800.

In tourist third there were certainly sheets and quilts, but intending tourists, particularly Americans, knowing perfectly well that steerage had been steerage, needed to be reassured. White Star, for one, did so. Bathrooms were available at all times, and there were eighteen items on the breakfast menu. And, said White Star, there need be no anxiety about the shipboard companions one would find. In tourist third, only those of a congenial type were accepted. Most were teachers, college professors, and students. It cost about $150 return, as against the cheapest first-class return, on the *Aquitania*, of $1,000. Cunard distributed pamphlets about 'Crusades of Friendship', hoping to attract the Rotary Conference business, which was mainly tourist third. They quoted the Prince of Wales as telling the American Legion that it was the duty of the two great English speaking nations of the world to see that their links did not become mere sentimental associations, and General Pershing as saying, also to the American Legion, that thousands of Americans should go abroad carrying faith, goodwill, and friendship among all peoples. In 1927 thirteen Cunarders were reserved to carry Rotarians to Ostend, the American Legion to Paris, the American Guernsey Cattle Club to Guernsey, and the Missouri Brethren to Glasgow. American businessmen formed an Ancient Order of Tramps, which had as its sign a lapel pin of two crossed walking sticks, one supporting the tramp's tin can and the other his bundle. They let it be known that they were travelling tourist third in order to further international friendship and get to know the other man's point of view. Cunard ingeniously pointed out that people in tourist were a joy to meet from the very fact that they chose to travel simply and unostentatiously.

It was the American lines which made the biggest pitch for the tourist-third market. They had to. Cunard, White Star, and the French Line could have their share without trying very hard. So it was the United States Line which advertised a great deal, and came up with the figures intended to convince, and the guff intended to seduce. On one ship in 1923, said the line, though it did not say what ship, there had travelled in tourist third 470 college students, 205 school-teachers, twenty-eight college instructors, eighteen university professors, three university presidents, eight protestant ministers of the gospel, nine catholic priests, seven lawyers, nine doctors of medicine, six doctors of dentistry, ninety-five doctors of philosophy, thirty-seven members of Phi Beta Kappa, seventy-three American businessmen, and four writers of national and international fame. Again it did not say who these were. The United States Line had been adopted as the official fleet of the Intercollegiate Alumni Association, and in this fleet, so it said, the spirit of youth romped unbridled. 'Fresh, wholesome youth . . . the half-back for a few stirring moments is a matador . . . a flower chain girl from Vassar outdoes Helen Wills . . . four fraternity brothers from Ohio State address their harmony into the blue Atlantic . . . the professor shoots the shuffleboard disc into the square and scores against the auburn-haired school teacher from Terre Haute . . . the Recreation Director introduces the novelist to a charming blonde who lazes in a deck chair.' This lush stuff ended with the hard sell. You could cross on the *Leviathan*, *Republic*, or *George Washington* (all three, incidentally, seized German ships), and have fifty-five days in England, France, Switzerland, Italy, Austria, and Germany for $858 dollars the lot, all accommodation, meals, and fares included. It was a bargain. You could pay five times this just for a first-class suite, one way, on the *Aquitania*.

To give substance to its claims, the United States Line took to giving free trips to reporters, so that in 1926 the New York *Herald* had a story from their own man aboard, about an Austrian baron travelling tourist third who was invited to the first class but came back fed up and full of Austrian curses. In tourist third he habitually sat next to a porthole and, his own name being unpronounceable, was known as Baron Porthole. Furthermore, on this same ship, the reporter overheard one gorgeous first-class young man say, at the beginning of the voyage, 'Look at the cattle down there,' but before the trip was over he was being led around by a sweet little girl from among the tourist-third cattle as if he himself were a tame bull with a ring in his nose.

Another American company, the American Transport Line, tried with its new but much smaller ships *Minnesota* and *Minnetonka* to offer ships carrying only tourist third. 'The whole ship is yours,' said the advertisements. 'Steamers of distinction but without distinctions.' Tourists got the best on board because there was no other class. They offered London-New York £40 return. White Star offered the same single class on their *Cedric* and *Celtic*, but these were much older ships, which had once upon a time, though briefly, been the largest in the world. But that was back in 1903, and by the late twenties they were shabby.

Tourist third was the principal American contribution to the Atlantic passage between the wars. The companies also tried to attract the English to travel tourist third to America, but there was not the impetus. Parties of Selfridge's shop assistants and Cambridge medical students did go, and so did the Rhondda Glee Club for a ten-month singing tour, but when the companies advertised in England the democratic American tone evaded them. In 1926 Canadian Pacific were trying to sell tourist third, from £35 return, with a picture-story pamphlet showing Jack meeting Ralph in the City of London. Both seem to be clerks. Ralph says he is going to Canada for twenty-one days.

JACK: 'Come into a fortune?'

RALPH: 'Not steerage at all, but third-class cabin arrangement. The food's good, and the people — well, just ordinary folk like us.'

They settle to go as a party of four, taking their wives Peggy and Nell. Peggy loves the nice little washstand in her cabin, and at one time is allowed a peep into the first-class dining-room. 'Pardon,' she says, 'dining *saloon*. It was simply IT written big, with about six knives, six forks, and six spoons for each guest. How much *do* they eat?'

As an example of how not to do it, this advertisement could hardly be improved — 'just ordinary folk', 'nice little washstand', the mere mention of steerage even to deny it, and the awed peep into the first class. American tourists were *not* ordinary folk; they were Phi Beta Kappas and international novelists, or Austrian barons, or at least auburn haired school teachers from Terre Haute.

It must not be overstated, but it is true, that one reason why Americans liked to be on board ship in the 1920s was that they could get a drink there. From 1920 to 1933 the Constitution of the United States forbade the sale of intoxicating liquor in all territories subject to its jurisdiction. This may have been, as President Hoover believed, an experiment noble in

The *Mauretania* at speed. From 1907, until she was at last beaten by the new German liners in 1929, she was the fastest liner on the Atlantic or anywhere

motive and far-reaching in purpose, but it was one more nail in the coffin of American steamship companies whose vessels, even on the high seas, were subject to federal jurisdiction, and dry. Of course it did not work. Lord Dewar, the whisky man, asked as he disembarked at New York what he thought about prohibition, replied, 'Well, it's better than no drink at all.' It was possible to get a drink on board an American ship, but it required ingenuity or dishonesty or both. An American ship's doctor became the most popular man on board. Passengers lined up as soon as the ship left quarantine.

'I got a sore toe.'

'That's too bad. What kind of medicine shall I give you?'

'How about two bottles of Scotch?'

Basil Woon, author of *The Frantic Atlantic*, a bestseller of the 1920s, reported that one film magnate, wanting to give a party, procured for the cure of a toothache four bottles of Rhine wine, six of claret, four of burgundy, six of champagne, one of Napoleon brandy, and a case of Scotch. Mr Woon is a wit and therefore not perhaps to be implicitly believed, but he was stating a part truth. Still, such subterfuge was not worth the trouble, and most Americans simply took to French and English ships. An officer of the *Mauretania*, watching an American passenger saluting the disappearing Statue of Liberty as the ship moved up New York bay to the open sea, was then addressed in these words, 'Say, that statue's gone. The bars will be open, won't they?'

As it happened, when the marvellous *Ile de France* entered New York on her maiden voyage in June 1927 she had the biggest bar on the Atlantic — twenty-seven feet long. The French Line could be relied upon for panache. 'Bon Voyage,' they said, 'is always French,' and their liners of the earlier 1920s, though technically not outstanding, always had a sophisticated following. Of their liner *France*, the French Line said she was not just a boat, but had a soul, in the same way that France itself was not just a country but a spirit of dauntless courage and flawless gaiety. 'She

isn't as big as the biggest, but neither is the Ritz.' When the *Ile de France* came along they called her the face of victorious France reborn and the glory of France personified. She certainly became one of the most successful liners that ever sailed the Atlantic, but what her attractions were it is not easy to describe. She was neither the biggest nor the fastest, and outside she looked an ordinary traditional three-stacker which could have been built before the war. But she was the first very big liner to be built in the nine years since the end of the war. Vessels of 20,000 tons had been built, but the *Ile de France* was more than twice that tonnage, a liner the size of the *Aquitania*. In that sense she was a revival. But though her exterior was traditional, her interior was not. Inside, there was nothing like the *Aquitania*'s Palladian lounge after Sir Christopher Wren, or her state-rooms after Queen Anne, or her swimming-bath after the best examples of Egyptian ornament to be found in the British museum, or her garden lounge after a garden. 'To live is not to copy,' said President Piaz of the French Line. 'It is to create.' On the day of her first sailing he asked the astonished Frenchwomen sitting in her saloon, women rather taken aback by the furniture around them in a style which would now be called advanced Odeon, 'Why, ladies, with your short hair and your short skirts, should you wish to sit in copies of Louis XVI armchairs?' Still, they did not at first take to the tubular concealed lighting, and blond wood veneer, and everything modern. Not that the *Ile* could have been called *severely* modern. She was eclectic. Her 390 first-class state-rooms were furnished in 390 different ways. After her maiden voyage Vincent Astor said he had taken two days to get used to the beautifully bizarre quality of his rooms, and that he had been much amused by his bathroom which had been decorated with monkeys instead of the expected gulls. The one thing every cabin had in common was wood veneer, which throughout the *Ile*'s career creaked and danced incessantly, in any sea at all. But she was a much-loved ship. She had panache. For years she carried more first-class passengers than

Dancing on board the *France*. She was not, said the French Line, the biggest, but neither was the Ritz

The *Ile de France* in heavy seas. She had an elegance that made many passengers prefer her to faster ships, and stay faithful to her for passage after passage

any other liner. It was aboard her that Toscanini met the young Yehudi Menuhin.

The *Ile de France* did not long remain the only new ship on the Atlantic. North German Lloyd, expressing its *Wille zur Tat*, will to action, had laid down two ships which were intended to be not only beautiful, and an expression of Germany, but to take the blue riband which the aged *Mauretania* had held since 1907. The *Europa* was launched on 15 August 1928, and the *Bremen* the next day. Just as the *Mauretania* in 1907 had looked like a cruiser, the *Bremen* and *Europa* resembled sleek destroyers. They were in fact huge ships, of 50,000 tons, larger than anything afloat except Ballin's old trio, low in silhouette, with twin funnels so low indeed that they soon had to be raised to prevent the decks getting covered in smuts, and everywhere streamlined. Their bows were raked, but bulbous, not fine cut like the cruiser bows of British ships. Their hull plating overlapped forward, which the ship-builders had proved in their testing tanks to lower resistance through the water and increase speed. North German Lloyd said their design laid great stress on purity of form, and that the ships gleamed like new planets. Professor Fritz August Brehaus de Groot of Munich University wrote and produced, and the company then distributed, a book which must be the most lavish give-away ever handed out by a shipping company. The red hull of the *Bremen* gleamed forth from a rich gold cover. The preface said, 'The architecture of the *Bremen* emancipates us from a time which is not our own, and leads us into the grandeur of our present age, in which we desire to breathe and not to suffocate.' This is, in principle, not so far from the president of the French Line telling women that if they wore short skirts they should not want to sit on Louis XVI chairs, but the tone is different, the *Wille zur Tat* stronger. Around the walls of the *Bremen*'s library were tablets bearing stirring texts in German, French, Spanish, Italian, Russian, Chinese, and Arabic. Goethe said: 'It does not suffice to know, one must also apply; it does not suffice to will, one must also do.' There was a shooting gallery where a cinematograph projected on to larchwood walls the images of creatures to be

Cecile Sorel, celebrated actress, on board the *Ile de France*

The *Europa*, sister ship of the *Bremen*, 1929; they were the first large German liners to be built since the war and for a while the fastest on the Atlantic. North German Lloyd said they gleamed like new planets

German 'will to succeed' in the gymnasium of the *Bremen*

shot. As soon as the bullet struck the wall the strip of film was automatically brought to a stop and the spot where the bullet entered illuminated, so that the sportsman could accurately judge whether his shot was good or bad. In the restaurant, Rhine maidens watched by men sported on the walls, and this is the only way in which the *Bremen* and the old *Imperator* had anything in common. The *Bremen* had a ship's hostess, Dr Gertrude Ferber, the first to be appointed by any shipping line to such an office. The ship's surgeon, Dr Dammert, offered the Dammert Inhalation Treatment for seasickness, price two marks. The patient had to inhale a mixture of oxygen and atropine, the oxygen to revive the system and the atropine to

calm the nervous inner ear. This treatment could not, however, be administered in the cabin: it was first necessary for the sufferer to have the will to go on deck to receive it.

The *Bremen* took the blue riband on her maiden voyage in July 1929, both ways, as it was inevitable she would, but her speed of 27.83 knots was only one-and-a-half knots more than the *Mauretania*'s. In a last gesture, Cunard allowed the *Mauretania* to steam all-out for two crossings, and she achieved almost 27 knots, the fastest passages of her long career but not quite fast enough. That was in August. In the last week of October 1929 the New York stock market broke, and the great depression began. Both the *Berengaria* and the *Ile de France* were at sea, and many of their passengers learned over the ships' wireless that they were ruined. This was also very bad news for the shipping companies.

It was the very worst of luck for North German Lloyd, who had fought back from nothing to build the two fastest ships in the world only to find, first, that feeling against Germany was still so strong that many people would not sail in German ships, however fast; and that, second, after the crash, those who would have sailed in them could no longer afford to. They were later to find, when the market had recovered a little, that many who would and could have sailed North German Lloyd then refused to do so because of Hitler. But in 1929 Hitler was a few years in the future. The crash was hard on Italy, who were building their own new liners, one of which, the *Rex*, would take the blue riband from the *Bremen*. It was hard on the American lines, whose tourist-third passengers were suddenly unable to afford Europe. It was hard on Cunard, who were still attempting to run the *Berengaria*, the *Aquitania*, and the *Mauretania*, but with fewer passengers. Perhaps the *Mauretania* still had the most faithful following of all, including some people who had transferred their loyalty to her after the *Lusitania* was sunk. It became not unusual for one Cunarder to make a crossing at its usual and uneconomical speed, the last knot always costing the earth, and then have

The work of a Cunard artist, the soft sell, not so much as mentioning a liner, only suggesting the kind of girls who tended to travel first class in the 1920s

R.M.S. "Carinthia" – Cunard Line

Above: the *Normandie* approaching New York.
Watercolour by J. Simont

Above left: the Aquitania at Southampton. In the
1920s she was the most fashionable Cunarder

Below left: Postcard of the *Carinthia*, built in 1925
and intended for cruising, though she did make
slower, and therefore cheaper, Atlantic crossings
out of Liverpool. The card, as was customary, was
signed by those who met on the passage and kept
a souvenir

Right: the *Bremen*. A North German Lloyd poster,
1928

CUNARD ~ CHRISTMAS ~ 1931

Job number 534 on the stocks at John Brown's yard in the Clyde, 1931

The *Mauretania* at Cowes in 1929 when she had just lost the blue riband and was coming to the end of her career on the Atlantic

to remain laid up at its New York berth from Monday of one week to Wednesday of the next.

The *Berengaria* was sent on $50 cruises, known as booze cruises, from New York up and down the coast of Nova Scotia, and became known as the Bargain Area or the Dead and Bury'er. The *Mauretania* was painted white and sent on permanent cruising, which the crew called yachting. Sometimes on Bahamas cruises, with the Gulf Stream, she would do 31 knots for an hour or so to please the passengers. White Star sent the *Olympic* on one-day bank holiday cruises from Southampton. Canadian Pacific, which in 1931 had introduced its brilliant *Empress of Britain*, another liner of the first rank and the best ever to run up the St

Lawrence, found themselves unable to fill her and began to advertise cross-channel services from England to France, saying, 'An impression exists among many who have no occasion to make an Atlantic crossing that the great ocean liners are to them "forbidden ground". But travel CP and be just as welcome as trans-atlantic passengers.'

On her transatlantic services, *Empress of Britain* passengers could read in the ship's paper not only advertisements for Helena Rubinstein's pasteurized face cream at $1, or for her Youthifying Tissue at $1, but also hints on how to pronounce the names of the famous.

Aldous (Huxley). All-dus. Similarly the *al* in John Galsworthy (and in the Chicago and Alton Railway) is pronounced *all*.

[137]

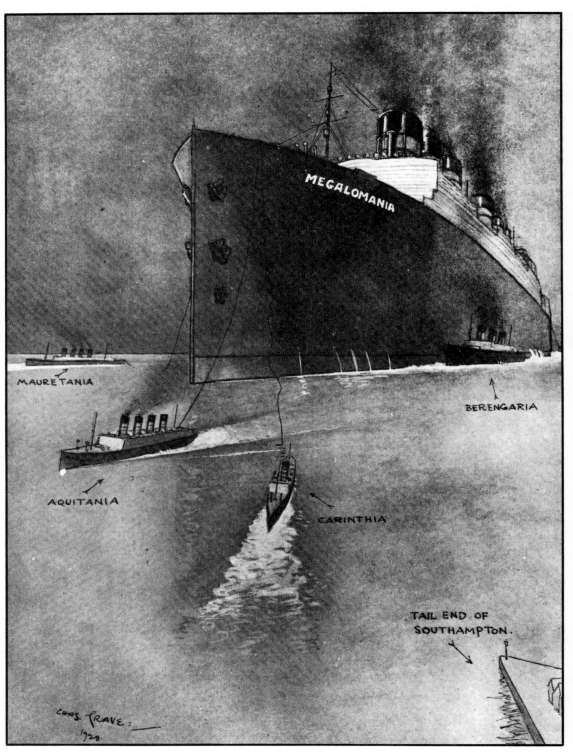

MEGALOMANIA

MAURETANIA

AQUITANIA

CARINTHIA

BERENGARIA

TAIL END OF
SOUTHAMPTON.

CHAS GRAVE:
1928.

The Canadian Pacific *Empress of Britain*, 42,350 tons, the fastest liner ever to sail the Canadian route, and also the first to be designed to be a cruise ship in the winter when the St Lawrence was impassable

Dunsany (Lord). Second syllable accented and pronounced *say*.

Maurois (Andre). *More-wah*.

Meynell, Alice. Rhymes with kennel.

This was no longer quite the high style of the twenties. Things weren't what they used to be. In the *Empress of Britain*'s newspaper for 3 November 1933 there were three news stories. From Sault Sainte Marie, Ontario – that a man had choked a bear with his hands. From Sacramento, Calif. – that among the 1,039 machine guns recorded in the state was one owned by Douglas Fairbanks, forming part of the 'defensive equipment' of Pickfair, his Hollywood estate, and that the list prepared by the State showed that thirty-nine of the machine guns were covered by permits and the other thousand not. From Berlin, Germany, there came a suggestion that foreign visitors should wear badges to prevent their being attacked for failing to give the Nazi salute.

It was a very bad time. The *Olympic* was taken out of service and brought home to be broken up. At Jarrow, where she was to be scrapped to give employment to shipworkers who otherwise would have had no work, her fittings were first sold at auction. Mr Arthur Knight, of Messrs Knight, Frank, and Rutley, the London auctioneers, said he had in his time broken up many a noble and historic home, but

◄ The urge to build bigger and bigger derided by a Cunard artist of 1928 who has four Cunarders of the time acting as tugs to RMS *Megalomania*. This was all very well, but the Cunard board were already thinking of laying down the *Queen Mary*, which was to be half as big again as any liner then afloat.

The brilliant *Mauretania* in her last days, painted cruising white, somewhere in the Mediterranean

now he had the unhappy task of performing the last rites for this magnificent ship and it was impossible for him to be unmoved. The magazine *Shipbuilder* said it was not exposing anything in the nature of a secret to say that over the last few years British shipping on the Atlantic had been slowly forced into a position of palpable inferiority to the French, the Germans, and the Italians. This was true. No single British liner of any size had been launched since the First World War. Furthermore, the flagships of both principal British lines and of the United States Line were ex-German. In 1930 the world's five biggest ships were *Majestic* (ex-*Bismarck*), *Leviathan* (ex-*Vaterland*), *Berengaria* (ex-*Imperator*), *Bremen*, and *Europa* — all German built. The *Mauretania* continued cruising. Her crew did not dislike this, even though they thought that in her cruising white she looked like a wedding cake. In 1933 the pay of Cunard first officers was £1 a day. If

they were ashore, between ships, they received an allowance of one shilling and sixpence a day out of which they had to feed themselves. If they were cruising, they had abundant food, and an allowance for white hot-weather uniform. There is a no doubt apocryphal story that one obscure and insolent island in the French Caribbean would regularly signal to the *Mauretania* asking 'What ship are you?', as if she could be mistaken for anything else, to which the *Mauretania* would regularly reply with the signal, 'What island are you?' In the autumn of 1934 the *Mauretania* had completed her last cruise, three months in the West Indies, and made her last such signal. Cunard had no further use for her, and she too was up for sale to the breakers. She left New York for the last time on 26 September 1934, to many mournful good-byes. It was a bad time. But that same day the *Queen Mary* was launched.

CHAPTER SIX

534 and T6:
Queen Mary
and *Normandie*

On the Clyde, 534 was the shipyard number of the *Queen Mary*, and at Saint Nazaire T6 was that of the *Normandie*, and these were the two ships that dominated the 1930s. They were both beautiful, and neither could possibly be afforded. They took turns beating each other for the blue riband by margins of about one-third of a knot. They were designed, sailed, and boasted about, all with great style.

There are two delightful legends about the *Queen Mary*, which arose before she was ever launched, and one of these legends is even true. She was to be propelled by four screws, each twenty feet across and each weighing thirty-five tons. Anyone making the slightest error in their casting would have cost the shipbuilders £15,000, and when they were cast they had to be mounted so delicately as to permit of their being turned by a man's hand. Because of this, while the workmen laboured to mount the screws into her steel hull, no woman was allowed to visit the yard for fear that a man might for a moment glance away from his work and ruin the essential balance of a screw. The second legend concerns the name of the ship herself, how 534 became the *Queen Mary*, because with her as with the *Normandie* there was great secrecy about the name until the very moment of the launch; but that is a story that can wait.

Cunard themselves never boasted about their ship. Others did, but Cunard went in for understatement. Sir Percy Bates, chairman of the company, did call her 'the inevitable ship', but he went on to explain to his shareholders precisely what he meant by that. Cunard, he said, was 'projecting a pair of steamers' – the other was eventually to emerge as the *Queen Elizabeth* but not to sail as a liner until after the war – which, though they might be very large and very fast, were in fact the smallest and slowest which could do the job. He meant that 30 knots was the slowest the two could sail if they were to be able to maintain a weekly service between them, so that the company could rely for its express Southampton-New York service on two vessels instead of the traditional three. It followed also that if there were to be only two ships they had to be that much bigger, to carry the same number of passengers as used to fit into the old three. So the day of the 80,000-tonner had arrived, and once again a new generation of liners was being built almost exactly half as big again as its predecessors – just as the *Lusitania* and *Mauretania* had been half as big again as the German liners before them, and as the *Olympic*, *Titanic*, and *Britannic* had been half as big again as the *Mauretania*. It is interesting that as late as 1930 Sir Percy should refer to his great liners as 'steamers': this was an old usage, but one that persisted in Cunard advertising up to the beginning of the Second World War.

But in 1930, at any rate, only one of his pair of steamers stood any chance whatever of being built, and by rights even she should not have survived. In 1930 Britain was in the middle of a depression. There was no money to build the ships. What was more, the slump was getting worse in America, where the millionaires came from. In Wall Street every day the millionaires were becoming fewer. So the ships there was no money to build would, if ever built, very likely find themselves ships without passengers. The White Star company had already laid down a 60,000 liner at Belfast, to be called *Oceanic*, but then cancelled her, and bits of her hull were cut up to use in smaller ships. But at least one great new British liner had somehow to be built, principally for reasons of national pride and because across the Channel at the Penhoet shipyards the *Normandie*, although facing equally dismal prospects, was taking shape. Something had to be done. There had to be a British rival to the *Normandie*. At the same time, it was obvious that there was no room for two competing British steamship companies in the north Atlantic passenger trade. If Cunard and White Star would merge, and only if they would do so, the British government would lend the combined company the cash to build two fast new liners, £3 million to complete the first straight away, and another £5 million to build the second eventually. This was accepted because there was no option. It seems extraordinary to write about the demise of a great steamship company, White Star, as if it were just a necessary incident in the building of the *Queen Mary*, but that is a large part of the truth. White Star had been going through a very bad time. In 1926 the Royal Mail Group had bought White Star back into British ownership from the American I.M.M., which had been shedding its foreign interests. But this had been done at exactly the wrong time. The White Star fleet was old, the brilliant German competitors were soon to appear, and so was the slump. By 1930 White Star was making large losses. If one of the two big British companies had to go, it would be the weaker. Nominally Cunard and White Star merged, but it would be fairer to say that Cunard took over White Star. After the merger on 1 January 1934 the Cunard services continued and those of White Star ceased. The names were combined as Cunard White Star, and White Star vessels kept their old colours, but two years after the merger there were only two of them left to do so. The rest had been sold

[142]

or scrapped, including the splendid old *Majestic*.

As soon as the merger was agreed, work on the *Queen Mary*, which had been stopped, began once again. Cunard's house-magazine said how typical it was of Old England to set about a huge job like this at such a time, when her back was said to be against the wall, when some asserted that she was done. 'A dangerous hour, this, for England's traducers. It is then that we become most ominously busy. Listen to the snarl of steel on steel.' It was not so much Old England that was setting about the job as Old Scotland. The *Queen Mary* was being built on the Clyde. And as it happened, throughout her career, when Scotch beef was served on board her, it was described on the menu as English. John Brown, the builders, made a model of the ship, and a film of her going through a simulated Atlantic storm. In a 60-knot gale the pitching and rolling were almost negligible. The model must have been inaccurate.

The *Queen Mary* was launched in September 1934 among much jingoism, some of it very pleasant. This was the launching of one ship costing in real money little more than two jumbo jets would cost today, but the London *Times* said it was a national event of deep significance, and an event whose real importance depended on its being regarded not as something singular and unusual but as a normal happening in the life of the nation. 'It is customary for Great Britain to construct from time to time such ships as are necessary to maintain her ancient predominance on the seas.' From time to time indeed: the last such customary event would have been the launch of the *Aquitania* in 1913. However, it *was* an event of deep significance, and this was not only because of international rivalry but because the Atlantic was the voyage of voyages. *The Times* then continued, in the kind of leading article prose for which it was justly admired by school-masters, to remark that the first successful accomplishment of this voyage, by Columbus, had been the most romantic sea exploit since Jason brought back the Golden Fleece, and that in the centuries since Columbus the voyage had only gained in dignity what it had lost in strangeness and danger. The leading article went on to call Samuel Cunard an Englishman, which he had not been, and to mention that the first Cunarder, the *Britannia*, could be placed in any single one of the *Queen Mary*'s three funnels, which, as Cunard's publicity brochures had shown, was true. Cunard White Star, said *The Times*, took upon itself the burden and the splendour of the national fame in a way that had been permitted to only one or two private companies through all the centuries — to the Merchant Venturers, the East India Company, and the Bank of England. This was a just claim. Cunard did hold just such a position. There was also, in this article, one little echo of the *Titanic*, which was never forgotten. The new Cunarder's defences against the perils of the ocean would be 'so complete as almost to permit that absolute immunity which the nature of the sea does not allow'.

On the date of the launch itself *The Times* was at it again, this time calling her A Tall Ship and 'the people's ship', whatever that meant, and saying that she had twenty-two lifts, that each voyage was an adventure, and that she was an example of the mystic belief of an island people in its own sacramental union with the sea. That same day, before the launching, John Brown's presented the Queen with a decorated casket in gold and silver gilt, the principal design upon which was an ornamental map of the Atlantic surrounded by boldly chased waves in turbulent motion. Cunarder 534 was shown in mid ocean, bound for New York, leaving behind her a wake extending to the English Channel. On the North American seaboard were shown polar bears, icebergs, and the Aurora Borealis. The southern waters were enlivened by mermaids and dolphins.

On Clydeside it was raining hard for the launch. The B.B.C. commentator saw the side of the ship like a great white cliff, and the heads of the crowd, covered by a multitude of wet umbrellas, like so many black stones on a beach. King George V and Queen Mary appeared behind a glass-fronted canopy, he in naval uniform and she in powder blue. When the proceedings began, the crowd at once lowered their umbrellas and stood uncovered in the rain. The King said it was still less than a hundred years since Samuel Cunard had founded his service of mail paddle-steamers, and there must still be a few people, alive that day, who as children would have heard those little ships spoken of as evidence of man's mastery over nature. 'Today,' he said, 'we come to the task of sending on her way the stateliest ship now in being . . . Today we can send her forth no longer a number on the books, but a ship with a name in the world, alive with beauty, energy, and strength.' The time had come for her to be named and launched by the Queen, but at that moment she was still 534, and her name had been a properly kept secret. Here is the time for the story. It goes that the Cunard directors had brooded over the name and, having decided, had asked Lord Royden, one of their number, who was also a personal friend of the King, if he could obtain the royal assent to their suggestion. Royden agreed, and a little later found himself a member of a royal shooting party at Balmoral. 'I say, Royden,' said the King, 'how's that ship of yours coming along?' Royden replied that she was coming on well, and that he wished to ask permission to name her after the most illustrious and remarkable woman who had ever been Queen of England. The King was moved and said, 'That is the greatest compliment that has ever been paid to my wife. I'll ask her.' Royden could do nothing but express his gratitude and keep quiet. Only he and the rest of the Cunard board knew that he had meant to ask permission to name the ship *Victoria*. Now this is a lovely story. It is even a likely one. Cunard ships in modern times had always been given names ending in -*ia*, and there was a rumour that, on the merger of Cunard and White Star, the first new express steamer being subsidized by the government would be named *Victoria*,* with the Cunard -*ia* ending, and the second *Oceanic*, with the White

---

* *Victoria* was one of the names which nearly thirty years before had been considered and rejected for the *Lusitania–Mauretania* pair.

Star's traditional *-ic* ending. The source was also a good one – Captain Harry Grattidge, who was to become commodore of the Cunard line and who said that in August 1934 only a few of them in Cunard, including presumably himself, had known. It is *very* likely, but it is not the truth. The truth emerges, though with some furtiveness, from the personal letter files of Sir Percy Bates, which are now in the Cunard archives at Liverpool University. On 30 May 1934, Bates was writing to the Board of Trade thanking them for their letter explaining the difficulties about ship's names, and saying, cryptically, that he was rather dismayed to observe that they saw no way of insuring against blackmail. In consequence, he said, he would have to be very careful in his dealings with Buckingham Palace. At this stage no ship's name at all had been mentioned in the letter, and indeed throughout the series of letters no name was ever mentioned; when it became inevitable that a name should appear, Bates's secretary simply left a blank in the typewritten sheet which perhaps he filled in in his own hand in the original copy he sent to the intended recipient. All this talk of blackmail and care in dealings with Buckingham Palace could delightfully suggest, taken on its own, that the King wanted to call the ship one thing and Cunard did not, and if this were the only letter that would be a far-fetched but reasonable explanation.

But there are other letters. On 10 July 1934, Bates wrote a letter, marked 'Personal and Secret', to Hugh M. Macfarlane of Williamson Buchanan Steamers Ltd, Glasgow, saying he much appreciated Macfarlane's courtesy and consideration in the matter, and would do all he could for Macfarlane. That is all the letter says, but it then becomes easy to discover that Macfarlane had a Clyde steamer called the *Queen Mary*, that he was unwilling to change her name because the Clyde business was a competitive one and he feared that if his ship lost her name she might lose some of her attraction, and that what Bates was promising to do was to intercede with the Board of Trade to let Macfarlane give Cunard the original

name and call his own steamer the *Queen Mary II*. At any rate, thus it was settled. What blackmail Bates was referring to in his earlier letter is still anybody's guess. Perhaps he thought Macfarlane might stick out for a price, which would not amount to blackmail. Or perhaps he thought someone else might get in before him and register the name *Queen Mary* for something else. But in another letter of the same date, 10 July, Bates wrote to Sir N. Warren Fisher, barrister, asking him to approach their majesties and explaining, without mentioning the name explicitly, why he wanted it. He said one of the most difficult things had been to reconcile the opposing wishes of the merger companies, who had these two traditional and different endings to their ships' names. It would be a happy event if 534 could be given a name definitely marking a breach with the past and the beginning of a new future era. 'If the name can be approved, I think it will help me in my work as chairman of the company, and in addition I am confident that approval will give pleasure and pride to thousands of His Majesty's subjects.' By July 21 the Palace had approved, and so, when in September the Queen launched 534 with a bottle of Australian wine she named the ship *Queen Mary*, and then turned to the king and said, 'Was that right?'

It was. The ship slid down into the Clyde. Cunard had asked Kipling if he would care to write something for the occasion, with or without remuneration as he chose, but in the end it was John Masefield who wrote an ode for her launching, calling her long as a street and lofty as a tower, ready to glide in thunder from the slip and shear the sea with majesty of power. He ended with this couplet:

> I long to see you leaping to the urge
> Of the great engines, rolling as you go.

Roll she did, notoriously; her crew said she could roll the milk out of a cup of tea.

While the *Queen Mary* lay fitting out, the *Normandie* had already been launched, celebrated in verse of a more exalted, French kind, and then shriven by a cardinal of the Roman Catholic Church. She was more than a ship;

An invitation card to the launching of 534, still known only by that number until the Queen launched her

The Chairman and Directors of
Cunard White Star Limited
and of
John Brown and Company Limited
request the honour of the company of

at the Launch of
Q.S.T.S. N.º "534"
in the presence of
Their Majesties The King & Queen
on Wednesday, Sept. 26ᵗʰ at 3.15 p.m.
Her Majesty The Queen
has graciously consented to perform the naming ceremony.

Clydebank,
August 1934.

An early reply is requested to
Cunard White Star Limited,
Liverpool.

The *Queen Mary*, a Cunard artist's impression

The first-class dining saloon of the *Normandie*, three decks high, lined with hammered glass, and a hundred yards long, slightly longer than the Hall of Mirrors at Versailles

The swimming pool of the *Normandie*

Queen Mary launching the ship which she had just named for the first time. After she had said the form of words which sent the liner down the slipway, she said, 'Was that right?' and King George V (on the left, in naval uniform), smiled. The shading on the photograph is heavy rain on the glass-fronted canopy

she was a floating piece of France. The French Line said their ship *spoke* for France, and spoke for all that was best in the national life – the cuisine, the welcome, warm but without familiarity, the decor with nothing *de trop*, and above all the grace and ambiance of France. The cuisine was of course magnificent. Table wine was always free aboard the *Normandie*, and so that the wine should properly settle in it was stowed in her holds no less than six months before her maiden voyage, and in such a way that if she should, by some unforseen chance, ever roll, the rolling would least upset the wine. As for the French ambiance, that was undoubted too. Announcements on board her were generally made only in French, even though most of her passengers were American. As for the decor, though nothing may have been *de trop*, everything was magnificence. She had the largest dining hall ever seen on any ship, one hundred yards long in an unbroken run three storeys high, lined with glass, and *slightly* longer, as the French Line modestly remarked, than the Hall of Mirrors at Versailles. She had the grandest interiors since the *Imperator*, and vaster than hers. The French Line spent on her interior decoration one-tenth of the total cost of the ship. A tenth of that tenth would have been enough, but it would not have been magnificent. She was all in all a most originally beautiful ship. Her hull was designed by a Russian emigré named Vladimir Yourkevitch,

The clean, uncluttered foredeck of the *Normandie*. She had the simplest lines of any great ship

who had before the Revolution designed warships for the Tsarist navies. At full speed, *Normandie* had the cleanest entry of any ship her size. When his ship and the *Queen Mary* were cutting each other's throats for the blue riband, Yourkevitch would proudly show around aerial photographs of both ships at speed, proving the turbulence round his hull to be much less.

French men of letters considered it their duty to exalt her. Jean Giraudoux wrote that this great work which was the *Normandie* was characterized not only by the strength of the men who had built her, and the mass of the materials that had made her, but also by the unanimity of the country that had willed her

construction. It was the will of France that she should be built, and the grand undertaking had created a spiritual unity that vividly revealed the qualities of the French nation. Perhaps. There were others who so opposed her construction, and considered it so extravagant, that they called her France's floating debt; and it was a debt which, as it happened, she was not to have the time to repay. In the same spirit as Giraudoux, André Dumas wrote a poem 'O Normandie!', which shrinks in translation and really requires the heightened words of the French to do it justice, but rhapsodizes about a ship-of-light cleaving through blue immensities at such a rate that one saw that in spite of those thousands of miles there wasn't really any Atlantic left any more between Europe and America. But the fear of hubris still hung around, not in Dumas but in the minds of the French Line, whose president, at a ceremony to consecrate the chapel on board, sought reassurance from Cardinal Verdier, who had come to bless the ship. 'Eminence,' said the president, 'those who built this fast and luxurious liner have not committed the sin of pride. They desired that, in international competition, France should be represented by an *unité* worthy of her.' The cardinal assured them that they had not, in the circumstances, been guilty of sinful pride.

Normandie was nearly not called *Normandie* at all, and indeed there was much more real doubt about her name than about the *Queen Mary*'s. One suggestion was to call her the *Jeanne d'Arc*, which would not have been a good omen considering the natural tendency of French Line ships to burn at their moorings, as will appear; or *La Belle France*, or *Maurice Chevalier*, or *Aristide Briand*, or *Pax Napoleon*, or even, in the American interest, *General Pershing* or *Benjamin Franklin*. (The Americans, when they briefly took her over during the war, gave her the very French name of *Lafayette*, though he was a Frenchman more celebrated in America than in France.) But when the French were originally naming her, the worst danger was that she would be called *Paul Doumer*, after a president of the French Republic who was assassinated by a madman in 1932. The French Minister of the Merchant Marine had even gone so far as to make the blunder of virtually making the offer to M. Doumer's widow, which irritated the French Line, who could not conceive of their ship being named after a murdered man however grand. It would not have been lucky, and the Americans, who were thought by the French to be particularly superstitious, would not have liked it. The widow was assuaged by having a smaller ship in the Indo-China trade named after her late husband, and everyone in the end was pleased by the choice of *Normandie*, which happened to be not only a maritime province but also that represented in the French assembly by the Minister of Merchant Marine

himself. *Normandie* was also thought to be a name the Americans would remember. The New York office of the French Line put out a leaflet saying how, more than 1,000 years before, Rollo the handsome Norseman had come to Le Havre in quaintly shaped Scandinavian galleys. Not loot but a kingdom and a home had been his ambitions, and he took to wife Gisela, daughter of Charles, and that was the beginning of the historic Normandy everyone knew and loved.

The *Normandie*'s maiden voyage from Le Havre was on 29 May 1935. The *corps de ballet* of the Paris Opera arrived on board, and so did Madame Lebrun, wife of the living President of the French Republic; she was to make the crossing in the Trouville suite, of four bedrooms, living-room, dining-room, and kitchen. It was not quite ready; as in many of the other first-class cabins, the hot running water was not yet running and water had to be brought in pitchers, but though the plumbing might have failed, the panache had not, and Madame President's suite was guarded by a sailor with a pike. The other of the two great suites, Deauville, was occupied by the Maharajah of Karpurthala, who, however, offered an unjustified slight to the *Normandie*'s 200 chefs by bringing his own cook with him. Colette was on board, writing for a Paris newspaper, but even her sharp observations collapsed into lofty prose and she wrote about the great liner struggling for the record, and the ocean obeying the ship in silence, and so on. There never was any struggle. The sceptics had said she might break in two, but no liner, however large, had ever done so badly as that even on her maiden voyage, and the *Normandie* did easily what she had been built to do, and took the blue riband at the first attempt. She sailed from Bishop's Rock to the Ambrose light in four days, three hours, fourteen minutes. She had not been officially trying for the record. No liner of breeding ever openly did. But as soon as she happened to break it, little commemorative medals with blue ribbons were spontaneously produced and there were just enough to go round, one to each passenger. A blue pennant thirty metres

The *Normandie* approaching New York soon after having taken the blue riband on her maiden voyage

The *Normandie* in the North River, New York, very near the French Line pier, attended by a flotilla of small craft and an airship

long, one metre for each knot of her speed, also appeared immediately, and the *Normandie* docked in New York flying this pennant and with the Marseillaise blaring from a loudspeaker flying overhead in an aeroplane. From the Manhattan shore 30,000 watched, and from New Jersey another 100,000. Visitors were charged fifty cents to look round her in dock. Madame Lebrun, at a banquet, gave the Mayor of New York a cheque for $500 for the city's poor, and the *Petit Journal* of Paris remarked that New York had shown itself to be a city on the scale of the *Normandie*. Cunard said that the *Normandie* appeared to have done pretty well.

They were later to do pretty well themselves, as they very well knew. By May of 1936 it was time for the *Queen Mary*'s maiden voyage. A week before, Cunard hired the Trocadero restaurant in London and tried to make it look like their new ship. The foyer was made to resemble Southampton docks, and a corridor was dressed up to be a gangplank. There was a bridge, bells, lights, lifeboats with orchestras playing in them, and guests eating dinner in deckchairs served by waiters got up as stewards. The guests were newspaper reporters and travel agents. Members of Parliament were taken round the ship herself at Southampton. Princess Elizabeth, later to become Queen, and then a child of ten, made a royal tour, and was delighted with the Sinbad the Sailor pictures in the third-class nursery and by the tank of tropical fish in the first. She played with the toys, slid down the slide, telephoned on toy telephones, played the toy piano, and was shown a Mickey Mouse film. The *Queen Mary* sailed on her maiden voyage on 27 May, and by 8.55 in the early morning of 1 June was off the Ambrose Light. Coney Island was visible in the haze. Carrier pigeons had been released earlier, at dawn. As she sailed into New York bay a B.B.C. microphone was suspended over her stern to allow listeners in Britain to hear the turbulence of her propellors. The bands played 'Goody Goody'. As she came to her mooring, crowds watched her from canvas stands aboard the old laid-up *Leviathan*, which was then good for nothing more than a grandstand.

The *Queen Mary* had not been faster than the *Normandie*, but she would be, and when she was, on her sixth voyage, the Paris correspondent of the London *Daily Telegraph* reported that in France the general reaction to the news was 'most sporting'. Until 1938, the *Normandie* and the *Queen Mary* went on beating each other now and again by a third of a knot, or sometimes by even as much as half a knot. On one such occasion, in 1938, when the Cunarder had regained the blue riband yet again, the London *Daily Mail* chartered a small plane to overfly her as she passed Bishop's Rock, and the reporter said, 'We cried, "Well done, *Queen Mary*".' Not of course that Cunard even acknowledged the existence of anything called the blue riband. Let the *Normandie* fly pennants thirty metres long when she was that shade faster, but the *Queen Mary* never did. In 1936, speaking in Liverpool at a dinner given by British marine insurance companies, Sir Percy Bates said, 'We are not racing. We will not go into the racing business . . . Our business does *not* consist essentially of racing.' That was a tactful thing to say to a gathering of marine insurance men, whose gift of a silver rose bowl on that occasion he accepted, as he never would accept the silver trophy of the blue riband. Just so, in August 1938, having on one crossing just happened to have been that bit faster in his turn again, the master of the *Queen Mary* made nothing of it, saying he had merely steamed at the speed necessary to catch the right tides at Cherbourg and Southampton. Geoffrey Marr, who in 1938 was third officer of the *Queen Mary*, and later became commodore of the line, called this sort of thing a polite fiction. He said that to give an air of verisimilitude to the company's statement that a record crossing had just been routine, which the ship could repeat at any time if circumstances justified it, the time table was altered to allow the ship to do crossings at over 30 knots on the next two or three voyages, though the normal service speed was 28·5.

The speeds did not matter. The *Normandie*'s fastest crossing was 31·20 knots, and the *Queen Mary*'s 31·69. In so many ways, there was nothing between the ships. Their tonnages were a game too, as if any tonnage was ever accurately measured anyway. The *Normandie* was built as 79,301. A little later the *Queen Mary*, when nearly completed, came out at 81,235. Certain alterations then found necessary abaft the *Normandie*'s third funnel had the unforeseen effect of raising her tonnage to 83,102 at a time when similar alterations to the *Queen Mary* would have been too expensive. So the *Normandie* was, that way, slightly the larger vessel, though Cunard had a later opportunity, which they took, of making the *Queen Elizabeth* a little larger still. The *Normandie* was a bit longer than the *Queen Mary* too, though about that the Naval Correspondent of the London *Daily Telegraph* had some hard words to say. The Cunarder, he wrote, was 990 feet long, while the *Normandie* had been given the impressive length of 1,029 feet. *But* the French ship had clipper bows and, at the stern, a thirty-eight-feet overhanging counter. Subtracting these useless projections at bow and stern, said the Naval Correspondent, the *Queen Mary* came out longer, and furthermore the English ship was built with all the strength of a battle cruiser. This was an unfortunate turn of phrase for a Naval Correspondent, who ought to have remembered that the last time British battle cruisers had seen action was at the Battle of Jutland, when three of them, almost brand new, had mysteriously blown up. He might also have remembered that one of them had been called the *Queen Mary*.

The comparison that brings most vividly home the size and speed of the two liners was made by Frank O. Braynard, the American writer and authority on shipping. It struck him that a taxi darting out of the old Pennsylvania railroad station in New York at 32 miles an hour on to Seventh Avenue would cause no surprise, but imagine Pennsylvania Station itself coming out and following the taxi at the same speed and you would have an idea of the vastness and power of the *Normandie* and the *Queen Mary*.

The two companies' own publicity of their ships tended to be a little less vivid. 'The French Line,' said the French Line, 'is aware that perfection is a very difficult achievement and would welcome any suggestion for making the ship as agreeable as possible.' The company, in the same brochure, had already mentioned that there was naturally an orchestra in the grill at all meals, and that furthermore a *symphony* orchestra played every day in the main lounge. Cunard went rather for the hard sell, which was perhaps partly because they carried fewer first-class passengers, and did not insist on such a rigorous separation of the classes as the French Line. In the first year of her sailing, Cunard were offering tourist returns on the *Queen Mary* '25 per cent down and the rest over a year', and the off-season return was only $52.84 down and eleven monthly payments of $18. 'Have you ever,' they said, 'read about Cunard White Star's crack express ships with a secret determination to make one of them your magic steed to Europe?' On the other hand, you could pay up to $2,411 for a suite for six, or $1,633 for a suite for two, cabin class, one way. Here is one Cunard advertisement:

Queen Mary is just about the most beautiful ship afloat (*New Yorker*)
Unsurpassable . . . the basic good taste is invariable (*New Yorker*)
Ease . . . takes the sea without vibration or uncomfortable roll (New York *Herald Tribune*)
Elegance unmarred by ornateness (*Brooklyn Eagle*)
Not one garish note has been allowed to intrude (*Brooklyn Eagle*)

Many wisdoms went into her making (New York *Herald Tribune*)
A new peak in luxury at sea (*New York Times*)
Regal a ship as ever ruled the waves (*New York American*)
You find yourself secretly grateful there are no screaming colours . . . (*New York American*)

This same ad went on to fit in other testimonials for which it had been able to find no introductory initials in the ship's name, quoting the *Newark Star Eagle* (which is scraping the barrel a bit), as saying that the *Queen Mary* like the Grand Canyon was essentially indescribable, and the

Dancing in the main lounge of the *Normandie*

Cleveland Press as asserting she was a noble vessel, 'as sweet as English air could make her'. She was, as we have seen, made in Scotland.

Both Cunard and the French Line continued to make much of their passenger lists, which were eagerly fed to the press and eagerly published. The *Normandie*, on her 100th crossing, carried many notables of the Screen, including Douglas Fairbanks Snr, Olivia de Havilland, Walt Disney, and Fred Astaire; some of the Stage, like Noël Coward; many of Diplomacy (all forgotten); and many of Society, among them H.R.H. the Grand Duchess Marie of Russia, who mysteriously ranks before the Duke of Marlborough, who was at least still real. Beaverbrook and Hemingway were on the same list. Cunard could do every bit as well,

though they tended to be more selective of celebrities, not for instance listing so many who are now so infallibly unknown. Thus they have Viscount Astor, R. C. Sherriff, Mrs A. A. Milne, John Barbirolli, and Rebecca West. Cunard's press men were also better at the off-beat. There were delegates to the Mothers of the World Peace Movement in Los Angeles, and also Sidney Freemand, described as 'buyer of lucky sweepstake tickets'.

Both lines courted the famous. Aldous Huxley, boarding the *Normandie* at Southampton in 1937, had paid tourist rate but was shown to a large and luxurious cabin, compliments of the French Line, and told he had the freedom of the ship. 'Everything,' he said, 'was entirely unreal. We wandered about the vast and brand-

[153]

new ship, crossing and recrossing public rooms, a gilded, throbbing, overheated limbo.' It was just like an Englishman to think the place overheated: the *Normandie* was heated for Americans. Harold Nicolson was another Englishman who found the *Normandie* unreal, the whole interior like something by Le Corbusier, like an *exposition des arts decoratifs*, like a setting for ballet choruses of stewards, sailors, stewardesses, and fifty lift-boys flying along bright corridors. It was all gold, Lalique glass, and scarlet; very gay, but he thought it would drive him mad after a week. Both Nicolson and Huxley are unkind. Photographs show the *Normandie* to have been very beautiful. And both no doubt would have been equally scathing of the *Queen Mary*. Clive Bell called her interior 'teddy bear', meaning cosy. Others thought she was a maritime version of the then quite new Dorchester Hotel, London. What of her interior now survives can hardly be called teddy-bear, though it may be extravagant. Eurythmic women fly across mirrors, streamlined trains and aeroplanes fly across walls, but everywhere the wood veneers are delightful. Cunard at the time called her, among other things, The Ship of Beautiful Woods, and said she had no clumsy baulks of timber but veneers of angelim (deeper yellow than primrose), ash, avodire (in some lights grey and in others gold), beech, cedar (to line the cigar-shop), cherry burr, tiger oak from England, pear, satinwood from Ceylon (in former days considered too precious for anything larger than a jewel case), sycamore, and synara (called Lemon wood).

They were both lucky ships, with few troubles. There was at first the *Normandie*'s vibration, which was pretty well as bad as the old *Mauretania*'s had been. In the calmest seas, glasses were never much more than half filled, or the wine spilled. Nicolson said that in the circular grill room in the stern the flowers in little vases on the tables wobbled dreadfully. It was either the hull which needed strengthening, which would have been bad and could have encouraged no end those marine critics who said that any ship of 80,000 tons was going to fall in two eventually, or it was the screws.

The bronze doors to the dining-room of the *Normandie*, which are now at the Church of Our Lady of Lebanon, Brooklyn

On the *Mauretania* it had been the screws. So the French Line cast a set of new screws, each with four blades rather than three, and when these were fitted and tested, the vibration disappeared. After this small refit, the *Normandie* was due to go back into service, and a routine underwater inspection was made. The diver reported that all was well and that all *three* screws were in excellent condition. He was then told the *Normandie* was a quadruple-screw steamer. One of the new screws had fallen off, and there were no more of the four-bladed kind ready. But the *Normandie* was ready to sail, and the French press was already full of her new smoothness. There was only one thing to do; if she was to sail at all, two of her old three-bladed screws had to be refitted, and this was done. She vibrated as merrily as ever, to the French Line's embarrassment, until more new screws could be cast. The company's New York office, trying to be loyal

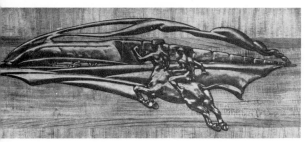

Typical motifs from the decor of the *Queen Mary* — an aeroplane with winged horse, a small boat with flying fish and gulls, and a streamlined locomotive attended by a centaur. All are by Maurice Lambert

and helpful, and perhaps not to disclose more than was necessary, then put out this statement explaining the new steadiness: 'What did it? Good old flannel, the common or garden variety of flannel, which wraps every upright, stanchion and joint, and even lines the walls.'

The *Normandie* turned out to be a better ship than the *Queen Mary* in a heavy sea, and the French Line made much of this, saying that in the winter storms of 1936 when her rival had to slow down, and still arrived with much damage and with some passengers hurt, the *Normandie* had maintained her speed and had moreover been so steady that she had never once even had to empty her swimming-pools. This may have been true, but if it was, then the water in them must have slopped around a fair bit, because though the *Normandie* did not loll on the roll like the *Queen Mary*, she did at times possess the opposite characteristic, and when she did lean, she whipped back to the vertical like a destroyer, very sharp and snappy. Still, it was true that she kept to her timetable in the worst storms. The English magazine *Engineering* said she was often only five hours late compared with the twenty-four to thirty-six hour delays of other liners.

The war was coming. Americans in Europe wanted to get home, and westbound crossings were crowded. The *Queen Mary* left Southampton for her last pre-war crossing on 30 August 1939. Temporary berths were rigged up in the libraries and swimming-pools. The upper-deck lights were blacked out. The commander was warned that two German pocket battleships might be in the Atlantic. Commodore Marr recalls that on 3 September, which was a Sunday, they were steaming down the coast of Nova Scotia and just beginning morning church service as Mr Chamberlain was making his wireless announcement that England was at war with Germany. At noon the look-outs reported the masts and funnels of two warships on the horizon, and the officers thought of the German pocket battleships. But they were the British cruisers *Exeter* and *York* searching for the *Bremen* which had slipped out of New York two nights before. Commodore Marr does not say so, but had the warships been German, then the *Queen Mary*, which was not running empty but with more than 2,000 passengers, could only have tried to run, and then, failing, would have had the choice of surrender or being shelled to pieces. But next day she came safely to New York, and there she stayed while she fitted out as a trooper.

The *Normandie* was in New York too, and there also, in June 1940, came the new *Queen Elizabeth*, having made a secret maiden voyage across the Atlantic to join her sister ship. For two weeks the three largest liners in the world were tied up at neighbouring New York piers. First the *Mary* left and then the *Elizabeth*, leaving only the *Normandie*. Almost all the French crew left for France via Canada. Miles of carpets were taken up. The three funnels were covered with canvas shrouds. She was still a French ship, a skeleton French crew remained, and every morning and evening the tricolour was raised and lowered. But by 1940 the French were thought to be doubtful allies. Paris had fallen. Half of France was occupied by the Germans. Half was ruled by a puppet Vichy government. Those French who could be called Free French were either in London or in Africa. The New York *Herald Tribune* began carrying letters suggesting that the *Normandie*'s crew might sabotage her. On 15 May 1941, at 7 o'clock, a captain of the United States Coast Guard presented himself on board with orders to protect the ship from sabotage from within and without. Commandant Hervé Le Huédé of the *Normandie* received him and said, 'I give you my word we shall never sabotage the *Normandie*. But if we wanted to do it, nothing would be easier; all we should have to do would be to leave the ship, and hand her over to you.' He did not mean to be all that insulting. It was just that only the *Normandie*'s own crew understood the complexities of her structure, or her fire drill. In the summer of 1941 the French wine on board ran out and was replaced by Californian. On 7 December the Japanese bombed Pearl Harbor. Five days later the *Normandie* was seized by the United States government, and her French crew left singing the Marseillaise. The *Normandie* became the USS *Lafayette*. The first idea, rapidly abandoned, was to convert her to an aircraft carrier. Then, more reasonably, they decided to make her a

George VI's letter to Lord Aberconway, Chairman of John Brown, Shipbuilders, explaining why he was unable to attend the launching of the *Queen Elizabeth*. The ceremony was performed by the new Queen whose name the ship was given. The worrying situation the king refers to in his last sentence was the Munich crisis. The day before the launch, the British fleet had been mobilized

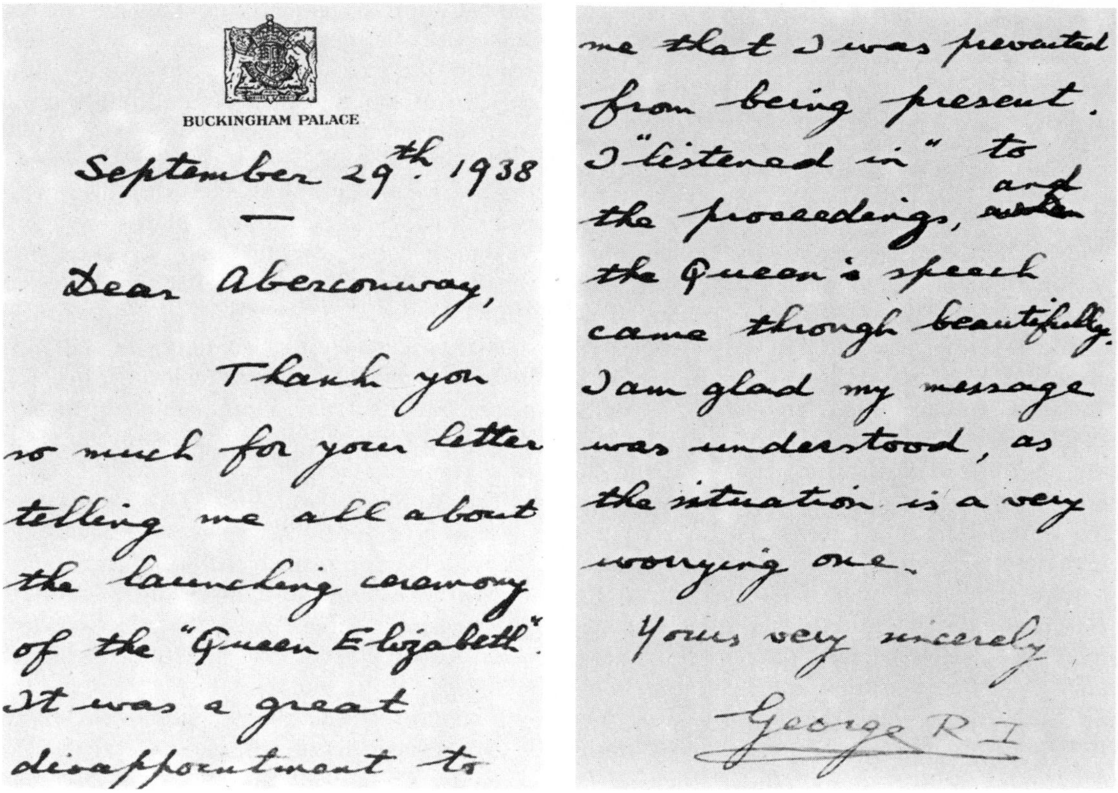

BUCKINGHAM PALACE

September 29th 1938
—
Dear Aberconway,
Thank you so much for your letter telling me all about the launching ceremony of the "Queen Elizabeth". It was a great disappointment to me that I was prevented from being present. I "listened in" to the proceedings, and the Queen's speech came through beautifully. I am glad my message was understood, as the situation is a very worrying one.
Yours very sincerely,
George R I

The *Normandie*, in February 1942, burned out and capsized at pier 88, Manhattan

troopship. Into the grand salon were dumped many thousands of kapok lifevests, which are inflammable, and at 2.37 on the afternoon of 9 February 1942 they did catch fire, probably from sparks from an acetylene torch removing the bases of lamp standards that had once supported chandeliers. Perhaps the common or garden flannel wrapping every stanchion and lining every wall, if it existed, helped the blaze. The direct telephone line to the New York Fire Department did not work. Over the next many hours, 3,500 tons of water were pumped into her. It froze. She listed, and, at 2.45 in the early hours of 10 February, capsized at pier 88, where she remained until November of the following year when she was at last righted and her ruins towed away by fifteen tugs. She had been one of the sights of New York, visible from the upper storeys of every skyscraper in central Manhattan. The Superman comic strips put forward ideas on how to save her. Her designer, Yourkevitch, went round insisting

to the end that she could be restored. She was sold for scrap. In her brief career, the most brilliant of ocean liners had cost the US government eleven million dollars, in seizing her, botching her up, attempting to refit her, sinking her by incompetence, and then raising her. She had also cost the French Line – or in effect, since she was so heavily subsidized, the French government – 863 million francs to build and run, of which they had recovered only 168 million. In her 129 crossings from 1935 to 1939 she had been on average no more than half full. But she *had* been, and this is with apologies to the *Queen Mary*, who survived to sail again another day, the most brilliantly original of ocean liners. The *Queen Mary* was the stateliest ship, but she had evolved, and could plainly be seen to have evolved, from all the Cunarders of the previous thirty years, from the *Mauretania* and *Aquitania*. Except that she was bigger and better, she was nothing much that they had not been in their time. She had their lines. The *Normandie* was no evolutionary ship. She was like nothing before, and of course it helped her immortal reputation that she died young.

Her dash and gaiety are perhaps best captured by Ludwig Bemelmans, who travelled aboard her and wrote a short story about it. In her decor, he said, she leaned towards excess. There was something of the *femme fatale* about her. Everybody was satisfied, particularly with the Lalique ashtrays. The great hall — silver, gold, glass, and high windows — was as large as a theatre. On the sun deck, children rode the merry-go-round that was built inside the first funnel, which was there for no purpose except decoration and proportion. On the outside of that funnel was a small plaque, like the charm on a bracelet, elegant and right. On it was inscribed: *Normandie, Chantiers Penhoet, Saint Nazaire*, and the date she was built. A young widow aboard travelled with an icebox full of flowers which helped her bear up through the voyage. She appeared with fresh blooms at every meal. Each lift had not only one operator, but also a second man whose purpose it was to squeeze himself into the car, pushing the first one against the wall. The second man then asked the passenger his destination, and passed this information to the first. The second man also opened the door and then rushed ahead to guide the passenger to whatever room he had asked for. When Bemelmans went to buy railway tickets at the ship's travel bureau he told the man there he wanted to go to Zuerrs in the Tyrol, and started to add that Zuerrs was on the top of the Arlberg between . . . But he got no further. The man at the bureau stopped him and explained, 'It is I, Monsieur, who will tell you where Zuerrs is found.' Bemelmans thought that the tips on that crossing amounted to more than the whole price of the voyage.

In 1942, at the seizure docks of the New York Customs, a sale was held of the furnishings that had been removed before the *Normandie* caught fire. Four wooden hobby horses went for up to $30 each. One man paid $310 for 8,534 life preservers (though why were that many ever needed?), explaining that they could be sold as beach souvenirs. Six pianos fetched from $80 to $700 apiece. 'La Normandie', the statue of a peasant girl from the staircase of the ship's smoking room, now stands in a pool in front of the Fontainebleau Hotel at Miami Beach. The doors of her first-class dining-room, that splendid space which was slightly longer than the Hall of Mirrors at Versailles, are now at the church of Our Lady of Lebanon, Brooklyn.

CHAPTER SEVEN

The War and Other Hazards

In a history of the 1939–45 war the carrying of troops by liners would be an important chapter. Churchill said the *Queen Mary* and *Queen Elizabeth* had shortened the war by a year. But in a history of ocean liners, the war is only an interlude.

At the end of August 1939, with war only a few days away, the *Bremen* was at her New York dock ready to sail. The United States customs and other agencies did all they could to delay her. She was searched to see that she was not carrying arms. In a purely routine inspection to see that the safety regulations were being complied with, she was formally required to lower and raise all her lifeboats. These stratagems kept her for nearly two days, and then she slipped out of New York with her portholes blacked and her crew lining the rails giving the Statue of Liberty the Nazi salute and singing 'Deutschland Uber Alles'. She carried no passengers. Rumours flourished. Her decks were reputed to be stacked with explosives, which presumably had eluded the search for arms, and she was said to be under orders to destroy herself if intercepted by British or French warships. She was at one point reported to have scuttled herself, and lifebuoys bearing her name were washed up off the Massachusetts coast. She was otherwise reported to have gone to Mexico. She had really gone north, with her crew painting her grey as she went. The British cruisers *Exeter* and *York* searched for her but all they found, on 3 September, the day war broke out, was the *Queen Mary* bound westward and steaming flat out for New York. That was off the coast of

Nova Scotia and by then the *Bremen* was far north, making for the North Cape and the Russian port of Murmansk. Part of the way she flew the Hammer and Sickle, though she resembled no conceivable Russian ship. From Murmansk she later crept down to Bremerhaven. She and her sister ship *Europa*, which had been safely in Germany all the time, then became part of Hitler's Operation Sealion, the proposed invasion of Britain. Large ports were cut in their sides through which soldiers could rapidly disembark. Sealion was abandoned, which was as well for the two liners since stationary ships of their size could only have presented the most unmissable targets to any stray allied aeroplane. The *Bremen* was still lying at her home port of Bremerhaven in 1941 when she was set on fire, apparently by a member of the crew with a private and not even a political grievance, and became a total wreck. There were thoughts of converting the surviving *Europa* to an aircraft carrier, but the Germans, having no suitable aircraft she could carry, and, by 1943, having no waters in which she could safely sail, abandoned that idea too. The *Europa* remained at Hamburg under camouflage and somehow survived the bombing of that port throughout the war.

Early in the war, the *Columbus*, the third of the large German liners but much inferior to the other two, was found by an English destroyer as she tried to get home from Mexico and scuttled herself off the coast of Virginia. A new turbo-electric liner of 35,000 tons, no longer one of the very largest, but after all the size of the *Mauretania*, was hastily launched at Hamburg in 1940 to clear the shipyard for other work, but then was destroyed in an air raid without even having been named. German plans for a super-liner faster and larger than any British or French ship were naturally abandoned at the outbreak of war, and so the *Viktoria*, to be 1,000 feet long, with five screws, and a speed of 36 knots, was never started. The two large Italian liners, *Rex* and *Conte di Savoia* were both sunk by bombing, the first by British planes near Trieste and the second by the Americans near Venice.

This is a record of disaster, and at first the Allies did no better. The *Normandie* foundered, out of incompetence it is true, but she was as final a loss as if she had been bombed. The Canadian Pacific *Empress of Britain*, 43,000 tons, homeward bound from the Middle East via the Cape, was attacked by a German bomber off Ireland, and then finished off by a U-boat. She was the largest allied liner to be lost, but since she was homeward bound there were mercifully few troops aboard her. Her master, reporting the loss, filled in, presumably for want of any other form, an ordinary Board of Trade death certificate, normally used to certify the death of a seaman.

The printed form read: '*Relating to the death of . . .*', and the name *Empress of Britain* was then typed in, and the captain wrote: 'I, Charles Howard Sapsworth, 57, of 24 Belgrave Crescent, Edinburgh, Master, *Empress of Britain*, do solemnly and sincerely declare . . .' What he declared was that on 26 October 1940, off north west Ireland, she was hit by five bombs. 'The ship was completely on fire,' he said, 'and every living person was taken off.'

The greatest allied shipping catastrophe of the war occurred when the Cunarder *Lancastria*, an old, slow, small ship, was embarking retreating troops from the beaches of St Nazaire in 1940, under heavy dive-bombing. One bomb exploded inside a hold, killing a number of soldiers never to be known but guessed at 3,000. Churchill, in his memoirs of Gallipoli, in the 1914 war, mentioned that an unnamed Turkish transport was sunk with 6,000 killed. These terrible figures would have been nothing if

either the *Queen Mary* or *Queen Elizabeth* had been sunk, but the miracle of the war is that they were not, although they were scarcely more difficult targets to a U-boat than the *Lusitania* had been, and of infinitely greater value.

It was a distinct allied advantage, and one of the few British advantages apparent early in the war, that they did possess a great number of the most splendid troop transports. Early on, when Britain was so desperate that she gratefully bought ancient American destroyers of the First World War, the Americans also offered the *Kaiser Wilhelm II* and the *Kronprinzessin Cecilie*, North German Lloyd blue-riband liners dating from 1903 and 1907 which had been interned in the First War and had never crossed the Atlantic since 1918, but had lain rotting in the Chesapeake. This offer was declined. The fastest liners of the Cunard and French Line fleets were again used as they had been in the First War, to steam alone and very fast, relying on their speed to keep them safe from U-boats. These great liners were fast, but all the same it is astonishing that they so completely escaped. It only needed a sighting from one German long-range reconnaissance aeroplane, and a U-boat pack could have been summoned up and had at least an even chance of killing the equivalent of an entire army division with one torpedo. By 1942 the Queens were regularly carrying 15,000 troops each. They were the capital ships, but there were also the *Aquitania*, the new *Mauretania* launched only in July 1939, slightly larger than the famous old one but slower, and later the *Ile de France*.

Soon after the outbreak of war, the *Queen Mary* was already in New York and was painted grey. The *Queen Elizabeth*, her sister ship and the largest liner ever built, had been launched in 1939, had barely been fitted out at all, and in September 1939 was still in the Clyde. She too was painted grey. It was put about that she was to move to Southampton on trials, and she moved out to sea. But a King's Messenger who had come by train from London to the Clyde handed the master sealed orders to make directly for New York. So in March 1940, a few weeks

The *Queen Elizabeth*, painted troopship grey, landing soldiers in the Middle East, July 1942

before the date of what should have been her maiden voyage had there been no war, she made for New York flat out and practically empty, except that she had on board a few workmen who had confidently expected their next port to be Southampton. They formed a club known as the Unruffled Elizabethans. At New York she tied up alongside the *Queen Mary*, which left within two weeks for Sydney to fit out as a trooper. That November the *Queen Elizabeth* also sailed to the Far East, to fit out at Singapore. Until Japan came into the war late in 1941 they ferried Australian soldiers to Suez, taking German prisoners back with them. With wounded prisoners, the story was the same as on the *Mauretania* in 1915. An Atlantic liner is not built for great heat. In the Red Sea

in 1941 many prisoners died. There were burials every four hours. Then the Queens ferried American troops from New York to the Pacific by way of Rio de Janeiro. On one voyage, General Marshall asked if the *Queen Mary* could take 15,000 men. The Cunard officers calculated that this would increase her draught to forty-four feet six inches, which would mean she was sailing well below the Plimsoll line. Not only that, it meant that as she left New York she would barely have enough water to scrape over the Hudson Tunnel, and if she listed at all would certainly be unable to do so. The ship was balanced, and then the 15,000 soldiers were ordered to stand exactly where they were, unmoving, as the *Queen Mary* crossed the tunnel. It worked. Once again, at

[161]

Nurses disembarking from the *Queen Elizabeth* at a Middle East port in 1942

Rio, where the increased draught was dangerous, the orders were that no one should move. On previous voyages, with fewer soldiers, the *Queen Mary* had always listed heavily when GIs crowded the rails to look at the women in passing ferry boats. Later, when American troops were being moved to Europe, 15,000 men were often carried from New York to Scotland. Henry Morgenthau, Secretary of the United States Treasury, visited the *Queen Mary* one day in 1942. Treasury money was being spent on her, and he wanted to see on what.

He asked to be shown the worst living accommodation on board, and was taken to the first-class swimming-pool where bunks were stacked in tiers of seven. There was little light and less ventilation. The Americans carried out time and motion studies, filming each embarkation so that delays could be seen, and avoided next time.

'The ship will be very crowded,' said the American troops' standing orders. 'Officers and men should not view this trip as a vacation; it will be anything but that.'

The Old World and the New, joined by the Atlantic. This panel, by MacDonald Gill, was and still is in the restaurant on C deck of the Queen Mary. A crystal model of the liner, electrically lit and synchronized with the ship in speed, showed passengers where they were. In this picture the model is just visible, in mid ocean

The theatre of the *Normandie*

The *Queen Mary* running down the *Curacao*, one of her escorting cruisers, October 1942. As she was ordered, the *Queen Mary* steamed on. A court of inquiry divided the blame for the accident. Painting by Rigby

Cunard White Star *Georgic*, sister ship of the *Britannic*. Both were motor vessels, only of 27,000 tons and slower than the bigger liners, but both had a reputation for steadiness. They were the last White Star ships to survive in the Cunard fleet. *Georgic* here still retains the White Star pink funnels

'As long as the ship floats your best place is on board. Have your life jacket properly adjusted.'

To serve the officer passengers, Cunard stewards were still on board, and these officers were even told how much to tip them. The U.S. Army advised its officers to give the bed-room and table stewards one dollar each. British officers were advised to tip the bed-room steward five shillings and the table steward sixpence less. Thus the English carried a proper distinction of class on to even a troopship in wartime. But as the dollar was then worth four shillings and twopence, the British were slightly the more generous.

The Atlantic crossings were a gamble. Until late in 1941 the *Queen Mary*'s only armament was one four-inch gun and one anti-aircraft gun. Then she was given some rockets. Until 1942 she had no radar. Captain Harry Grattidge, her staff captain on many of these wartime voyages, said no self-respecting gambler would have betted too heavily on her chances of survival. Across the Atlantic she was unescorted. Near either coast she was escorted by warships. On the morning of 2 October 1942, nearing the end of her passage to the Clyde, she was met off Bloody Foreland by the old cruiser *Curacao*. A few destroyers also appeared seven miles distant. Cruiser and liner kept company for four hours, zig-zagging for safety. At two in the afternoon, in sunlight, one ship or the other misjudged its zig-zag and the *Queen Mary* cut the cruiser in two. Fifty feet of the *Curacao*'s stern were sheered off and sank immediately. The rest of her floated for twenty minutes. For fear of U-boats, the *Queen Mary* was under orders to stop for nothing, ever, and she did not. Her master had no choice. The destroyers came in seven miles for the survivors and saved 102: 338 men died. The *Queen Mary*'s forepeak was awash, and her stem was crumpled, but the collision bulkhead held and she steamed on at 24 knots. A court of inquiry divided the blame.

The Queens between them carried nearly two million soldiers. The *Queen Mary* made eighty-six Atlantic crossings. The *Mauretania*, given that she was half the size, did as well. In 1945, on a variety of trooping passages, she sailed round the world on a course of 28,000 miles in eighty-one-and-a-half days. The *Aquitania* brought women and children from Pearl Harbor to San Francisco, and later crossed the Atlantic with troops many times. But it is the Queens that are most remembered. Here is the briefest log of one passage of the *Queen Mary*:

New York to Gourock (Clyde), 16,683 souls aboard. New York 25 July 1943. Gourock 30 July, 1943. 3,353 miles. 4 days 20 hours 42 minutes. 28.73 knots. The greatest number of human beings ever embarked on one vessel.

In January 1946, just after the war, but before she had made her maiden voyage as a passenger liner and while she was still on trooping duties, Winston Churchill crossed on board the *Queen Elizabeth*. The day before they reached New York, he made a speech to the troops over loudspeakers. 'Yesterday,' he said, 'I was on the bridge, watching the mountainous waves, and this ship – which is no pup – cutting through them and mocking their anger. I asked myself, why is it the ship beats the waves, when they are so many and the ship is one? The reason is that the ship has a purpose, and the waves have none. They just flop around, innumerable, tireless, but ineffective. The ship with the purpose takes us where we want to go.'

It was not revealed until later that year, 1946, that in the winter of 1942 a mountainous wave had very nearly sunk the *Queen Mary*. She was making for Scotland and was seven hundred miles out with a full load of American soldiers, in a gale, when a wave struck her and put her broadside. She listed until the upper deck was awash, and those who had sailed in her since she first took to the sea were convinced that she would never right herself. Had she listed another five inches she would have foundered. How the figure of five inches was arrived at is not explained, but the information was given at a widely reported press conference intended to give an account of the Queens' war service, which had up to then remained more or less secret.

The *Great Eastern* rolling in a gale, 1861, smashing her grand saloon to pieces.

This is probably the nearest that an ocean liner has come to being simply overwhelmed by heavy seas since the *President* disappeared in 1841. Certainly no liner has been lost from such a cause this century, but at least two have come near it and others have been badly smashed about. The war was an interlude, and that is enough of it, but it is as well to remember that there were other hazards than war, which were there all the time and inherent in any Atlantic crossing, particularly in winter. These dangers were no more constantly in the mind of passengers or crew than the prospect of crashing is in the minds of passengers in an airliner nowadays, but they nevertheless existed. They were fog, fire, collision, and, rarest of all, calamitous seas.

In 1841 the *President*, a wooden paddle-ship owned by the same company as the *British Queen*, left New York in March with 136 souls aboard. She was notoriously top heavy. On that passage she ran into a famous gale, was last sighted labouring heavily and shipping water, and was never heard of again. In modern times, the two liners which have come nearest to disaster, apart from the *Queen Mary*'s one incident when she was, after all, grossly overloaded, are the *Carmania* in 1912 and the *Leviathan* in 1926. The *Carmania* was a big ship for her day, a Cunarder of almost 20,000 tons, the immediate predecessor in that line of the *Lusitania* and *Mauretania*. On 4 January 1912 she was so thrown around that she rolled fifty degrees, some of her lifeboats were blow to pieces, chairs in the dining-room came away from the deck though they were screwed down, and beds were thrown through the walls of one state-room into the next. And she had a reputation of being one of the steadiest ships on the Atlantic. The *Leviathan* had no such reputation. Like all of Ballin's huge trio, which were the largest in the world until 1932, she was known as a tender ship, which rolled a great deal and hung on the roll. In a spring gale of 1926 she ran into waves more than a hundred feet high. They broke over her. Her captain, Commodore Herbert Hartley, had to manoeuvre her aslant, so as to ride up and over the waves at forty-five degrees. He believed that to have ridden the seas head on would have broken her apart, and that had she been brought broadside on she would have been swamped and capsized. Portholes were smashed a hundred at a time. Hartley remained on the bridge for seventy-two hours. He said that aside from avoiding the probability of the *Leviathan* breaking up, and probability was his own word, his greatest fear was that the passengers might panic. At the height of the storm a woman climbed the exposed and vertical ladder to the bridge. Her clothes and hair were drenched.

'Captain,' she yelled, 'are you afraid?'

He grabbed the rail with one hand and held her round the waist with the other to prevent her being washed away. 'I'm not afraid,' he said.

'How far are we from land?' she asked. She was obviously out of her mind.

'About three miles,' he shouted over the howling wind.

She was insane. It took five sailors to carry her screaming to her cabin, and it was weeks before she was normal again. As for being three miles from land, Hartley had told her the truth. As he later remarked, in one of the most heroic throwaway lines of Yankee seamanship, 'Land was three miles straight down.'

That was such a crossing as a captain has to face once in a lifetime at sea. The size of the ship seems to make no difference. In 1852 George Wilkes wrote a travel book called *Europe in a Hurry*. He forecast ships of 10,000 tons, in which he was right; and this means that, since this was as early as 1852, he was already thinking as boldly as Brunel. He forecast that Liverpool would give way to Southampton as the principal English Atlantic port, and in this he was also right but sixty years before his time. He also forecast New York would give way to Newport, Virginia, in which he was as wrong as a man could be. And in his boldest prediction he was most wrong of all. He believed that ocean travel would soon be as steady as railroads on land, and gave his reasons. Monsters of the deep would progress steadily over the great bed of the sea because their draught would be so great that their hulls would be beneath the motion of the waves, that *surface* of agitation, the greatest depth of which had been ascertained to be only twenty-five feet, with an average of eighteen. He was soon proved wrong. By 1861 Brunel's *Great Eastern*, a ship of twice ten thousand tons, although exceptionally steady in smooth seas, was pitching and rolling in a gale as badly as any tiny early Cunarder, and much more out of control. Much later, and much bigger, the *Mauretania* could still, as a marine engineer put it, cause acute disturbance, and he thought it strange that anyone should expect otherwise. 'A few more thousand tons,' he said, 'does not intimidate the ocean.' The *Olympic* came into New York in 1921 with two men killed in a storm. The *Queen Mary* was at first not even fitted with handrails for passengers to hold in a sea, but after her first storm they were rapidly installed. In 1956, two years before she was fitted with stabilizers, she came into Southampton after a March crossing with four passengers and two crew to be taken to hospital. On the second and third days of her passage she had been forced to slow to twelve knots. The captain said the worst roll had been only twenty-four degrees. The new *United States*, after one or two stormy passages, printed this advice on passenger lists: 'When the ship is pitching or rolling . . . do not stroll about the ship unnecessarily. If your chair should move in the dining-room while at meals, hold on to

A recurring nightmare — steamship nearly running down sailing ship in deep fog

the table — do not attempt to save table utensils or equipment.' In 1966 the new and elegant *Michelangelo* of the Italian line, crossing on the calmer southern route, shipped a sea that smashed her fore-superstructure and killed two passengers. Even the *QE2*, a much bigger ship and stabilized beyond the dreams of marine architects in the heyday of the Atlantic liners, rode out such a gale in April 1972 that her passengers were given storm certificates as souvenirs. On this certificate Captain Mortimer Hehir recited that waves fifty feet high and winds of more than one hundred miles an hour had obliged even the *QE2* to lie hove-to for twenty-one-and-a-half hours until the storm abated. He commended all passengers in 'sharing this unique experience with great cheerfulness and calm'. One of the officers

later said they just could not get out of the storm. She rolled twenty-two degrees to port and starboard and two pianos shot across the floor. £2,500 worth of crockery smashed. No one was badly hurt, but a year later cracks sustained in the gale — superficial cracks in an inner wall, nothing to do with the structure of the ship — could still be seen.

Collisions with icebergs need nothing more to be said about them. The *Arizona* rammed one head-on in 1879 and survived. The *Titanic* glanced one in 1912 and did not. Collisions between ship and ship are much more ordinary, and the strange thing is that it is generally the larger, sometimes very much the larger, of the two ships that founders. In 1895 the North German Lloyd *Elbe* was struck by a Scottish coasting steamer and sank with the loss of 303 lives. In 1898 the French Line's *La Bourgogne* was rammed by a sailing ship and foundered in a few minutes, drowning 549 people. In 1909 the White Star *Republic*, 15,400 tons and the largest ship to sink before the *Titanic*, was holed and sunk by a small Italian steamer. All the *Republic*'s passengers and crew were saved. In 1914 the Canadian Pacific *Empress of Ireland* was struck by a Norwegian collier: it was the liner that sank and 1,011 died. She foundered immediately; it was night and her passengers were asleep below. And in 1956 when the *Andrea Doria* and the *Stockholm* collided west of Nantucket it was the Italian liner which foundered with the loss of fifty lives, and not the Swedish ship, which was not much more than a third her size and the smallest liner on the Atlantic.

And so the list of wrecks could go on, from many hazards. There are coincidences. White Star were surely the unluckiest of all the great companies. The *Titanic* was theirs, and the *Republic*, and also the *Atlantic* of 1871 whose wreck cost 546 lives: and the verdict of the Board of Trade inquiry on the *Atlantic* was as damning as that on the *Titanic* thirty-one years later. The *Atlantic* was lost because 'she was run at full speed, engine and boilers all in perfect order, upon well-known rocks, in fine weather'. And of all companies, the French

Line suffered most from fire, but always in dock, never at sea. The *Lafayette* burned at Le Havre in 1938, the *Paris* also at Le Havre in 1939, and the *Normandie* in New York in 1942.

Then there is fog. The Cunard orders to masters of vessels have always been very clear. Safety was always to be put before speed. It was Samuel Cunard himself who insisted on this, saying that though he had very great confidence in his captains, nevertheless in fog the best men often attempted to push through where prudence would indicate patience. And yet here is Geoffrey Marr, who rose to become commodore of the Cunard line, writing in his memoirs about the navigation of the *Queen Mary*, which he joined in 1938 as junior officer. Looking back, he said, he found it almost impossible to understand how they managed to maintain such very high speeds on a North Atlantic which had just about as much foggy weather as today, but which was then being used by a large number of passenger liners of all nationalities. It may, he says, have been a bit 'By Guess or by God' at times. 'It simply meant that captains and senior officers were prepared to gamble their professional reputations on the mathematical improbability of two ships arriving at the same spot on this large ocean at the same time. We all knew then, from near misses (or rather near-hits) when the visibility was only slightly reduced, how very close a ship had to be before her whistle could be heard.' This was particularly noticeable on the *Queen Mary*, because when she was running at high speed there was so much noise on the bridge from the whistle of the wind through the rigging and superstructure. But there were, he said, older and wiser heads than his to deal with the risk of collision, and when they ran into fog there was a standard procedure. Two extra look-outs were posted, the watertight doors were closed, the engines were put on standby, and the captain reduced speed to whatever he considered prudent. The captain and senior officer on watch then stationed themselves on opposite sides of the bridge and everyone listened intently. If a ship's whistle was heard and its direction con-

The White Star *Teutonic*, pitching heavily in icy seas, *c.* 1890

firmed, course was immediately altered forty-five degrees away from it. The new course was held for ten minutes when, providing the whistle could no longer be heard, the original course was resumed.

Marr also has vivid recollections of the *Aquitania*, which he says was a splendid sea boat. Her bow sliced through the Atlantic sending plumes of spray over her foredeck. But there was a little triangle just abaft the knights-heads which remained dry except in very bad weather, and so long as you could still see that dry spot there was no need to reduce speed. The *Aquitania* was the last liner to have four funnels. These were useful in fog off Halifax. It was either a two-, three-, or four-funnel fog, according to how many funnels could still be seen from the bridge.

A steamer of the 1880s, almost certainly the *City of New York*, rolling in moderate seas. The vigorous are promenading. Others lack the stomach for anything but lying in deckchairs

So in fog on the *Queen Mary* in 1938 everyone listened intently, which was just what they did on the White Star *Cedric* in 1903. Shortly after she left Queenstown, westbound, fog came down and everyone was told to keep quiet and forbidden to go forward of the centre of the ship. A young American girl on board, keeping a journal of the passage, said it was really exciting, deathly still, and she enjoyed it. Then they stopped and anchored and rang a bell incessantly. This same rich young American woman had been doing the grand tour in ships of several lines, and another thing she noticed but did not enjoy was the seasickness, another of the natural hazards, not in the still of the fog on the *Cedric*, but earlier when she and her mother had left New York in the *Umbria*. She was not sick herself, but was expected to be. 'An awful Cook's

tours man' came and asked her if she 'hadn't thrown up yet' and related his own experiences before she could get away from him. She left him abruptly and walked round the deck, only to see 'at least six horrible exhibitions'. At Gibraltar, joining a German liner, she went below for the first time and there in her stateroom renewed acquaintance with what she called that cold, musty, seasick smell.

It is, alas, a fact that a good many passengers, even on the most splendid ocean liners, were seasick. The Collins line, which was the first to equip Atlantic steamers really sumptuously, rolled up the carpets while its liners were still making their way up the bay to the open sea. It is a long time now since seasickness has been advertised by the steamship companies. The daily newspaper printed and distributed on board the *QE2* does run a discreet paragraph

Again probably the *City of New York*, again rolling, this time at dinner. Cutlery is sliding off the table (right), the steward is balancing the soup, and two of the women look as if they wish they had not left their cabins. The men of course are bearing it well. This was a myth. Women were often better sailors

on an inside page saying that injections against motion sickness can be obtained from the ship's hospital, and little blue pills are dispensed free if you ask for them, but that is all that is said. It was not always so. Before about 1910 the shipping companies made it clear in their guides that seasickness was to be expected. Commodore Hayes of the White Star line said passengers used to be so glad to land that they never grumbled at their sufferings on the way over but on the contrary seemed to take a pride in relating the awful experiences they had come through. And a White Star guide of 1896, in a chapter of what are intended to be humorous hints, devotes ten out of forty-five of them to the business of seasickness.

'Don't deny that you are ill when you are.' 'Don't go to the table unless confident of your ability to stay there.' 'Avoid looking at the water as much as possible, and occupy the mind with some interesting book. If a contribution to Neptune becomes unavoidable, do not become discouraged, but continue to eat . . .' The guide also contained a cheering item called Master Tommy's Diary, which reads in part:

May 14. Orful ruff. Most all is Sicker than expected.

May 15. ruffer than yesterday an Only 6 too dinner.

May 18. I didn't rite in my Diarie yesterday. But i am Better now But will not rite no More Until i get home as My Head Akes me. still ruff.

Cunard, in their guides of the same period, gave a jumble of advice. You should put your trust in no so-called remedies. On the other hand, some people suffered more crossing the English Channel than all the way to America, and

'Rolling', on a French Line ship

Laces, jewellery, ribbons, and all other knick-knacks of feminine toilet became 'vexatious and vanity of vanities'.

Lieutenant-Commander J. D. Jerrold Kelley, United States Navy, a frequent writer on shipping matters, reassured travellers that they could as a general rule count on disagreeable weather in the Western Ocean, which tried the temper of people who might be saints ashore; and, say what you would, women were out of place on a ship. However, he added, towards the end of a voyage all but hardened cases and mental dyspeptics enjoyed themselves. This was the tone of the *Etruria*'s daily newspaper at sea on 26 December 1903. 'Some of us have been chastened by that mischievous devil *Mal de Mer* (with capitals please for that is the way it feels), but only for our own good. But for the preliminary period of fasting and self-retrospection, would we have appreciated our Christmas dinner half as much?' This shows signs of Christianity, as did the suggestions, in an article in the *Illustrated London News* on the prevention of seasickness, that in effect it was unpreventable and that very likely the animals in the Ark had suffered from it; but the author of this article also believed in self-help and thought Dr Kappmeier's electric helmet, of which this appears however to be the only known mention, might provide temporary alleviation.

There were appeals to imperial power, one passenger saying that if Britannia ruled the waves he wished she would rule them straight. There were appeals to divine power, as of the passenger on the *Olympic* when she was pitching into a head sea, who prayed, 'Good Lord, if you can't help me, you might bring this sea to attention.' There were imprecations, as of Vesta Tilley, the male impersonator, who, having finally got home, swore she would never face the Atlantic again. There were, if not cures, at least Triscuits which were advertised in Hamburg–Amerika ships' newspapers of 1912 with the jingle:

> A life on the ocean wave,
> A home on the rolling deep.

There were shredded-wheat wafers, a boon to

anyway the worst sailors rarely suffered *mal de mer* for more than a few hours. If you felt a little rocky, lager beer was a capital preventive, but on no account eat ice cream. Recovery was a natural process which could not be hurried, though it might be delayed by over-much giving way. And — ominously — ladies should provide themselves with a bodice or jersey that fastened simply and easily and was devoid of all elaborate neck or waist arrangements. Only those who had experienced the struggles of the dressing hour when seasick knew what ludicrous importance every unnecessary button, tie, or hairpin suddenly assumed on such occasions. The American Line concurred, saying hairpins at sea became involved in disordered masses of flowing tresses.

'An Ocean Steamer's Great Wave'. The steward is amused. The gentlemen succour the ladies

travellers, and obviously meant for those who could face nothing else. There were jokes, like that of the steward: 'Rough, sir? A bit *fresher* perhaps, sir. She did put 'er foot in a few 'oles lahst night.' There was resignation, as of the woman passenger who, urged by the stewardess to put on her lifejacket for boat drill, turned her face to the bulkhead and moaned, 'Let her sink.' There was also a poem by Kipling.

When the ship goes wop (with a wiggle in between)
And the steward falls in the soup tureen,
And the trunks begin to slide;
When Nursey lies on the floor in a heap,
And Mummy tells you to let her sleep,
And you aren't waked or washed or dressed,
Why, then you will know (if you haven't guessed),
You're 'Fifty North and Forty West'.

But by the 1920s seasickness was no longer written about so often. Perhaps it was because it was assumed that full-grown liners as big as the *Olympic* and *Berengaria* were so stable there was no longer any need for seasickness. This was false. The *Olympic* as it happened was stable, but even ships of her size move in a seaway; and as for the *Berengaria*, she was as tender a ship as ever was. The steadiest ships of those days were not the very biggest, but the White Star's *Homeric*, of 34,000 tons, and that line's two motor ships *Britannic* and *Georgic*, both of 27,000 tons and not fast, but with the reputation of sitting like ducks on the water. Perhaps there was less written about seasickness when passengers could be seasick in private. On the earliest liners there was no

[173]

chance of this, even in first class, where the cabins were shared and led off the main saloon. Even in 1907 the *Mauretania* went into service with only thirty-five single cabins. *Olympic*, *Aquitania*, and the biggest German liners had more space and privacy. Perhaps there was something, but not much, in North German Lloyd's contention, when they launched *Bremen* and *Europa*, that seasickness was by way of a vanishing complaint, because it was no longer the fashion, and that, like swooning, it had been one of the specialities of the nineteenth century. But obviously, fashionably or not, people were still seasick. Why else should Dr Dammert devise his atropine and oxygen for that very North German Lloyd that asserted seasickness no longer bothered many people? Why else should Canadian Pacific advertise its *Empress of Britain* as taking the '39% less-ocean route', meaning that the last

'The First Breakfast at Sea'. Another ferocious illustration calculated to encourage passengers

[174]

day and a bit more were spent in the sheltered waters of the St Lawrence?

Commander J. G. P. Bisset, who later became Sir James and Commodore of the Cunard line, augmented his salary by writing, himself publishing, and selling for two dollars a copy a book called *Ship Ahoy*, which was a passengers' primer of sea travel. He said waves one to two feet high made a smooth sea; eight to twelve feet high a rough sea; and forty feet and above a precipitous sea. Heavy rain in a storm, however, tended to keep waves down. The seasick passenger should lie down, preferably in the fresh air, as near the centre of the ship as possible. He should eat no food for twenty-four hours. After this period of starvation, some benefit was usually to be had from iced champagne. As to the clothes to be worn by the patient, he said, 'Some authorities also advise Kayser silk for certain items, but I'm getting into deep water now and guess I'll drop the subject.'

So there was one ship's officer advising the superstitions of champagne and silk. Another Cunard officer, Geoffrey Marr, who also became Commodore in his turn, offered no remedies, but just admitted that throughout his career he never reached the point when he did not feel squeamish in rough weather. He remarked stoically on one voyage of the *Carinthia* that the weather was so bad, and the crockery breakages so great, that Cunard was reduced to serving tea in paper cups.

Many passengers did not need weather that was all that rough to make them sick. In the Second World War it was important to land soldiers in a condition to fight, and some effective anti-seasick drugs like Dramamine were found. But even after the war, and dosed with these drugs, Alexander Korda and Noël Coward were bad sailors even in calm seas. Danny Kaye made crossings dizzy with Dramamine if not with seasickness. The captain of the second *Mauretania*, in a memorable phrase, recalled seeing on one crossing 'two lovely but pale girls crouched wanly over large china bowls'. First-class passengers had the great advantage of cabins amidships, where the ship moved

A spectacularly rolling ship of the French Line, *c.* 1925, and in by no means a heavy sea

least. In heavy seas, three-quarters of the *Queen Elizabeth*'s third-class passengers, whose cabins were nearer the bow and stern, were sometimes sick. As the marine architect said, a few thousand extra tons did not intimidate the ocean. John Masefield, apart from writing that he longed to see the *Queen Mary* leaping to the urge of her great engines, rolling as she went, was also the author of 'I must down to the seas again, to the lonely sea and the sky'. Once when he arrived in New York a reporter asked how he had enjoyed the crossing. His wife replied for him, 'It was too uppy-downy, and Mr Masefield was ill.' When steamship company publicity writers, writing after all to reassure passengers, mention that, though there may be storms, in even the worst of them 'the soup does not elude the diving spoon', then it is fair to deduce that the steadiest liner will sometimes feel like a ship at sea.

CHAPTER EIGHT

High Days and Valhalla

In 1946 the *Queen Elizabeth* brought back the copy of Magna Carta which had gone to the New York World's Fair of 1939 and then, for safety, had stayed in America for the war. The captain was presented with a metal box lined with copper and sealed with lead, and invited to sign a receipt for 'One Tin Box Containing the Magna Carta'. This he altered to 'One Tin Box alleged to Contain the Magna Carta', and then signed. Of the two Queens, the *Elizabeth* was released first from war service, and was fitted out for the first time as an ocean liner, her entire previous career having been that of a troopship. The master's cabin was lined with Waterloo elm, from piles driven under old Waterloo bridge in 1811 and recently recovered when the new bridge was built. During the eighteen months after the war the *Queen Mary* carried 12,886 G.I. brides to America, who were naturally welcomed by bands aboard New York tugboats playing 'Here Comes the Bride', but then she too was handed back to Cunard and refitted with the 10,000 bits of furniture that had been stripped from her and stored in New York, Sydney, and the New Forest. One-hundred-and-twenty female French polishers were brought in to restore the woodwork in which American soldiers had carved their initials. Very soon the two Queens were running the weekly Southampton–New York service they had been designed for. The new *Mauretania* was also running to New York, and the old *Aquitania* to Canada, and Cunard were thriving. Aboard the *Queen Mary*, Henry Ford II and Greta Garbo dined, incommunicado and separately, in the Verandah Grill. On the

Queen Elizabeth, Crown Prince Akihito of Japan won the ship's table-tennis tournament. On the *Mauretania* Miss Lana Turner, on honeymoon, required for breakfast minced raw beef beaten up with egg-yolks, and champagne to wash it down. The Queen of England, returning from New York on the *Queen Mary* after visiting the United States, watched the nightly film shows on three evenings of the crossing, asking to be called just before the main feature began because she did not like cartoons. In the first-class dining-room, passengers were as pampered as ever they had been, and earnestly invited not to limit their choice to the enormous menu, but to ask for anything else that took their fancy. An American oil magnate asked for rattlesnake steaks for four. His order was gravely taken, and his party was served eels in a silver salver born by two stewards shaking rattles. There were sixteen kinds of breakfast cereal every morning, and each liner, on each crossing, carried fifty pounds of mint leaves to make mint juleps. A very few extravagances were moderated. It was noticed that the best people now required smaller suites. Before the war it had been nothing for Count Rossi of Martini Rossi to book a suite of twenty cabins. After the war, the largest suite demanded was only of twelve rooms, by Sir William Rootes, the car manufacturer. Even King Peter of Yugoslavia, no longer having a kingdom, made do with the simplest of royal suites consisting only of three rooms, bathroom, and pantry. But otherwise the tone was maintained. The Marquis and Marquise de la Falaise exacted the same suite with the identical furnishings every crossing, and there was a bed-room steward whose greatest pride it was to store such details in his memory. Mrs Fern Bedaux, at whose château the Windsors had been married, liked quarts of lilac scent to be sprayed round her suite before she came aboard. The Duchess of Windsor herself always sent advance details of the colour schemes she required to be executed throughout her suite, usually electric greens or blues. Stewards were still stewards, working all hours, travelling light with only two shirts to their name, receiving up to £50 a passage in tips and themselves tipping the pantrymen to ensure their particular passengers got the quickest service, the pantrymen in their turn tipping the chefs. Cunard stewardesses, whether married or unmarried, were according to long custom addressed by other members of

the crew as Mrs, though by the passengers of course by their surname alone, with no prefix.

It was all as it had been. All continued. The Duke of Windsor continued. He had been a passenger longer than the Duchess. As Prince of Wales, in the early 1930s, it was he who had come aboard the *Berengaria* one midnight when she was tied up empty at Southampton, bringing with him a ragtime band called the Blackbirds, whose music he conducted in the great ball-room. When the officer of the watch, roused by a watchman, presented himself deferentially in the ball-room, he was just in time to hear the Prince conduct a final tune, thank the band, and promise that there would be cheques in the post for them in the morning. The officer asked why the Prince had chosen the *Berengaria*, and he replied, 'It was very con-

The *Queen Elizabeth*, newly painted and fitted out after her war service, makes her first peacetime voyage

The second *Mauretania*, in cruising colours

venient of course, and — well, I thought we shouldn't be disturbed . . . Sometimes, you know, it's very hard to find a place where you can be alone.' After he became king and then abdicated, Cunard tactfully removed his picture from the ward-room and substituted that of his brother, the new King George VI, as the *Queen Mary* left Southampton. On the Duke of Windsor's first return to England after the war, and therefore the first after his abdication, it was the captain of the *Queen Mary* who noticed that at Sunday service hymn 304 was on the list, which was 'Crown Him With Many Crowns'. At the last moment a tactful change was made. At the end of that first crossing after the war the Duke came on to the bridge to see the Isle of Wight and the Solent for the first time after many years, and was moved to see Osborne, where his great-grandmother Queen Victoria had lived for so long. Cunard captains got on well with the Duke. They noticed that he always went to watch the bellboys attending roll-call at seven in the morning under the second steward. They noticed that he was restless

and felt the cold, and played endless games of canasta with the Duchess, and that after dinner she would allow him only one glass of brandy. Captain Marr said the Duke always came on to the bridge for a few minutes before going to bed, and seemed to be happy in the quiet male atmosphere on the bridge of an ocean liner in the middle of the night.

The passenger lists were mostly as grand as ever. For three years the only bedside reading of Captain Grattidge, who commanded both the Queens, was *Who's Who* and *Who's Who in America*. He had to be a master of protocol. He appeared to have made an error one evening, however, when he invited to his cabin for drinks the many United Nations delegates who were his passengers. Among them were Sir Alexander Cadogan, Paul Spaak, and Andrei Gromyko, and at first the party did not go at all until the captain's steward unwrapped on the cabin floor a parcel of two dozen opulent toys sent as the gift of an American manufacturer. There was a bear that walked, a donkey that rolled its eyes, and a doll that rocked itself to

Publicity pictures on board the *Queen Elizabeth*, c. 1950. The decor, as in the nymph and fawn mural, was less subtle than the *Queen Mary*'s. The model accepting a drink from a waiter is Roger Moore, who later went on to play the Saint on television and James Bond in the cinema

sleep. 'Gentlemen,' said the captain, 'you may be interested in these.' There was instant amiability, with only one disagreement, over Cadogan's bear. 'It's my turn now,' said Spaak. 'No, it's mine,' said Gromyko. 'You promised.'

It is fashionable, but quite untrue, to believe that the grand days of the ocean liner were over by the 1920s, and certainly by the Second World War. The fact is that the twelve years after 1946 were the most profitable years ever on the north Atlantic, for those companies who had ships. It so happened that Cunard possessed far and away the fastest, biggest, and most famous liners of those days, and that they resumed regular services sooner than any other line, and so the greatest share of the prosperity was theirs. The Queens were running full, which the *Queen Mary* and *Normandie* had never done before the war. In 1949, the *Queen Mary*'s tourist berths were sold out for a year ahead, her cabin class for six months, and first class for two months; furthermore, if a passenger wanted a particular first-class cabin, a deposit was demanded six months in advance.

Each ship was making more than £100,000 profit each round voyage. That year Cunard showed a gross profit before tax of £7 millions. Since England after the war was poor, and the hard currency of those days was the United States dollar, the most impressive figures are that for three years running the two Queen liners made between them an annual profit of $50 millions. Cunard had at last lost the *Aquitania*, the oldest liner on the Atlantic and the last with four funnels. After the war she went into the Halifax service, carrying to Canada the likes of Colonel Sadler, on his way to represent the British Empire in a tuna-fishing contest. One rainy afternoon in 1949, at Southampton, one of her decks split in a rainstorm and the resulting deluge washed out the Board of Trade surveyors who were lunching below, having just given her a certificate of seaworthiness. She was broken up. The *Aquitania* was thirty-five years old, and the only liner to have served in both wars. She had sailed three million miles, and completed 884 Atlantic crossings. At the end she was tatty.

So was the *Britannic*, the last of the White Star ships still to sail for Cunard, but even she was booked solid. Her smoking saloon was done up with mock-Tudor beams, and logs burned in her open fireplaces, before which dogs were allowed to sleep.

In the years immediately after the war, Sweden, Holland, and Italy built new ships, none of them of great size or speed. The two other companies to share most of the profits with Cunard, though a little later, were the French and United States lines. The *Normandie* had gone. The *Ile de France* survived and, having been refitted for two funnels instead of three, sailed again for New York in 1949. Next year she was joined by the *Liberté*, which was nothing but the North German Lloyd's *Europa*, the only great liner ever to be twice raised from the dead. In 1929, when she was fitting out, she was severely damaged by fire, but restored. At the end of the war she was the only first-rate German liner left. The Germans had intended to destroy her rather than see her taken, but in the chaos she was forgotten and seized by the Americans. They found her structurally weak, having been much patched up in her pre-war record-breaking days. An American admiral told a commission of inquiry he did not know how she had hung together in Atlantic winter weather. So she was given to the French Line and taken to Le Havre to be rebuilt. There she broke loose and ran into the wreck of the old *Paris* which had burned and capsized in 1939 and was still where she had foundered. The *Europa* too settled on the bottom, which was not deep. By 1950 she was raised, refitted, and sailing through the narrows into New York. She was much slower than in her German days, but had been given the name *Liberté* and two most elegant new funnels. The French Line at least had a first-rate pair, though not in the same class as the Queens.

Then there was the United States Line. The history of American-built liners is an astonishing one, mainly because there were, for most of the time, no American-built liners at all, although a good three-quarters of first-class

Atlantic passengers had always been American. Partly this was because one of the great steamship companies, White Star, had been American controlled, though running British ships and flying the Red Ensign. This was so from 1902 until 1926, when White Star was sold back to Britain. The story of White Star and I.M.M. has been told. There also existed, quite separately, the United States Line, which did fly the American flag. By 1929 this line had one splendid extravagance, the ex-German *Leviathan*, and some other liners of no consequence. Wheeling and dealing then took place. The line was bought by a concern which agreed, as part of the deal, to build in America two new 45,000-ton liners. In a world slump this was a hopeless promise, and it was not carried out. Part of the line was then sold again, this time to I.M.M., who had at least a lot of experience of running ships and, having got rid of their English subsidiaries, wanted more American shipping. The United States Line then built two liners, *Manhattan* and *Washington*, medium liners in every way, of medium size and medium speed, but incredibly the first Atlantic liners to be built in America since the *St Louis* and *St Paul* in 1895. After the *Leviathan* made her last voyages in 1934, it was proposed to replace her with a new but smaller ship, the *America*. This was done, but she was not completed until 1940. This was no date to put an Atlantic liner into service, and so she spent the war as a trooper and only began commercial crossings in 1946. She was only the third decent liner to have been built in America in more than forty years, but she had some distinction and was in speed and size very like the new *Mauretania*, only with a bit more dash. After the war she and the *Washington* did good enough business.

Then in 1950, at the height of the boom, the United States Line laid down a liner of the most surpassing distinction, certainly one of the greatest ever to cross the Atlantic, and by far the fastest. This was the *United States*. She had about her everywhere the stamp of originality. She cost the earth and was worth it, particularly since most was paid by the

The *United States*, far and away the fastest liner ever to cross the Atlantic

American government. She was supposed to be first a troopship and after that a liner, and on this pretext the American government paid four-sevenths of her cost of $77 million. It was a convenient way of ensuring that America should possess the world's fastest liner, and, as a pretext, really nothing new at all. Great ships had almost always been built with some hidden government subsidy – loans at nominal interest for the *Mauretania* and the Queens, outright subsidy for the *Normandie*. The *United States* was built out of national pride. A troopship of her size could by 1950 have been of no possible use to anyone. In the Second World War the two Queens had just got away with it. By 1950, when any imaginable enemy would have been equipped with jet aircraft able to fire rockets, a troopship like the *United States* would have been the surest way that could have been devised of losing a division of soldiers at one swoop. She never did carry troops, but she did have a nominal capacity for 15,000 of them. She was of 53,000 tons but no more, since a larger liner could not have passed through the Panama canal. She was subdivided like a warship, though again for what reason it is difficult to imagine, since no warship, however subdivided, had ever withstood determined torpedo attack. Her machinery was placed in two separate watertight compartments, so that with one engine completely out of action she could still steam at 20 knots. Full out on her trials she is said to have achieved more than 40 knots, though what even such speed could do to protect a troopship against air attack is not clear: but it could, of course, although incidentally, easily win the blue riband. At any rate, the result was a beautiful ship, and probably the safest passenger liner ever to sail. William Francis Gibbs, her designer, made her entirely of steel and aluminium, and permitted on his ship nothing that would burn.

[181]

Prophetic *Punch* cartoon after the maiden voyage of the *United States*

Wood was forbidden. Funnels, masts, cabins, rivets, decorations, lifeboats and lifeboat oars, were all of aluminium, and so were the thousand flower vases on board. But Steinway declined to make aluminium pianos for her, and so pianos were the only articles of wood she carried. Bed-clothes were of some uninflammable concoction allied in its nature to glass fibre. Gibbs did, however, as he prowled round his lovely aluminium ship, infallibly carry in his pocket a small piece of wood to be touched for luck.

The *United States* was not launched but built in dry dock and then floated out when she was completed. On her maiden voyage in July 1952 she ran from Ambrose Light to Bishop Rock in three days, ten hours, forty minutes at an average speed of $35\frac{1}{2}$ knots, a clear four knots faster than the *Queen Mary*, and she completed her passage in a sixty-mile-an-hour gale that was hardly made for speed records. Most of her passengers stayed up dancing through the last night to be awake the moment the record was broken, which was at a quarter past six in the morning. Margaret Truman, the president's daughter, sounded the ship's whistle. Those who were still dancing stood and sang the national anthems of the United States, Britain, and France.

The *Spectator* of London made an ass of itself by remarking: 'We surrender the blue riband and no one can deny we have done it with good grace . . . British liners have been supreme on the Atlantic for a century [which showed how much marine history the *Spectator* knew]; we have no need to begrudge the honour to the Americans.' *Punch* simply said, and this was the entire extent of its comment; 'After the loud and fantastic claims made in advance for the liner *United States* it comes as something of a disappointment to find them all true.' But it did publish a full-page cartoon showing the liner breaking its record on the ocean below, while overhead flew a British jet airliner, a Comet, doing 500 miles an hour and spelling out in its vapour trail the message 'Congratulations sister'. The irony of this was seven years in the future; in 1952 there were no jets on

the Atlantic. The meeting must have been over the English Channel, and the Comet was flying the old British Empire route from England to India. Turning round, the *United States* broke the record westbound, also by four knots. It was exactly one hundred years since an American-built ship, a Collins liner, had held the blue riband. The United States Line was thereupon booked up for months ahead. The captain of the *Queen Mary* cabled the USS *United States*: 'I LOVE BEING FOLLOWED'. The Duke and Duchess of Windsor, after all those years, left Cunard and thereafter travelled American.

The extraordinary prosperity continued throughout the fifties. Cunard was finding that not only the two Queens but the other ten ships of its fleet were always very well-filled, fuller than ever before. This prosperity needs a few figures to illustrate it. In 1902, 205,000 passengers crossed the Atlantic. In 1929, at the height of the twenties just before the crash, 1,069,000 made the passage. After the crash these figures fell badly to 685,000 in 1931 and to 460,000 in 1934. In the late thirties, business was bad. Even the brilliant *Normandie* sailed on average little more than half full. But after the war, for many years, any berth could be sold, and by 1958 more people crossed the Atlantic by sea than had ever done so in one year before – 1,200,000.

The chairman of Cunard in the 1950s was Colonel Denis Bates, brother of Sir Percy Bates who in the 1930s had seen the vision of the two Queen liners sailing together and pressed for their building. He died in 1946, the evening before the *Queen Elizabeth*'s maiden voyage as a peacetime liner. Colonel Bates, in the 1950s, was so strong-minded a man that, although he relied on getting three-quarters of his passengers from America, he never set foot in that country. The chairman of the most successful company on the Atlantic, at the time of its greatest success, never made a crossing in one of his own ships. By then there were of course many piston-engined aeroplanes making Atlantic crossings every day, but a man of such stubbornness of mind as Colonel Bates could be forgiven if he still thought of aeroplanes as no threat at all. He probably thought of them in the way his older brother, Sir Percy, would have in 1936, the year the *Queen Mary* entered service. In those days no aeroplane crossed the Atlantic at all, and there were few flights going anywhere. The London *Times* published a short column of small print headed 'Aircraft Movements'. On 2 May 1936, there were three Air France planes entering or leaving London, and one K.L.M. plane. Nine of Imperial Airways craft, all with names, were on their way to or from some part of the Empire. *Hannibal* was outward bound. *Hengist* was homeward bound, having left Karachi the day before. *Heracles*, from London, had arrived at Paris on the first. The ports of call of these aeroplanes were Capetown, Baghdad, Alexandria, and Brindisi. No times were given, only dates. By 1958 the first jets were flying the Atlantic, not the pioneering British Comets but American Boeing 707s. The Cunard chairman's report for that year was not concerned. Why should it have been? After all, 1958 was the year when more passengers crossed the Atlantic by sea than in any year before; or, ever would do so in any year after, but that could not be known. As for air travel, the chairman said 70 per cent of Cunard clients travelled on holiday or for pleasure. The Cunard motto was 'Getting there is half the fun'. The chairman told the story of an American travel agent trying to sell an American couple an air ticket to London, and receiving the reply, 'We've waited twenty-five years to make this trip and we're certainly not interested in getting there in any six-and-a-half hours.' As for the extensive advertising campaign by the airlines, Cunard thought that it might certainly encourage travel by jets, but that it would also increase the general lust for travel from which the sea as well as the air would profit.

It did seem likely. But if there was an omen that year it was the sale, and then the death, of one of the great liners, the *Ile de France*. She was thirty years old, and worn out. The French Line received a bid from Sheraton Hotels, who wanted to moor her at Martinique, but refused,

saying they would only sell her for scrap. In 1959 she was sold for rather more than one-and-a-quarter million dollars to a Japanese firm. Captain Souhie Komasi was sent to Le Havre to take her to Japan. The French Line captain moved out of the master's quarters, which however Capt. Komasi declined to accept, saying that in the Shinto religion a ship had the soul of a gallant warrior, and that her old captain should stay in his quarters. She was registered as the *Faranso Maru*, which simply means the *French Ship*, but while she was still in a French port the Japanese declined to paint this name on her or fly the Japanese flag over her. At sea the Japanese flag was run up to the masthead, but was kept furled while the French flag, below, was allowed to flow in the wind. When the liner reached Osaka a last scrupulous ceremony was observed in the first-class dining-room. A Shinto altar was erected, with offerings of food to the Gods, and a thousand guests attended a ceremony of purification so that the *Ile de France* could approach the Gods with her soul immaculate. That night it rained in Osaka and by dawn the last cherry blossom had fallen. In Shinto mythology, the cherry blossom is the symbol of the warrior spirit. The blooms of other plants hang on and rot, fearing death, but the warrior-spirited cherry flower leaves the stem cleanly and with courage, and reaches the ground still fresh.

It is strange that the Japanese should insist explicitly that a ship has a soul. Roosevelt said much the same of the old *Mauretania*, and the idea does exist, though less explicitly, in the west. A ship is not just an artifact, but has a being of sorts, which is perhaps why children born aboard ship were often named for her, though always as their middle name. Thus children were named Joseph Imperator Schnapp (1914), and Regina Ile de France Rosenberg (1929); and a little girl born on board the *Mauretania* in 1931 to an American mother and a Czech emigrant father was given the Christian names Anna Mauretania, and, because she was born on a British ship, acquired British nationality.

Cunard publicity pictures, posed with models on board the *Queen Elizabeth*, and aimed at the American market ▶

LUNCHEON

Juices: Grape Fruit   Pineapple   Sauerkraut
Sea Food Cocktail
Smoked Irish Salmon with Capers

HORS D'ŒUVRE
Cornet de Jambon en Gelée   Œufs, Rémoulade   Matjes Herrings
Antipasto   Salade Landaise   Asparagus, Vinaigrette
Tomato, Windsor   Filets d'Anchois   Salade Beaucaire
Boneless Sardines   Roll Mops   Herrings in Tomato
Saucisson: Cervelat, Salami, Liver, Lyon, d'Arles and Mortadella
Olives—Green, Ripe and Farcies
Salted Almonds and Peanuts

SOUPS
Consommé Brunoise   Potage Malakoff
Jellied Madrilène

FISH
Fried Scallops, Cole Slaw, Tartare Sauce
COLD: Crab Flake Salad, Mayonnaise

FARINACEOUS
Gnochis, Piémontaise

VEGETARIAN
Celery Fritters, Tomato Sauce

EGGS
Poached, Florentine   Sur le Plat, Lyonnaise
Omelettes (to order): Mexicaine and Limousine

ENTREES
Fried Chicken, Southern Style   Frankfurters with Sauerkraut
Navarin of Lamb, Jardinière

CONTINENTAL SPECIALITY
Entrecôte sauté, Chambord
Sirloin Steak seasoned and cooked in butter, served with Bordelaise Sauce and
garnish of Sliced Beef Marrow, Cèpes Provençale, Parisienne Potatoes

GRILL (to order)
Escalope of Sweetbreads, Béarnaise   London Mixed Grill
Pork Chop, Apple Compote

AMERICAN SPECIALITY
Corned Round and Brisket of Beef
(Cabbage and Dumplings)

SUGGESTED MENU
——
Hors d'Œuvre, Variés
——
Consommé Brunoise
——
Pétoncles frits, Sauce Tartare
——
Côte de Porc grillée, Compote de Pommes
Haricots Verts   Pommes Sautées
——
Tarte aux Pommes à la Suisse
——
Fromage   Café

Passengers on Special Diet are especially
invited to make known their requirements
to the Head Waiter

VEGETABLES
Garden Peas   French Bean
Young Carrots au Beurre   Buttered Vegetable
Stewed Tomatoes

POTATOES
Baked Idaho   Sautées   Creamed-Purée   Fren

COLD BUFFET
Roast Ribs and Sirloin of Beef, Horseradish Cream
Boiled American Ham   Home-made Brawn   London Pres
Roast Turkey, Cranberry Jelly   Roast Lamb, Mint Sauce
Terrine of Duckling   Rolled Ox Tongue   Jell

SALADS
Hearts of Lettuce   Baltimore   Sliced
Mixed Bowl   Française   Snowflake   Fre

DRESSINGS
French   Chantilly   Figaro

SWEETS
Rusk Custard Pudding   Fresh Swiss A
Pineapple Shortcake, Hawaiian   Deep Fresh Rhu
Gâteaux : Boston Cream Pie   Caramel Lay
Hot Lancashire Eccles Cakes
Compote of Apricots, Plums and Cherries—Whipped

ICE CREAM
Vanilla   Peach   Burnt Almond   Ne

CHEESES
Edam   Roquefort   St. Ivel   Gorgonzola   P
English Cheddar and Cheshire   Stilton
Old Blue Cheshire   Gruyère   Camembert   Pont

Fresh Rolls

FRESH FRUIT
Apples   Oranges   Tangerines   Pears

Tea (Hot or Iced)   Coffee (Hot or Iced

Queen Mary luncheon menu in 1959. The dinner menu offered a little more variety

After the Shinto ceremony, something less generous then awaited the *Ile de France*. The contract had stipulated she should be scrapped, and so she would be, but there was no clause to prevent the Japanese owners, having first committed her soul to the Gods, from leasing her to Metro Goldwyn Mayer to assist in her scrapping and incidentally shoot some film. Andrew Stone, an M.G.M. producer, explained that he was making a film called *The Last Voyage* which required as its climax the sinking of a liner. He explained that after the sinking she would be salvaged and returned to the scrappers, who 'planned to chop it up anyway'. The French Line intervened to ensure that at least the name *Ile de France* would not be visible in the film, but that was all. According to the film script, the liner should have been in mid Pacific when a boiler exploded, but Mr Stone conceded that this would make salvage difficult, and agreed to sink her in coastal waters, whereupon she would be raised by a firm of salvagers who had worked for the Royal Navy. The film would be a story of dramatic suspense, showing in one-and-a-half hours the disintegration of the captain's character as well as that of the ship. 'We do everything for real,' said Mr Stone. 'When a boiler explodes, a boiler explodes. When a funnel collapses, busting in the front deck, a funnel collapses and bashes the deck. Bulkheads really explode – and so on.' All this for a ship which the Japanese contended had a soul, and which the French pointed out had been awarded, for her war service, the Croix de Guerre with Palm.

By the time the *Ile de France* was being sacrificed by M.G.M., the French Line already had the *France* on the stocks, intended to be a new *Normandie*. She very nearly was. She was faster, longer, as powerful, but of lesser tonnage, 66,000 against 83,000. The French Line called her a last refuge of the good life. She had been laid down in the high days of the late fifties, and was launched by Madame de Gaulle with a Nebuchadnezzar of champagne, seven litres, and with a resounding sentence from General de Gaulle, who said, 'May this ship accomplish her destiny.' But by the time of her maiden voyage in 1962 the high days were already over. She was the last pure Atlantic express steamer, built as a ferryboat between Europe and America, designed to make thirty-four round voyages a year and to work that route alone. Between her laying down and her sailing, the decline had been rapid, and it had been brought about by the jets which the Cunard report of 1958 had so reasonably dismissed. American tourists were by 1962 being persuaded to book a westward crossing taking only six-and-a-half hours, even if they had saved for twenty-five years for it. Speed, which the steamer companies had always sold, was now cutting them out. 'I would point out,' a Cunard commodore had told his passengers, 'that what you are paying for is speed.' Fuel oil cost £10 a minute; even in first class the food cost Cunard only 35 shillings per head per day. What was costly was the extra few knots that the very fastest liners had in hand over the rest, but this was worth little when the jets were cruising at 500 knots. What, for that matter, had a few knots difference meant when propellor-driven airliners were crossing at 250 knots? But the jet did more than suddenly double the speed of air travel. Jets are much smoother. Rough flights became very rare. Jets were cheaper. This new cheapness attracted yet new passengers. Since the war at least,

the liners had not been absolutely the only way to cross. But after 1959 they were no longer the rational way to cross. In that one year the steamship companies lost a quarter of their trade. Suddenly all the liners could offer, which had been built for speed, was leisure, and, in first class, opulence. But to travel first class by British Overseas Airways or Air France was as opulent as any liner if not as spacious. Many of the younger Cunard and French Line stewards joined the airlines: on airliners stewards more or less traditionally serve the first class, leaving stewardesses for the tourist.

By 1962, aboard the maiden voyage of the *France*, Charles Clore the London property owner and financier, known to have been interested before, vigorously denied that he was planning to bid for Cunard; he was off to America to look at a textile mill, a hotel, and the biggest office building in New York. The same year Cunard announced a loss of £1,728,000, and no dividend. They also sold seven Merseyside warehouses, as they were, later in the decade, to sell ships. Plans to build a third *Queen*, the *Q3*, of 75,000 tons, had been abandoned. The London *Times* said it was hard not to shed a tear.

In the early 1960s the old Queens were often criticized. Magazines ran articles with headlines like 'Cunard-on-Sea', comparing the deserted Queens to deserted English holiday resorts in rainy summers. In 1962 John Rosselli, an English journalist and historian, crossed the Atlantic both ways in the Queens, one way on each, with his wife and two children. He travelled tourist, and wrote an article entitled 'The Notion of Steerage'. He suspected that the fall of 7 per cent in the numbers of passengers carried by these ships in the previous year had come about partly because some of the missing 7 per cent had heard what it was like from previous passengers and had decided to try the jets instead. The tourist-class decorations reminded him of the Winter Gardens at Hoylake, near Blackpool. The crew seemed helpful in an Ealing Films way, courteous at all times but noticeably at their best in an emergency.

The *France*, the last pure Atlantic liner ever built — that is to say for speed and the Atlantic crossing all the year round, and not for cruising half the time

The surest way to get magnificent service was to be seasick from the moment you went on board. But he and his family were not seasick, and found the Queens rather a trial. The ships tended to superimpose on the seedy grandeur of the Odeon the trade-union demarcation lines of the sixties. He wanted to bath his children but found the bathroom doors locked. He called the stewardess who called for the Lady Bath Attendant, who, in turn, when she discovered that he wished to bath the children himself, and was a man, said in that case the Male Bath Attendant was required. After another wait, they all had to go to the deck below, where the Male Bath Attendant had his bathroom. Later, in the restaurant, the wine waiter had never heard of a carafe, though the

menu said there was one for nine shillings, and the bottle of wine they ordered instead did not arrive until after the meal. The tiny deckspace for tourists on both Queens suggested that the notion of steerage died hard. On the *Queen Mary* there was no covered deck space where you could sit and look at the sea. It was wind and view, or no wind and no view. The *Queen Elizabeth* did have a small lounge on the top deck, a bit dingy, but with a view. Rosselli suggested fewer waiters and simpler meals. Passengers should be allowed to open their own bathroom doors and fetch their own drinks from the bar without having to wait for a steward to serve them. And generally Cunard could do a lot to make its ships pleasanter and cheaper.

The *Queen Mary* at Southampton in 1966, late in her long career

About the same time, passengers in first class were claiming that the service there was not what it used to be, saying that some of the stewards did not even speak English and sounded like the Real Madrid football team. 'Do you gents want something to drink?' though uttered in a perfectly friendly manner, was not quite the way for a wine waiter to address first-class passengers. It could also have been said that some of the passengers were not what they used to be either. In 1963, only forty-two took their own manservants or maidservants with them at the special rates traditionally offered by the company.

But Cunard, though having abandoned the idea of a third Queen, had after all decided to build a new liner, the *Q4*, by no means so big as the old Queens, with only two screws instead of four, a vessel which could earn its living both as an Atlantic liner in the summer and as a cruise ship in the winter. She was to cost almost £30 million, of which the government would lend £24 million. This ship was laid down in 1965, and at much the same time, Cunard, having bravely decided to continue the weekly transatlantic service, sent the *Queen Elizabeth* for a big refit. She was said still to have ten good years in her, and plainly Cunard must have thought so too or they would not have spent so much. The refit was not easy. After four months on the Clyde, the three hundred cabins supposed to have been equipped with showers and lavatories were not ready, not one of them. She had also been pilfered. It was a hallowed tradition on the docks. The most profitable trade was in copper piping, which was sold in the local pubs for whisky. If a man saw a bit of copper pipe he first hammered a nail into it to see if there was water running through it. If not, he ripped it out and sawed it into lengths short enough to fit into his trouser legs as he walked out through the dock gates. The panelling cover was then replaced. Later, when the water was turned on, there was flooding.

The refitted *Queen Elizabeth* did not prosper. Even with bathrooms and air conditioning she did not attract the cruise passengers that had been hoped for. When one cruise was cancelled she made a double crossing of the Atlantic instead, carrying 70 passengers one way and 130 the other. It was possible to go down for afternoon tea and find you had the vast first-class lounge to yourself. In 1966, Cunard lost nearly £7 million.

On 8 May 1967, the masters of both the Queens, at sea, received wireless instructions to open sealed envelopes and to read the contents to their crews. The sealed letters said each liner had been losing three-quarters of a million pounds a year and that Cunard was going to scrap them, the *Queen Mary* in the autumn of that year, and the *Queen Elizabeth* a year later.

That September there were two great events. On the twentieth the *Q4*, christened the *Queen Elizabeth 2*, with an arabic number *2* and not the Roman *II*, and ever after to be known as the *QE2* anyway, was launched. A week later, the *Queen Mary* came into Southampton Water at the end of her last crossing from New York. Passengers sang 'Auld Lang Syne'. The dockside crane drivers were on strike, so even the first-class passengers had to carry their own luggage, which the *Queen Mary*'s master said was a damned bad show. Lynn Redgrave, a young film actress, said, 'The voyage was lovely. You almost expected Ginger Rogers and Fred Astaire to appear and dance any minute.' At the last lunch, the chef's choice was Cherbourg sole, and on the captain's table there were autumnal chrysanthemums. One thousand four hundred passengers had come from New York, but another five hundred

were trippers from Cherbourg who crossed the channel on the liner as part of a two-day package deal, from £11 up, with a chance of duty-free liquor thrown in. A Southampton taxi driver said, 'I have seen them all come and go. The *Aquitania*, *Mauretania*, and *Berengaria* sailed on Saturdays. The *Olympic*, *Majestic*, and *Homeric* on Wednesdays.'

The *Queen Mary* was not, as it happened, to go for scrap. Cunard said they did not wish her to be bought to sail in competition with their own new ship, and nor did they wish her to be bought for a degrading use. The City of New York offered two million dollars to set her up as a floating high school in the abandoned Brooklyn Navy Yard. So strong was this possibility that John Lindsay, Mayor of New York, paying a visit to his tailor, had to deny that he was going to be fitted out as captain of the *Pinafore*. In the end *Queen Mary* went, for $3,400,000, to the City of Long Beach, California, who hoped she would be an attraction to rival Niagara Falls. Her passage to California round Cape Horn was organized as a cruise, with suites for two costing up to $9,000. 'Be one of the few modern-day sailors to circumnavigate storied, historic Cape Horn,' said the handout. Cunard declined to handle the cruise. The Americans did it themselves. It was not an elegant voyage. She was not air conditioned, so many passengers preferred to sleep on deck as she passed slowly through the tropics on half power. Cockroaches appeared. Rats were seen. The captain denied this. In a radio-telephone call from somewhere in the tropical Pacific he said the cruise had gone well, there was enough soap, and there were no rats aboard, only a few trouble-makers among the passengers. As the *Queen Mary* came into Long Beach, £1,000-worth of flowers and plants were dumped overboard because California state law forbade their importation. Eric Littaur, for twenty years the ship's gardener, said it was a bad moment for him. The *Queen Mary*'s last stowaway was detected, Jane Miletich, aged twenty-two, who had got on board at Acapulco where she had been working as a waitress. She said she just wanted

SPECIFICATION

for Produce and Manufactures of the United Kingdom exported

NOT to be used for goods on which drawback is claimed or which are subject to restriction.
(See Note A overleaf as to delivery of Specification)

X.S. 29
(formerly No. 29 (Sale))

C.D.3 Number, or insert "N.R." if C.D.3 is not required   N.R.

DIVISION (See Note B)   7.73

H.M. CUSTOMS AND EXCISE

Port of Shipment........Southampton

Dock and Wharf or Station....107 Berth

Particulars of process, if any, which the goods have undergone since importation (See Note E)

Ship or Aircraft

Name or Mark........'Queen Mary'

Nationality of Ship (See Note C)........British

Date of Clearance....31 Oct 1967

Port or Place of destination....Long Beach U.S.A.

Country of Consignment of Goods (See Note D)   U.S.A.

FOR OFFICIAL USE ONLY

Specification No.

Ship's Rotation Number

* Marks	Numbers	Number and Description of Packages	This column for official use only	Particulars of Merchandise (see Note F)		Quantity (see Note G)		Export Value (see Note H) £
				Export List Statistical Code Number	Description	Number or Measure	Net Weights	
					'Queen Mary'			3,450,000
'Queen Mary'	One	One Ship		E.73589	SteamShip .Net Registered	One	33073.10	
					Tonnage;33073.10 Tons		Net.Reg.	
					Official No.164282.		Tons.	
					Registered in Liverpool			
					1936. No.7.			

I declare that all the particulars set forth above are correctly stated and that the goods entered above do not on account of their description, ultimate destination, or any other reason contravene export control regulations.

Signed: (see Note I) ....
(Adding Exporter or Agent as the case may be)

Date.....26.Oct.....196....

X.S. 29   FOR NOTES SEE OVERLEAF

Address:..The Cunard Steam-Ship Co.Ltd......
Southampton   Sec. F2206 (June, 1963)

(Countersigned)..
Officer of Customs and Excise

The *Queen Mary*'s export certificate, after she had been sold to Long Beach for $3,450,000.

to get back to the United States, and then go home to Brooklyn. Edwin Wade, Mayor of Long Beach, said the *Queen Mary* would become a national shrine. Supervisor Kenneth Hahn of the Los Angeles County office said she was a rusty bucket. Long Beach had expected to spend five million dollars converting her but it cost twice that. Gene Darcy, an interior decorator, paid $20,000 for the nuts, bolts, taps, doorknobs, chamber pots, and other junk of the *Queen Mary*, and then sold the lot for $3 million as souvenirs. His customers included Frank Sinatra, Dean Martin, and Lucille Ball. He sold chamber pots as champagne buckets. They bore the Cunard crest.

In 1968 the *Queen Elizabeth* carried out her Atlantic crossings alone. Cunard lost a million pounds. Towards the end of her last homeward

passage, crew and passengers crowded on to the dance floor and sang, again, 'Auld Lang Syne'; and the captain said it was hard to bear. While she was lying idle at Southampton, Queen Elizabeth the Queen Mother, after whom she had been named thirty years before, said she would like to vist the ship for the last time. The *Queen Elizabeth* was grimy, but Cunard got together a shore gang to wash down the funnels and the white paintwork on the side the Queen Mother would be able to see from the dock, the starboard side.

The *Queen Elizabeth* was not sold for scrap either, but to be a convention centre at Port Everglades, Florida. Commodore Marr took her there, and, when he had finished with engines, received a cable from Southampton office which read 'ACTS 27 VERSE 39'. This verse reads:

[191]

The former *Queen Elizabeth*, renamed *Seawise University*, burning in Hong Kong harbour in January 1972

'And when it was day, they knew not the land: but they discovered a certain creek with a shore, into which they were minded, if it were possible, to thrust in the ship.' To advertise the ship, her new American owners asked Marr to give talks at clubs in Tampa, Jacksonville, Orlando, Atlanta, Cleveland, and Cincinatti. He later said he felt like a used-car salesman.

So both Queens had been sold to America. There was an old joke, told again and again in the days of Cunard's prosperity, about the inevitable Texan millionaire who made the captain an offer for the *Queen Mary*. The joke used to go like this:

CAPTAIN: 'Awfully kind of you, sir, but she's not for sale.'

TEXAN MILLIONAIRE: 'Why not? My money's good.'

CAPTAIN: 'Yes, but you see, sir, she's part of a set.'

Well, the set had gone.

The *Queen Elizabeth*'s Florida owners went broke. At the bankruptcy sale she was bought by C. Y. Tung, a shipowner from Hong Kong who ran tankers and wanted to refit the liner as a floating university. In his honour, and as a play on his initials, she was renamed *Seawise University*. Under a Chinese captain and with a Chinese crew, the largest Chinese liner in the world was partly towed, and partly crawled under what remained of her own steam, to the island of Aruba in the Dutch West Indies, where

The burned out wreck of the *Queen Elizabeth*, half-submerged and unsalvageable

it took eleven weeks to repair her boilers, and then she limped via Rio de Janeiro and Capetown to the Far East. As she rounded the Horn she sounded like a ghost ship. As she rolled, cupboard doors in hundreds of empty cabins banged open and shut. By way of the Straits of Malacca, the South China Sea, and the Paracel Islands she eventually came to Hong Kong, floundering at 4 knots. There she was redecorated. Replicas of the Chinese Great Hall of the Sages were built on board, and of the Imperial Peacock Lounge, and of the Tang Emperor's Moon Palace – all, it was said, without destroying her English decor. Mr Tung

intended to cruise her. A seventy-five-day Pacific cruise was announced. On 9 January 1972 she was seen in Hong Kong harbour ablaze fore and aft, and she settled as a total wreck on the harbour bed. Her last Cunard commander, Geoffrey Marr, said he could not believe she would burn so quickly and completely unless fires had been deliberately started in several parts of the ship at the same time. A marine court of inquiry later brought in a finding of probable arson. Marr said that she had earned a Viking's funeral and that if there was a Valhalla for ships she was there.

CHAPTER NINE

QE2 and the Ship of the Sun King

By the time the old *Queen Elizabeth* was in Valhalla, the *QE2* had for two-and-a-half years been crossing the Atlantic in summer and cruising in winter. Cunard called her the Greatest Ship in the World, which was partly a response to the French Line who persisted in advertising the *France* as the longest liner in the world, which she was by sixty-seven feet. Greatest or not, the *QE2* was certainly the last great liner to be launched. No one will build another. She was built in John Brown's yards on the Clyde. The boss of John Brown was John Rannie, who was born a quarter of a mile from the yards, started work there as an apprentice boilermaker, and then became a naval architect. Some of Cunard's publicity men wanted to engage the Beatles to play a specially composed pop tune at her launch. It was reasoned that this would attract useful coverage in America, where most of her passengers would come from. John Rannie said that until the *QE2* was delivered she was his ship and not Cunard's, and he engaged the pipe band of the Singer Sewing Machine Company to play 'Scotland the Brave' as the last huge ship to be built in Scotland slid down the ways.

While she was fitting out, the *QE2* was duly pillaged by the dock-workers, who took carpets, doorknobs, screws, radios, moveable wallboards, and anything that could be moved. 'Piracy on the Clyde', said the London *Daily Telegraph*, reporting that lorries were flitting through the night loaded with the stolen goods. On trial the beautiful ship did 32.46 knots over the measured mile in the Firth of Clyde. Her

turbines gave such trouble that Cunard at first declined to accept her, but the turbines of ocean liners had often given trouble before. The demand for cabins on her eventual maiden voyage was so great that Cunard tentatively announced five voyages – a short trial cruise to Southampton; a four-day trip from that port; the maiden crossing to New York via the Caribbean; a West Indies cruise from New York; and then her first eastbound passage

The Cunard flag hoisted on the *QE2* for the first time when the company took her over from the ship-builders

◄ The *QE2* in dry dock at Southampton, 1969

The *QE2* entering New York on her maiden voyage, the last great liner to receive the traditional welcome of fireboats and sirens

from New York to Southampton. A reader's letter appeared in the London *Guardian*:

VIRGIN BERTH

Sir, – Can there be any more striking evidence of the influence of the new morality than the report that the new Cunard liner is to have five maiden voyages?

In May 1969, the brass fire nozzles having been fitted at the last moment so that they at least should not be pilfered, the *QE2* made her first maiden voyage. Philip Howard, the London *Times* reporter, a good classicist, said there was no moaning in the many bars, where hordes of voyagers were thirstily following Horace's advice to men about to cross a large patch of water, and that stewards in gaudy pink jackets chattered to passengers with that intimacy which hinted at the promise of reward. Terence Mullaly of the London *Daily*

Telegraph, an art critic, burbled that an Atlantic passage in the *QE2* would become as much a social necessity, as much a matter of prestige for the 'with it' of the age, as a visit to Carnaby Street or the King's Road, Chelsea. The *QE2* would come to be loved by Americans.

On the maiden voyage the ship stopped at eight o'clock one morning and committed the body of Ernest Sharpe to the sea. He had been with Cunard for thirty-one years, and had served with the crew of the old Queens. It had always been his wish to work on the *QE2*.

For a while that year there were three great liners crossing the north Atlantic, the *QE2*, the *France*, and the *United States*. Also, on the southern route, the Italian Line's *Michelangelo* and *Raffaello*, the biggest sister ships since the *Bremen* and *Europa*, sailed from Italy to New York via Cannes. But at the end of the 1969

The Italian Line's *Raffaello* (centre) in Genoa harbour. In the foreground is the *Reina del Mar*.

Two out of work Cunarders, the *Franconia* (front) and *Carmania*, laid up at Falmouth in 1972 before being sold to the Russians

season the *United States*, the fastest of them all, was withdrawn.* She had an American government subsidy of $12 million a year, but was still losing her owners $5 million. She held not only the notional blue riband, but also a silver trophy three feet high which, in the 1930s, a Member of Parliament, Harold Hales, had presented to go with this notional honour. Nobody was ever likely to cross the Atlantic faster than the *United States*, but her owners considered they ought to hand the trophy back. They could find no one to give it to. The trustees of the Hales Trophy were all dead. It now rests at the U.S. Merchant Marine Academy at King's Point, Long Island. Things were then coming to an end. No American ship crossed the Atlantic. The French had one. Cunard, which in 1957 had twelve liners, were reduced to one. In 1969 six million passengers crossed by air, five times as many as had ever, in the best year, gone by sea. In 1969–70, for the first season in peacetime since 1840, no passenger liner crossed the Atlantic in winter. In 1971 Cunard was sold to a property company, not to Charles Clore but to Trafalgar House Investments, whose chairman said the *QE2* was a problem. She was beautiful, and she was identified in the public mind with the name of Cunard, and the name Cunard was itself a great asset, but she was losing half a million pounds a year and there was a limit. He thought she might tie up at Miami for two months in the winter, where she could beat any hotel for style and price. It was seriously considered anchoring her three miles off the Florida coast and running the biggest floating crap game in the world, but the State of Florida was afraid of the mobsters she would attract.

So the *QE2* went on her usual ways, though in 1972 she was subjected to a bomb hoax and, worse, to a partial interior decoration by a firm of American kitchen suppliers who were let loose on more than the kitchens.

In May of that year she was in mid Atlantic, eastbound, when an anonymous telephone call was made to Cunard's New York office saying there were bombs on board which would be exploded unless a ransom of $350,000 in used $10 and $20 notes was left in a blue bag in a telephone box. The caller, who was a man, said he had two accomplices aboard the ship who did not care whether they died in the attempt. Cunard and the British and American governments took the threat seriously. Four bomb-disposal men were parachuted by the Royal Air Force into the sea near the liner and were hauled on board eighteen minutes before the bombs were due to go off. Leopold Stokowski, the conductor, aged 90, was a passenger. He said some people at first feared that everyone would be killed, but every twenty minutes or so the captain spoke a few calm words over the public address system, and gradually everyone realized there was no bomb. The bomb-disposal men searched but found nothing. The American press discovered that before the telephone call was made, but after the *QE2* had already sailed, a story about the hijacking of the *QE2* in mid Atlantic had been read to a creative writing class at Hunter College, New York, by Barbara Shalvey, a typist. In this story a woman dying of cancer, with only a few days left to live, and wishing to have done one great thing in her life, books passage with a young friend, somehow gets to the bridge, threatens the captain with a gun, and succeeds in extracting from him the biggest diamond in the world, which the ship happens to be carrying. She also demands and gets a provisioned motor-lifeboat to escape in. In the story the plot succeeds. In real life, no one came to the phone box in upstate New York to collect the used bills. A few months later in New York the owner of a shoe shop was convicted of making the hoax call and jailed for twenty years.

That November there were also reports of what C. W. Robbins, kitchen suppliers, of Miami, had been paid to do to the *QE2*. The

---

* She was laid up at Norfolk, Virginia, where she remains. The Federal Maritime Commission has tried three times to sell her, without success. At the last attempt, in February 1976, there were only three bids — one from a convicted swindler, and one from a man who said he was a Viking. She remained unsold.

Bomb disposal men parachute to the *QE2* in mid Atlantic after Cunard received a telephone call saying bombs were on board and due to explode

gallery of the grand ballroom had been filled with shops in the style of an airport lounge. The Blue Room, a quiet library, had been converted into a casino with fruit machines and gaming tables. The original grill-room, said by one architect to be the most beautiful room afloat, had been swallowed up by the enlargement of one of the two large restaurants. Part of the first-class promenade deck had been made into a car sale-room. Penthouse cabins were added. James Gardner, the structural designer of the ship, said he had tried to give her a quiet dignity, like a Bentley, but now lumps had been added and wholesale changes made without a thought to the character of

the whole. Dennis Lennon, who had done much of the original internal design, said the new casino was Miami with Georgian mouldings. Another designer said the penthouse suites were an appalling mixture of styles belonging to the Louis-the-Who? period.

The following April the *QE2* was chartered by Oscar Rudnick, a travel agent of Worcester, Mass., to take a party of Jews to Israel for the twenty-fifth anniversary celebrations of the State of Israel. At this, it was the turn of Arab terrorists to threaten to blow up the ship. The crew were offered £50 danger money, but a hundred of them declined to make the passage. The *QE2* was escorted in the Medi-

The *QE2* at Ashdod, after her cruise to Israel

terranean by British and American planes, Italian destroyers, and French gunboats. Israeli frigates were also there but were unable to keep up with the liner's 28 knots. In spite of all these precautions, the threat had been enough to scare off hundreds of passengers so that the ship was half empty. Mr Rudnick was stoical about the prospect of losing a million dollars on the deal. Everyone on board was checked and checked again, and required to fill in complex Israeli immigration forms. The party of rabbis aboard, and their kosher dietary assistants, at first objected to this, on the grounds that no truly Orthodox Jew does any work at all during the eight days of the Passover. Then they complied, for the sake of Israel. On board, the atmosphere was vigilant. Nine security men kept watch on the bridge night and day. One passenger, James Fatorini, a jeweller, learned that one of his racehorses had foaled during the cruise and named the filly Voyage of Peril. Manny Williams, an American comedian hired to provide Jewish entertainment,

reminded his audience that it was round about the sixty-first anniversary of the *Titanic* sinking. 'Well,' he said, 'at least there'll be no icebergs in the Med. Goldbergs yes, Steinbergs yes, but no icebergs.' Thus entertained, the *QE2*'s 566 pilgrims reached Israel and docked at the new port of Ashdod. Samson once toppled a Philistine temple near by. As the ship docked she was welcomed by 'When the Saints go Marching In' played by the youth band of Kiryat Gat, which was once Goliath's home town. Unfortunately it was the Jewish Sabbath. Devout Jews both on board the ship and through Israel were shocked at the desecration of the Sabbath by the arrival that day, and by the reception. Two ministers asked questions in the Israeli cabinet. Mrs Meir, the Prime Minister, soothed them.

That was not the end of the story. A year later President Sadat of Egypt said in an interview that he had at the last moment heard of a plan, by another Arab leader, whom he did not name but who was widely taken to be the rabid

[200]

President of Libya, to sink the *QE2* in the Mediterranean. Sadat said he had intervened to prevent this. After this revelation, the London *Daily Mail* published a serial, written by Maurice Edelman, a novelist and member of Parliament, which carried the known facts over into fiction, imagining what might have happened if the attack had not been stopped. In the story Mr Edelman unwittingly pays the *QE2* and her builders the finest compliment that can ever have been made to the seaworthiness of a liner. In his version, the *QE2* is found by an Arab submarine and struck by no fewer than six torpedoes, all of which explode, but she still remains afloat, suffers few casualties, and sails back to England.

To return to realities. The Israeli charter was at the end of May, so here was an Atlantic liner, at that time of the year, cruising in the Mediterranean, and not a liner at the end of her career, as the old *Mauretania* had been, but one of the only two great liners left on the northern Europe to North America run. Only part of the *QE2* is a liner in the classic Atlantic tradition, and Cunard make no bones about this. These are their words: 'QE2 is not a modern version of the former Queens. She is a resort hotel that has the advantage of being able to follow the sun . . .' The purser is called hotel manager. Cabins are called rooms. Each room, in both first and economy classes, has wall-to-wall carpeting, its own bathroom, six-channel radio, and a telephone. And here, again from Cunard, is another realistic admission: 'QE2 is not so much in competition with the air, which is transportation, as with

land-based resort hotels, which are holiday and leisure centres.' She has twenty-five miles of wool carpet, and two million square feet of Formica decorative laminate (and that, surely, is the first time any liner can have made that boast for herself). As a cruise ship she is splendid, but she also is in part an Atlantic liner, and she can, in that ocean, cross at $28\frac{1}{2}$ knots. That is the same cruising speed as the old *Queens*, far beyond the needs of a cruise ship, but a speed that was built into the *QE2* when she was intended to carry on the week-in week-out Atlantic ferry, in summer at least, with the old *Queen Elizabeth*. She can be a liner, and the way to see this is to make a crossing in her.

Voyage 124 (West) was an uneventful passage. The Ocean Terminal at Southampton, built for the Queens, is now as tatty as an English railway station. The ship itself, and this strikes one immediately, has two utterly different characters at the same time. The beautiful exterior — her hull and superstructure and decks — are British. So are her officers, who ought, quite apart from their seamanship, to be paid a substantial extra salary for the tone they give the place. As for the rest, *QE2* is an American ship. The interior is entirely that of an American-owned hotel anywhere in the world — Intercontinental, or Hilton, or Hyatt; the best, but nevertheless American. A 'Pocket Companion' given to all passengers said the *QE2* was graced with no fewer than nine bars, but that should the passenger feel like a glass of water it was nice to know that the faucet in his room flowed with perfect drinking water.

Section of the *QE2* as she was originally built, before the penthouse suites were added to the top deck

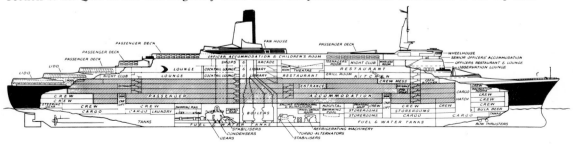

A glossary of nautical terms said bow meant the most forward end of a ship, and stern 'the back end of a ship'. Under Room Service there was a sentence which said, 'PS. If you leave your shoes outside your room at night, you'll find them there in the morning, gloriously polished by the night steward.' This was necessary information to Americans who, if they left shoes outside an American hotel room at night, would expect the next morning to find them gone. There was also a section headed, 'Tipping — it's not a problem!' This explained how one regular passenger calculated *his* tips, which he distributed just before disembarkation. He set aside about 5 per cent of his total fare for tips, divided nine-tenths of this between 'room service staff' and restaurant waiters, and gave the rest to anyone who had rendered special service. One-way fares on that crossing were £2,150 for the Trafalgar and Queen Anne suites, about £300 per passenger for a first-class room, and about £180 in tourist.

As for the service, in both the first-class and tourist dining-rooms it was too fast. Leisure, which is what Cunard is now selling, had gone from their dining-rooms. In first-class at least there is no reason for this. There are not two sittings to be got through, as in tourist, and there is all the time in the world. The tea ceremony is dead. Tea at four in the first-class lounge was served with paper napkins. Boat drill, which should be a serious business, was conducted at one station not by a ship's officer but by an unspeakable cruise director who addressed his passengers as 'Boys and girls'. First-class carpets are blue and tourist carpets reddish, but the QE2 is democratic. Except for meals, passengers wander anywhere. The tourist rooms must be far and away the best ever to be offered in that class.

On the first day out there were complimentary dance classes and a complimentary introduction to gaming. There was a swimkhana. The Ballantyne shop on board offered skirts 50-per-cent off. There was a social directress assisted by girls known as Q'nettes. There were two films a day in the cinema. There were quizzes offering fun for all the family.

When it did anything formally, the *QE2* did it supremely well, like the captain's or the officers' cocktail parties, but, apart from that, formality and quiet were difficult to come by. Peaceful bars were difficult to find, though there are two. One is in the centre of the ship, the One Deck Bar, which is peaceful because of its quiet decor which has escaped improvement, and because few people know it is there, and because on Voyage 124 (West) the bartender was a man who had been with Cunard for many years and liked to talk about it. The other is the Queen's Grill bar, at the top of the ship, near the apartments occupied by American millionaires, and American millionaires are reticent by nature. The drinks themselves were splendid. No fewer than forty-three cocktails were offered, including one called QE2 which consisted of brandy, orange juice, grenadine, vermouth, and curacao. Gimlets, Manhattans, Grasshoppers, Stingers, Side-cars, White Ladies, Kisses in the Dark, and Port and Starboard were also served. Only the London Ritz serves more. The wine list was also splendid, running to thirty-two pages, and offering anything up to Château Lafite First Growth, Pauillac, 1962, at £20 a bottle. There were also four other grand wines at the same price.

The additions by the Miami kitchen suppliers were not the most beautiful parts of the ship, though perhaps their critics have been a bit hard on them. It is depressing to see on an English ship thirty-one one-armed bandits taking only American quarters, but the gaming must please someone. At craps the minimum stake is $5 and the maximum $200. The new suites were high up where they got any roll and any wind that was going, and they creaked.

By far the most entertaining way to spend the five days at sea was to talk to the crew. Tom Davis, barman in the One Deck Bar, was with the old *Queen Elizabeth* for twenty years. At some times of year, he said, she would roll all the way home from New York, and four or five ambulances would meet her at Southampton. Sometimes even he was scared. But the most frightening sea he had ever seen was

2 CENTS
PAY NO MORE!

Chicago Daily Tribune
THE WORLD'S GREATEST NEWSPAPER

FINAL EDITION

VOLUME LXXXVIII.—NO. 28 C   FRIDAY, FEBRUARY 15 1929.—46 PAGES   ** PRICE TWO CENTS

TRACE KILLERS: LID ON CITY

SWANSON TELLS POLICE TO STOP GANGS' INCOME

Must Dry Up Chicago or Face Grand Jury.

WHERE SEVEN MEMBERS OF MORAN GANG WERE LINED UP AGAINST WALL AND KILLED BY RIVALS. The garage at 2122 North Clark street, on the windows of which appear the name "S. M. C. Cartage company," in which massacre took place. Two of the executioners wore the uniforms and stars of city policemen.

WARNS PEOPLE WILL RISE AND SMASH TYRANNY

Threatens to Expose 'Senate Hypocrites'.

Drinks Scarce as Cops Clamp Lid on Chicago

BY ORVILLE DWYER

RIVAL GANG CHIEF.
Al Capone, foe of Moran, as he appears in Florida, where he is now.

DETROIT FOCUS OF SEARCH FOR MASSACRE GANG

Hijackings Believed Clew to Killers

THE WEATHER
SUNDAY, FEBRUARY 17, 1929.

QUEEN ELIZABETH 2   COLUMBIA RESTAURANT

ROARING 'TWENTIES NIGHT DINNER
THURSDAY 23 AUGUST 1973

Appetisers
Choice of Chilled Fruit Juices
Chilled Melon with Lime   Delice de Foie Gras   Smoked Salmon
Calf's Head, Vinaigrette   Caviar Glace

Soups
Consomme Julienne   Potage Cressoniere
Chilled Cream of Mushrooms

Fish
FRESH CHERBOURG RED MULLET, MEUNIERE
POACHED SUPREME OF HALIBUT, VERONIQUE
Poached in a white wine sauce, garnished with muscatel grapes

Entrees
ESCALOPE OF PORK, CALVADOS
Thin escalope tenderly cooked in apple brandy-flavoured sauce

CREPES VERSAILLES
*Thin pancakes filled with diced chicken and mushrooms
blended with a cream sherry, coated with mornay sauce and glazed*

Roast Leg and Shoulder of Lamb, Mint Sauce or Red Currant Jelly

Grills
VEAL CHOPS, VERT PRE
FLAMED PEPPER STEAK

Vegetables
Okra and Tomatoes   Petits Pois, Flamande   French Beans
Chateau, Macaire or Parsley Potatoes

Cold Buffet and Salads
Roast Ribs and Sirloin of Beef, Horseradish Cream   Rolled Ox Tongue
Roast Turkey, Cranberry Sauce   Roast Duckling
Salads: Pineapple Slaw   Melangee   Waldorf Salad   Lettuce and Tomato
(Choice of Dressings)

Desserts
Orange Chiffon Pie   Grand Marnier Souffle   Crepes Montaigne, Flambees
Champagne Sherbet   Macaroons and Langues des Chats
Vanilla, Chocolate and Peach Ice Creams — Hot Chocolate Sauce

Fresh Fruit   Selected Cheese Board

Savoury
Croque Monsieur
A sandwich of ham and cheese dipped in eggwash and fried

Full Roast Coffee   Instant Coffee   Iced Tea or Coffee
Ceylon, China or Indian Tea

'Roaring Twenties' menu aboard the *QE2*

the storm of 1972 on the *QE2*. They couldn't get out of it. Fifty sailors were trying to board up windows. The new baby grand piano went crash. He remembers his old ship the *Elizabeth* with love. He says a bunch of wide boys from Philadelphia got hold of her, and calls her end shameful.

Ernie Breen, chief bar steward, was nine years on the *Berengaria*. Of course, he said, she rolled. You should have seen the fiddles on her – fiddles are raised edges fixed to the tables in rough weather to prevent the dishes flying off. They were the most beautiful things you ever saw. There was the *Berengaria* smile. The crew were encouraged to smile and be gregarious. In those days they were in competition with Claridges. But he said no ship in the world ever rolled like the *Queen Mary*. (That was a unanimous opinion.) She was run pretty exclusively as a first-class ship. On the *QE2* the tourists were good middle-class people. Tourist class had never had such opulent and lovely rooms. In his time he had seen the great people of the world – General Pershing and J. P. Morgan II. He said that if a ship moved, at mealtimes, you damped her down, and demonstrated this by taking a napkin, moistening it, and placing a glass on it. The glass stopped sliding, though *QE2* herself was rolling a bit. 'We talk American at times,' he said. 'We think American. I'm not English. I'm Cunard. Like a wooden leg, you get used to it.' He had an uncle who was in square riggers, and then in the *Lucania*, *Carmania*, and *Lusitania*.

Bob Wodehouse, chief deck steward, had been twenty-four years on the *Queen Mary*. She would roll, lie on the roll, and then roll a bit more. His father had worked for Cunard, joining the Company in 1912, staying with them for forty-nine years, and then retiring at the age of seventy. Now the *Queen Mary*, said Mr Wodehouse, she had a first-class smoking-room that was out of this world. It was like a businessmen's club. They didn't want to run around playing bingo. He had been to Long Beach to see the *Queen Mary*. He had looked into the Verandah Grill: 'That place is now a hot dog stand.' There had been nothing like

the library, with its polished mahogany, and now they sold novelties there. Then Mr Wodehouse said: 'The Atlantic crossing – which we know has gone now – you could pick up your passenger list and go down, and you could tick them all off, saying, this time of year, so and so should be here. They would take deck-chairs always in the same place.' The most famous name on the passenger list of the *QE2* on Voyage 124 (West) was Ronald Getty, the Texan oilman. 'Mr Getty? No, he doesn't take a deckchair.' Then Mr Wodehouse's mind returned to the *Queen Mary*. Though she could roll in a sea, when it was calm she would glide through: the *QE2* still had a shudder. He remembered the paying-off pennant they made when the *Queen Mary* was sold. All the boys in the ship made it, out of bunting, ten feet for each year, 310 feet. The girls from the purser's office all came and put a stitch in, and they laid it out on the promenade deck when it was done. It was red, white, and blue.

Captain William Law, who was captain of the *QE2* at the time of the bomb hoax, had retired earlier that month and was on board Voyage 124 as a passenger. He had been a Cunard officer since before the war, starting as third officer at £24 10s. a month. He too remembered the *Queen Mary* in 1938 crossing the Atlantic in fog, blowing the whistle all the way, going just that much faster than anyone else, and the captain on the bridge day and night. He had seen captains worried sick, silent, and so tired they did not know where they were. And eastbound the *Queen Mary* could pick up a westerly gale leaving New York and hold it all the way across, rolling until you got tired of it. In bed, they used to arrange the pillows as supports, to stop themselves falling out. One captain invented a gadget like a life-belt to lie in, with corks to support him either side. The best times Captain Law remembered were after the war cruising round the world on the *Caronia* with the same people all the time, and lots of racehorse owners among the passengers. He said that on the *QE2*, whenever their courses took them near enough, they tried to close the *France*, and when the look-out

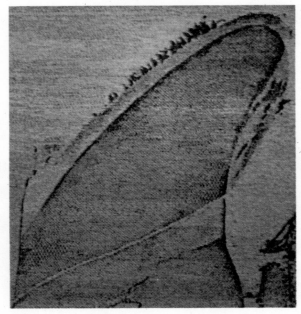

Brochure of the *Queen Mary* wedding chapel, which conducts ceremonies from $75 up

Tapestries showing the launching of the *QE2*, which are displayed outside the Columbia Room, her first-class dining-room

The *Queen Elizabeth* against the Manhattan skyline at night

[206]

The *Queen Mary* at Long Beach

saw her a Cunard fellow hummed the 'Marseillaise' over the VHF, and the Frenchmen replied with 'God Save the Queen'. Had he, when he retired, suffered the feelings of so many sea captains before him, that the voyage of his life too was coming to an end? He said he had not. He had been reasonably content. Many of his contemporaries had fallen by the wayside in these days of dissolution, with all the ships gone, and he had been the first to stay the course and retire at the proper age for retiring. So he was content.

On the fourth night out there was a Roaring Twenties dinner, with menus printed on a facsimile of the front page of the *Chicago Daily Tribune* of 15 February 1929, complete with a picture of Al Capone. But that night a real roaring gale with bursts up to Force Eight found the *QE2*, and so the dining-room was half empty.

Next day David Parkinson, bed-room steward, said she had not rolled more than ten degrees either way. The *Queen Mary* could do thirty, and he'd seen chairs falling all over the dining-room. His father had been with Cunard too, had served on the *Umbria*, and had missed going down on the *Lusitania* by one voyage. He himself had started in 1934 on the *Aquitania*, when he was just sixteen, for £1 16s. a month. All the silver cutlery had to be cleaned after every meal with Wellington powder, which was dark brown like cocoa. The *Queen Mary* experimented with a gold table service at first, but then abandoned it, not because it was stolen but because it stained terribly. If you cut a vegetable the knife went black. On the *Queen Mary*'s maiden voyage all the bellboys had new uniforms, biscuit-coloured jackets, red chevrons and red pillboxes. That voyage there was nothing but banquets. Even the crew

[209]

◀ The *QE2* at sunset, the only liner left on the Atlantic

THIS JEWELRY HAS BEEN CAREFULLY MADE FROM CHUNKS OF PAINT CHIPS THAT WERE REMOVED FROM THE R.M.S. QUEEN MARY DURING HER CONVERSION IN LONG BEACH.

'Carefully made from chunks of paint'. On board the *Queen Mary*, anything sells. From the jewellery shop aboard the *Queen Mary*

had champagne. The chief steward had his own bellboy. On the *Queen Mary* he had seen 5,000 tons of green water on the foredeck, and steel stanchions crumple like concertinas. Had the previous night's storm really been so slight? 'Well, last night I *knew* it,' he said. A bed-room steward sees little except his own passengers and his own quarters, but Mr Parkinson went on deck once a day. 'I make a point of going up every morning to see what kind of day it is. Because people ask me what kind of a day it is. At least I've got that.'

The morning bulletin said there had been rough seas and a heavy swell, but the ship had maintained a speed of 28.08 knots. At the captain's party, Mrs C. Reavis, an American, remembered that as a very young girl she had crossed on the old *Mauretania* with J. P. Morgan. He had brought his own grapes with him, and sent some over to her table. An officer said that on Voyage 124 an American woman talked to her dog in New York every night over the radio-telephone. It was a Pekingese. They telephoned the maid and the maid brought the

dog to the telephone, and the dog growled. It was good business for Cunard. In the casino, watching the play, John Sawyer, hotel manager, said he once saw an American lose $32,000 in one night. 'He didn't mind, and gave a champagne party at the end for the staff. And he was a brain specialist.'

At the end of Voyage 124 (West) the *QE2* slipped into New York bay very early one morning, passed under the Verrazano Narrows bridge at 6.59, and tied up at her North River berth at Pier 84, West 44th Street and 12th Avenue.

Three thousand miles away by jet, the *Queen Mary* lay in her fixed berth at Long Beach, California. She looked very grand. On board they sell cuff links for $8.95. 'Your cuff links,' says an explanatory cardboard notice, 'are not a reproduction. They are actually chunks of paint which have been removed from R M S *Queen Mary* in the process of converting her to a luxury hotel and museum . . . Treasure your Paint-Links as a memento, or a conversation piece, and remember their thirty-three years history as each coat was added. Some of it has perhaps graced the bulkhead of Winston Churchill's private quarters, much of it has felt the ping of underwater sound gear in the process of listening for enemy subs. Other parts have felt the spray on much of the Seven Seas.' The ship is run in parts. There is an excellent museum of *Queen Mary* history; there is a so-so hotel* which lets off some of the old first-class cabins; there are three dreadful restaurants which deserve to lose all the money they can; and then there are the franchises — the hamburger franchise, the kitsch franchise, the booze franchise, the wedding franchise, the entertainment franchise, and so on.

In the museum, a newsreel clip runs over and over again showing King George V saying she is the stateliest ship now in being, and Queen Mary naming and launching her ship. It is moving to watch, and as distant in time as if they were launching not the *Queen Mary*

---

* Since this was written the hotel has changed management, and other parts of the ship have been altered.

but the *Lusitania*. There is an invitation card to the launching. There is the Lady Astor Cup, presented by Nancy, Lady Astor in 1958 as an expression of gratitude to the crew, and afterwards competed for by them as a darts trophy. It is about the size of the trophy which used to go with the blue riband. Authentic ten-inch mooring ropes from the ship are on sale at $5.95 for four inches. Authentic cross-sections of the anchor chain are $4.95. Tiny sachets of Authentic Pacific Ocean Water, 'caressed by sandy beaches, flitted through by rainbow-coloured fish, and greatly admired', are sold at 35 cents each. And, which is a masterpiece of the salesman's art, sachets of Genuine Dehydrated Pacific Ocean Sea Water are also sold for 35 cents. Water with the water dried out. Each sachet contains what appears to be a fragment of white salt.

This is not the kitsch. That is on the promenade decks. There are suits of armour at $995.00, authentic coats of arms at $95.00, pirate flags at 39 cents, and a book containing the complete conversion story, and called *God Saved the Queen*, at $3.25. Fish and chips, of an enhanced and unrecognizable flavour, are 80 cents. Half the stalls have gone out of business. In the Verandah Grill, where Henry Ford and Garbo dined, cheeseburgers are 90 cents. In the theatre, a fifteen minute review is presented on the theme of '81,000 Tons of Fun'. 'Hail Britannia, Britannia Rules the Waves', sings a tired chorus, which then switches to 'Mary, Mary', and to 'London Bridge is falling down, and gone to Arizona'. They dance a bit, and end up,

> Enjoy the remainder of your trip
> To the Queen in all her glory.

One of those glories is the Queen Mary Wedding Chapel, which is not in the old chapel at all but in what used to be the second-class smoking-room. The chapel is open seven days a week, 9 am to 9 pm, and the fees are from $75 up, which includes chapel, minister, candelabra, and piped music. For $225 you can have real organ music. It is the done thing to be married on the *Queen Mary*. People have

QUEEN MARY

A day to remember aboard history's most famous ship.

"81,000 tons of fun."

Publicity brochure for *Queen Mary*, now one of the sights of California not to be missed

come from as far away as Arizona. They have had a Buddhist wedding and a Persian wedding. The Rev. Commander Pomeroy will perform marriages in his uniform, or there is the Rev. Lopez, of the universal church, who was not a minister before but became one specially for the chapel, or there are rabbis and priests and judges. 'To make your wedding day as lovely as possible,' says the chapel hand-out, 'the Chapel offers as a courtesy to you the service of gracious co-ordinators to assist you with your wedding arrangements, including the reception.' With the chapel's constant Muzak playing round her, Bobbi, a co-ordinator, explained that the electric candles could be dimmed on a rheostat, that all their upholstered pews were

In its last years, the France *too was trying to sell herself by an appeal to 1920s nostalgia*

The good old days are here again.

On the 'France' to New York.

Do you sigh nostalgically for the good old days ? Then take a trip down memory lane. Take the 'France' to New York.

We've cheated a bit of course. Because you'll also find all modern comforts. Like air conditioning. Stabilisation. Cabins with private bath or shower.

But we've kept the good old fashioned things. The *haute cuisine* as invented by the French. The *service de luxe* they've practised for decades.

Remember cocktails ? On the 'France' they'll mix you any one you care to name. Remember how you held your partner close when you danced ? On the 'France' you still can, to live music every night. Remember when nightclubs had atmosphere instead of noise ? On the 'France' the ambiance will match your mood.

So if you have the luxury of time, spend five days in the world of yesterday, and wake up in New York ready to face the world of tomorrow.

From 25th May, the 'France' leaves Southampton every other Friday night, and arrives in New York the following Wednesday morning. See your travel agent, or send for a sailing list to French Line, 20 Cockspur Street, London SW1Y 5BU. Tel: 01-839 9040.

FRENCH ▌ ▌LINE
it's the only way to go

extremely comfortable, that they had wall-to-wall carpets and air-conditioning, that the ship's real chapel had not been used because it was a bit dingy, and that after the ceremony the bride and groom were invited to sign the register with plumed pens. One bride had asked the vocalist to sing 'Proud Mary', which was a type of rock and roll song. Others had chosen the theme music from *Love Story*, and one had the theme from *The Godfather*.

Then a middle-aged couple came in to be married. 'Bob,' said the minister, addressing the groom, did he promise to honour and uphold his bride, and join with her to the utmost in exploring the meaning of love? Marge, the bride, then promised the same, and also to give herself completely to Bob. Bob then took Marge to be the wife of his days, the companion of his nights, and to keep together, whatever troubles their lives should lay upon them. The minister, declaring them married, and remembering no doubt that he was on what had been a ship, uttered a piece of free verse which hoped that the courage of the pounding surf and of the life-giving ocean might be in their hearts.

Newly married couples often go off to the hotel to a king-size bed (port side) for $30 a night, or to a king-size bed (starboard) for $32. A deposit of one night's rate is required. Some of the first-class cabins are almost intact, except that neon lights have been substituted throughout. The hotel is also trying to whip up convention business, pointing out that the *Queen Mary* is within easy driving distance of Los Angeles international airport, Hollywood, and Disneyland.

Part of the ship is like a fairground. Some of the franchise holders complain that the others are trying to run it like a five-and-dime. The great first-class dining-room is musty and not often-enough used. The engine-rooms are a rusting chasm. The swimming pool is derelict. But there are some signs of loving care. Some of the veneers of the ship of a thousand woods have been preserved. All the ship's clocks have been stopped at 12.16, which was the time on 9 December 1967 when her last captain gave his last order, 'Finished with engines'. The hull and superstructure are painted. It is better than Valhalla. There is still a little style left, and style was always part of what Atlantic liners sold.

Atlantic liners died because aeroplanes became an infinitely more efficient way to cross the Atlantic. Once the liners were no longer the only way to cross, when indeed they had become no sensible way to cross at all, no amount of *putting on* the style was going to save or help them. For the French Line, with so beautiful a ship as the *France*, to try and sell passages by promising five days back in the nostalgic twenties was just sad and never going to work. But in their great days, before the airliners, the different lines and different liners had a style of their own, which was not put on but was a natural part of them, and this, just as much as speed, was part of their attraction. An American pamphlet of 1953, offering advice to intending passengers, compared the various lines a bit crudely. On American ships you got the biggest helpings afloat, but service was buddy-buddy, and each class of passengers had to keep strictly to its own quarters. It is strange, but the democratic Americans were notoriously strict about this: the United States Line took care to see you got the privileges you paid good money for. On British ships, the food was not bad considering British cooking generally, and in all classes the public rooms were grander and more numerous then on the ships of any other nation. French ships were famous for being free and easy about class, and served wine free with meals.

All true, but there were subtler indications of style. One of these was the ritual of the captain's table. When Thackeray crossed on a Cunarder to lecture in America in 1852 all the cabin passengers dined with the captain. About seven or eight days out, said Thackeray, the captain came to dinner at eight bells, helped the soup, and went on deck again. Then he came back to help the fish, looking rather grave, and then absented himself again to go on deck for ten minutes. This time he returned looking pleased and in time to carve the sirloin. 'We have seen the light,' he said. This was a light-ship off Newfoundland. 'Madam, may I help you to a little gravy, or a little horse-radish? Or what not?' As liners grew, the captain chose his guests, who considered themselves privileged. It was a brave and rare passenger who would act as Van Veen does in Nabokov's novel *Ada* when, on a passage in 1901 on a mythical liner, Veen finds in his cabin an invitation to Dr and Mrs Ivan Veen to join the captain for dinner, and, remembering the captain as a bore and an ignoramus, calls the steward and sends the note back with the pencilled scrawl, 'No such couple.'

Cunard took much trouble over the ritual. The captain of the second *Mauretania*, about 1949, used to hold meetings in his cabin at 10.30 in the morning with the staff captain (his second in command), the chief officer, chief engineer, staff chief, surgeon, purser, and chief steward, to pore over the claims of the 160 or so passengers out of the 500 travelling first class who had been brought to the captain's notice by head office as in any way important. How were they to be entertained, and at which officer's table? On one voyage it was decided that the captain should entertain, among others, Prince and Princess Christian of Hesse, the Duc and Duchesse de Richelieu, and a rubber magnate. Occasionally, the captain admitted, he would suggest some people as his guests and the purser would murmur reproachfully, 'Oh no, sir, *they* are not for *you*. Leave them to me.' Having been promoted to command the *Queen Mary*, this same captain would still go painstakingly through the company's confidential list of up to 200 people, anxiously whittling down the names to those of the six or eight who would be invited to take their places at table 199. But in this matter, in modern times at least, the French Line has had more panache. Captain Raoul de Beaudéan of the *Ile de France* said it was a matter of delicately gathering, in a sensitive flower bed, those blooms most worthy of attention without bruising the others. 'No book of protocol touches on these subtle details, and in the end the more or less flattering

Raoul de Beaudéan, captain of the *Ile de France*

classification of the gentlemen will depend on their age, their rank in the Légion d'Honneur, or the beauty of their women.' Van Veen would not have declined Captain de Beaudéan's invitation.

The style of the British was in their bluffness. There was one chief engineer who in twenty years of Atlantic passages never set foot outside the New York dock gates, meaning no disrespect to the city but thinking that there were always things to be seen to in his engine-room. Theodore Dreiser noticed and much liked the aloof gravity of the Cunard stewards, who were actually civil, whose motions did not indicate that they were doing anything unwillingly, who did not make him feel as if they were doing him a favour by doing anything at all, who were, he said, men who carried none of the burden of serfdom that would have been felt by their American counterparts. They were like balm to a fevered brain.

It was de Beaudéan who devised the kindest way of not being seduced. 'If the man,' he said, 'has the least sense of gallantry he cannot, without being taken for the worst of

cads, disregard the lady's sensibilities in repulsing her spontaneous offer.' He had established this defence. First he assumed the tender air of one who savoured his good fortune, but then raised prudent and desolate objections. The captain, he would say mournfully, lived under the eyes of a vigilant crowd. He would seriously compromise the reputation of a woman so good as to offer him her favours. To be sure, a little rendezvous at night would not get into the ship's log, but nothing could escape such thorough surveillance, and the fear of a lamentable epilogue to a charming fling would make even a Satan careful, were he the least bit gallant. 'I don't know whether this is the most effective tactic for escaping from a spider in an evening gown without hurting the strands of her web. But I am waiting for someone to suggest a better method. How painful is duty, especially when one gets the reputation of being a cretin in its service.'

But of style or panache, or gravity on board, American ships had little. 'Standards maintained by the United States Lines,' said one of that Line's brochures, 'are American standards.' That was always the trouble. Here are extracts from the service manual compiled by the United States Lines for stewards and all

" *When is your next adventure cruise?* "

Cartoon from the London *Daily Telegraph* after the *QE2*'s turbines broke down and her passengers had to be transferred to another ship in mid Atlantic

ratings. Stewards should shave and have their shoes shined, never lounge on duty, and particularly avoid picking their teeth or snapping their fingers or hissing to attract attention. There should be no obvious attempt to get a passenger to tip. When a steward received a tip he should put it into his pocket without looking at it. He should never count his tips in front of passengers, or even take his money out of his pocket and look at it. Before coming on duty, waiters should avoid any smell of nicotine or liquor. They should have a clean handkerchief to wipe their face, at no time using a napkin or side towel. Then there are two sentences which deserve to be given verbatim:

To waiters taking orders: 'Never place your arm on the chair, table, or passenger.'

To bellboys bringing drinks: 'Always serve the drinks before presenting the bill.'

Furthermore, women should generally be served by stewardesses though, says the United States Line, in the nearest approach it makes to the sensibility of de Beaudéan of the *Ile de France*, it should be remembered that there were some women who did not want to be served by women.

To the end both English and French did preserve some style, the French probably more than the British, though Cunard's sea-going officers and some of her passengers kept the flag flying. When in the spring of 1974 the *QE2* had a little trouble with her turbines, so that she could not make way, had no drinking water, and had to transfer her cruise passengers in mid ocean to a Norwegian ship, the Cunard

The *France*, on her world cruise, at Circular Quay, Sydney. A suite for the cruise could cost up to £58,000

The *France* not quite at the end, but nearing it. Here she is tied up at Manhattan after it had been announced that she would be retired later in 1974

captain made light of this misfortune by supplying his passengers with unlimited champagne, in which some of them took the opportunity to shave. The *France*, which against its nature and purpose had also taken to winter cruising, calling at such unlikely places as Sydney, had trouble on a world cruise in obtaining fuel oil, which, in time of Arab crisis, increased sixfold in price. The French government could no longer afford her, and it was rumoured that she would be withdrawn and sold after the cruise. A group of passengers cabled the President of the French Republic in protest. Twenty millionaires were believed to be on board. The other passengers were not poor. It was reasonable to assert that if the French government wished to economize on the *France*, then it might with equal sense close down the Louvre and the Palace of Versailles, which also lost money. It was true, as the American writer Ted Morgan discovered, that

so much food was wasted that the *France* was followed by the best-fed sharks in the Atlantic, waiting for scraps. But it was also true, as Mr Morgan also remarked, that to cut down on the luxury would be like hiring inexpensive singers for the Metropolitan Opera in New York.

But later that year it was announced that the *France* was after all taken out of service. The French Line, witty as ever, advertised her last voyage with the headline, 'Not Au Revoir But Goodbye'. Martin Dugro Buttles, aged 57, an American citizen of Great Neck, Long Island, was left without an occupation, having for thirty years gone back and forth on French liners. His parents introduced him to the *Ile de France* in the thirties. He crossed more than thirty times on the *Liberté*. He went to see Madame de Gaulle launch the *France*, and crossed on her first passage, and made at least forty-seven more passages afterwards. Asa Briggs, the historian, aboard her on one of her last passages,

PLUSIEURS ACHETEURS POSSIBLES POUR LE «FRANCE»

Possible buyers for the *France* – the Arabs, for a floating Mecca; the Chinese, for surplus population; the late Aristotle Onassis and his wife Jacqueline Kennedy, for a yacht; or the Club Mediterranée, for a glorified holiday camp – *Paris Match*

WEATHER:
Cloudy, rain.
Lighting-up times:
7.54 p.m. to 6 a.m.
Details—Back Page.

Evening Standard

CITY PRICES

46,702   London: Thursday September 12 1974   5   4p

'She stays at sea until demands met'

MUTINY ON THE FRANCE

Crew seize giant liner

LE HAVRE, Thursday.

CREWMEN have hijacked the transatlantic liner France with 1266 passengers on board and have refused to berth the ship until a decision to take it out of service is reversed.

Today union representatives were said to be occupying the bridge. The liner " would stay at anchor" outside Le Havre until the French Government and the French Line

THE LINER FRANCE — Union representatives are " occupying the bridge."

agree to keep the massively-subsidised liner operating and ensure full employment in the French merchant service.

Marooned passengers were being transferred to a Townsend Thoresen car ferry in a calm sea.

A union spokesman said the decision to take over the liner was made by the crew during its last stop in New York.

The seamen were strikers, not mutineers, he claimed.

One of French President Valéry Giscard D'Estaing's first acts after taking office last May was to halt the £28,000,000 annual subsidy to the French Line to operate the France, the largest

Contd Back Page, Col. 3

5 British soldiers missing

THE Ministry of Defence in London said today that five British soldiers were missing after Nato exercise in which two other soldiers were killed near Kiel Canal in West Germany.

A paratrooper was killed in a parachute drop

Altogether 554 men from 1½ Parachute Brigade jumped as part of exercise Bold Guard.

Another soldier taking part in the exercise was found dead on the road near Heide in Shleswig Holstein. It was believed his death was the result of a road accident. The names of the dead soldiers have not been released.

A lovely tribute for Sammy

ACTRESS Joan Collins (left) actress Susannah York arrive at the New London Theatre . . . just two of the stars who turned out last night in tribute to the man whose songs turned many singers into stars.

Sammy Cahn, at one time the inspiration behind the legendary Marlene Dietrich, had a show about his works premiered at the theatre.

Among those who attended the premiere of Sammy Cahn's Songbook were actor Michael Caine and his wife, actor Peter Ustinov.

● Milton Shulman.— Page 25.

A Lord John credit account will be very fashionable this winter.

What it buys, and how it buys.
Choose your clothes from our new Autumn collection.
And whatever you buy regularly each month, you can have clothes immediately to the value of 24 times that amount.
Call in yourself or send in the coupon.

6, Warple Way, Acton, London, W.3.
Telephone: 01-749 3627.

Name_____
Address_____
_____ Tel:_____

LORD JOHN

OXFORD STREET, KINGS ROAD, CARNABY STREET AND BRANCHES   ES-4

Dave Willis

GOERING

Part 4 of Leonard Mosley's fascinating biography: Pages 26 and 27

Kidnap baby found in Blackpool

Property Scene   Page 40

Page 7   Entertainment - - - 22

'Lion of Judah is out'

HAILE SELASSIE — "Sent millions of dollars to Switzerland."

Standard Foreign News Desk

ETHIOPIA'S Emperor Haile Selassie was reported today to have been deposed by the country's ruling armed forces committee.

The news was given by the United States Embassy in Nairobi after receiving a telegram from officials in Addis Ababa.

The telegram merely said : "Emperor deposed. Airport closed." There were no further details.

All public communications between Addis Ababa and Nairobi have been cut since last night. Telephone and Telex circuits are reported out of order.

The Lion of Judah is 82. For several months he has been gradually stripped of his powers.

Daughter arrested

The committee said a week ago it would soon announce further action against the Emperor who has been accused of exploiting public funds and hoarding millions of illegally-acquired dollars and gold in Swiss banks.

For the first time in decades the Emperor took no part in yesterday's New Year celebrations.

Last night his only surviving daughter, Princess Tegnagne-Wong, was taken in armed troops from her home to an unknown destination.

Unconfirmed reports said other members of the Emperor's family had also been taken away by troops.

The deposing of the Emperor had been widely expected since the armed forces stepped up their campaign and started accusing him personally of maladministration and misappropriation of funds.

The gold which the Emperor is said to have sent abroad was mined by forced labour in Southern Ethiopia, according to the committee.

The Emperor has also been accused of taking millions of dollars illegally from Addis Ababa brewery — formerly owned by his family and now nationalised—and milking profits from the city's bus company.

Her crew seize the *France* in the English Channel in September 1974

In the last days of the *France* everything changed. Sailors and stewards so monopolized the bars with their talk of strikes that it was difficult for passengers to get a drink – *Paris Match*

said she was a floating Versailles of infinite social and gastronomic shades, where the unseen captain, like Louis XIV the Sun King, whimsically and omnipotently bestowed graces and favours like *crêpes suzettes* at dinner. Surely, said Briggs, at a fraction of the cost of the supersonic Concorde, she was worth saving.

But the ship of the Sun King was not saved, and her end was only hastened when, on the evening of 11 September 1974, her crew seized her as she lay in the approaches to Le Havre. For some months they had been muttering among themselves so much that it was hard for a passenger to attract a steward's attention to get a drink. To economize, a day had been added to the passage time across the Atlantic,

and the French Line had begun to charge for table wine. At the *France*'s last call in New York a plot was hatched between the crew and the seamen's union who hoped to coerce the French government into keeping her in service. The leader was Marcel Raulin, a cabin steward and former commando. When the ship reached Le Havre, a pre-arranged signal was received from the union leaders ashore. It sounded like the code messages broadcast by the B.B.C. to the French resistance in the Second World War, and it said: 'Good morning from Alfred. Send the oranges.' Raulin and ten others went to the bridge and told Captain Christian Pettré, known as the Pasha, that they were taking command of his ship and anchoring her in the main channel. He asked them if they were mad, but was afterwards impassive. At dinner, the passengers had reached dessert and coffee. The sailors told them what had happened, and then the orchestra played on.

Next day the director general of the French Line said he had been expecting *anything*, but hardly that the *France* would be occupied like a common-or-garden factory by its workers. The 1,266 passengers were taken off by a Norwegian ferry. The crew of 989 determined to stay on board until their demands were met. By the end of the month they had run out of wine, cigarettes, tobacco, and fresh vegetables. Because the weather got rough, the *France* had to move to a position off Cherbourg, and was therefore no longer blocking the main channel to Le Havre. The French government waited. On board, Captain Pettré, his officers,

The *France*, ship in a bottle. Cartoon by Chenez, *Le Monde*

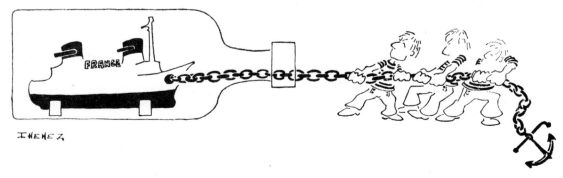

The occupation is over. Her crew give up the struggle and bring the *France* into Le Havre for the last time. Photograph by Stephen Moreton-Prichard

and some of the crew attended a last Mass in the ship's theatre. The French Line cancelled the voyages that should have been the *France*'s last. After a month the men took a ballot and four out of five voted to bring the ship back to Le Havre, which they did on 10 October. Three weeks later the French Line formally took the *France* out of commission. The men still picketed her until, in early December, they gave up. The ship of the Sun King was finished.

The *QE2* remained. Cunard, hoping to attract the *France*'s passengers, negotiated for the French Line to act as their agents in France. It was a time for obituaries, and not only that of the *France*. Commodore Robert Thelwell, former aide-de-camp to George VI, former captain of the *Queen Elizabeth* and *Queen Mary*, and a freeman of the City of London, died in Hampshire at the age of seventy-eight. Vice Admiral Harry Manning, who commanded the *United States* when she took the blue riband in 1952, died in New Jersey at the age of seventy-seven. He had an adventurous life. In 1940 he was in command of the American liner *Washington* off the coast of England when a German U-boat surfaced and ordered him to abandon ship, before being torpedoed. Manning said his was an American ship and told the

U-boat to go away, which it did. He was also an aviator. In 1937 he started to fly round the world with Amelia Earhart, as her navigator, but his leave ran out in Honolulu and he had to return home. She flew out alone over the Pacific, and disappeared.

And in 1974 there was also the death, at the age of ninety-three, of Mary, Lady Bates, widow of Sir Percy Bates, late chairman of Cunard. She was 'Pussie' to her friends, and was keenly interested in the evangelical work of the church. She was slight and nimble, and had been a beautiful skater. There were legends of the waltzes she danced on ice with her son Eddie who was killed in action over Germany on New Year's Day, 1945. She delighted in chamber music, and played her own full-toned Stradivarius until she was nearly ninety. Her husband died in 1946, the day before the maiden voyage as a passenger liner of the *Queen Elizabeth*. It was he, who, in the early 1930s, had explained that the two steamers which were to become *Queen Mary* and *Queen Elizabeth*, though they might be very large and very fast, were in fact the smallest and slowest which could do the job of giving a weekly service, the two ships crossing always in mid Atlantic.

SOURCES

Books: General Works

This is a selected bibliography. Many large volumes, typically entitled something like *Steamships and their Story* or *Floating Palaces*, contain little incident or information, and these I have omitted. A glance under the heading 'Titanic' in the catalogue of any large library will reveal several short poems on the disaster, and though I have quoted a few lines from some of these poems, I have not listed them. Between the wars, anybody who was anybody crossed the Atlantic, and the crossing was later mentioned in the autobiography or biography. Again, although I have quoted briefly from some of these works, I have not listed them in this bibliography, since they are concerned only incidentally with the sea. On the whole, only those books containing substantial information about the Atlantic crossing are included. I have made an exception with a few novels or short stories which, although not primarily about the sea, do convey the tone of being on shipboard.

ALLAN LINE, *Illustrated Tourists' Guide to Canada and the United States*, Liverpool, 1880. A lengthy bound book, as some early steamship line guides were.

ALLEN, FREDERICK LEWIS, *The Great Pierpont Morgan*, Gollancz, London, 1949.

ANDERSON, ROY, *White Star*, Stephenson, Prescot, Lancs., 1964. The standard history.

BARBANCE, MARTHE, *Histoire de la Compagnie Générale Transatlantique*, Paris, 1955. Standard history of the French Line, well illustrated.

BEAUDEAN, RAOUL DE, *Captain of the Ile*, McGraw-Hill, New York, 1960. Witty memoirs of the captain of the *Ile de France*.

BEAVER, PATRICK, *The Big Ship: Brunel's Great Eastern — a Pictorial History*, Evelyn, London, 1969.

BEESLEY, LAWRENCE, *The Loss of the S.S. Titanic*, Heinemann, London, and Houghton Mifflin, Boston, both 1912. The best eye-witness account, to which I am much indebted.

BEMÉLMANS, LUDWIG, *I Love You, I Love You*, etc., Viking Press, New York, 1942. Short story set on the *Normandie*.

BISSET, COMMODORE SIR JAMES, *Commodore*, Angus and Robertson, London, 1961. Memoirs.

BISSET, COMMODORE SIR JAMES (as Commander J. G. P. Bisset), *Ship Ahoy*, published by himself, Liverpool, 1930. A handbook for passengers.

BRAYNARD, FRANK O., *Famous American Ships*, New York, 1956.

BRAYNARD, FRANK O., *Lives of the Liners*, Cornell Maritime Press, New York, 1947.

BRAYNARD, FRANK O., *The World's Greatest Ship — The Story of the Leviathan*, Vol. I, New York, 1972. A massive work, magnificently illustrated. More volumes to come.

BREUHAUS DE GROOT, PROFESSOR F. A. (ed.), *Ocean Express Bremen*, North German Lloyd, Bremen, 1928.

BRINNIN, JOHN MALCOLM, *The Sway of the Grand Saloon*, Delacorte, New York, 1971, and Macmillan, London, 1972. A full social history, very good on the early days, before 1900.

BULLOCK, SHANE F., *A Titanic Hero — Thomas Andrews, Shipbuilder*, first published 1912, reprinted facsimile by 7C's Press, Riverside, Conn., 1973.

BUNIN, I. A., *The Gentleman from San Francisco*, translated by D. H. Lawrence and S. S. Koteliansky, Hogarth Press, London, 1922. Short story.

CANGARDEL, HENRI, *De Colbert à Normandie*, Nouvelles Éditiones Latines, Paris, 1957. A history of the French Line.

CECIL, LAMAR, *Albert Ballin — Business and Politics in Imperial Germany*, Princeton University Press, 1967.

CHORLEY, LORD, and GILES, O. M., *Shipping Law*, Pitman, London, 1963.

Cunard Steamship Co., a guide published by the company for the Chicago World's Fair, 1893. British Museum catalogue 8806.bb.25.

FORD, NORMAN D., *Your Ship — The Seafarer's Guide to Getting the Most from a Steamship Voyage*, Havian Publications, Greenwich, New York, 1953.

FROST, JACK, see POTTER, NEIL.

FRY, HENRY, *History of North Atlantic Steam Navigation*, Sampson, Low, Marston, London, 1896.

GOULD, JOHN H., *On the Ocean*, Ocean Publishing Co., New York, c. 1895. A Hamburg—Amerika souvenir.

GOULD, JOHN H., *Across the Atlantic*, Ocean Publishing Co., New York, 1896. Another substantial souvenir guidebook this time for White Star.

GRATTIDGE, CAPTAIN HARRY, and COLLIER, RICHARD,

Captain of the Queens, Oldbourne, London, 1956. Memoirs.

The Great Cunarder R.M.S. Aquitania, published by the Cunard company, London, 1921.

HAYES, SIR BERTRAM, *Hull Down*, Cassell, London, 1925. Memoirs.

HELMUTH, W. TOD, *A Steamer Book*, Carleton and Co., New York, 1880.

HODGINS, ERIC, *Ocean Express, Story of the Bremen and Europa*, published by North German Lloyd, New York, c. 1928.

HOVEY, CARL, *The Life Story of J. Pierpont Morgan*, Heinemann, London, 1912.

HULDERMANN, BERNHARD, *Albert Ballin*, Cassell, London and New York, 1922. Biography.

JORDAN, HUMFREY, *Mauretania*, Hodder & Stoughton, London, 1936.

Journal of Commerce Report of the British Titanic Inquiry, reprinted from the Journal of Commerce, Liverpool and London, 1912. See also *Titanic Disaster*.

KELLEY, J. D. JERROLD, LT COMMANDER, U.S.N., *The Ship's Company and Other People*, Harper, New York, 1897. Well illustrated.

KNAPP, PAUL, *The Berengaria Exchange*, Dial Press, New York, 1971. The *Berengaria*'s voyage at the time of the Wall Street crash.

LAWRENCE, JACK, (Ship-news reporter of the New York *Evening Mail*), *When The Ships Came In*, Farrar & Rinehart, New York and Toronto, c. 1920.

LEDOUX, MRS KATE REID, *Ocean Notes and Foreign Travel for Ladies*, Cook, Son, and Jenkins, New York, 1878. Dismal advice, very entertaining. Found only in Library of Congress, which identifies Mrs Ledoux as the author although only the phrase 'by K.R.L.' appears on the title page.

SS *Leviathan*, Catalogue of the auction of interior fittings at Rosyth, Scotland, 1938. In the New York Public Library catalogued under VM 383 LGM 5.

LEWIS, SINCLAIR, *Dodsworth*, Cape, London, 1929. A novel, set partly on shipboard.

LIGHTOLLER, CHARLES E., *Titanic and Other Ships*, Nicholson and Watson, London, 1935. Commander Lightoller was an officer on the *Titanic*.

LORD, WALTER, *A Night to Remember*, Longmans Green, London, 1956. The book from which the Rank film of the *Titanic* disaster was made. A revised, illustrated edition is to be published in 1976 by Allen Lane, London, and Holt Rinehart, New York.

MAEV (pseud.), *An Aristocrat of the Atlantic*, published by Cunard, New York, c. 1893. New York Public Library TRnc 7.

MARCUS, GEOFFREY, *The Maiden Voyage*, Allen & Unwin, London, 1969. Very good on the *Titanic* inquiries.

MARR, COMMODORE GEOFFREY, *The Queens and I*, Adlard Coles, London, 1973. Memoirs.

MAXTONE-GRAHAM, JOHN, *The Only Way to Cross*, Macmillan, New York, 1972, and, as *The North Atlantic Run*, Cassell, London, 1972. A comprehensive history from 1907 to the present.

MENCKEN, AUGUST, *First Class Passenger*, Knopf, 1938. A collection of short pieces by several hands.

MORGAN, CLAY, (ed.), *Fun en Route, the Bon Voyage Book*, Simon and Schuster, New York, 1934.

MORRISON, JOHN H., *A History of American Steam Navigation*, W. F. Samerz, New York, 1903.

PEABODY, MARIAN LAWRENCE, *To be Young Was Very Heaven*, Houghton Mifflin, Boston, 1967. Reminiscences.

POTTER, NEIL, and FROST, JACK, *The Elizabeth*, Harrap, London, 1965.

POTTER, NEIL, and FROST, JACK, *Queen Elizabeth 2*, Harrap, London, 1969.

POTTER, NEIL, and FROST, JACK, *The Queen Mary*, Harrap, London, in association with the San Francisco Press, 1971.

These last three works were compiled with the assistance of Cunard. The late Mr Frost was for many years shipping correspondent of the London *Daily Telegraph*.

ROBERTSON, MORGAN, *Futility*, published by M. F. Mansfield, New York, 1898, and republished, as *The Wreck of the Titan, or Futility*, by McKinlay, Stone, & Mackenzie, New York, 1912. A short story which has been seen as a premonition of the Titanic disaster.

Service Manual, Stewards Department, compiled by the United States Lines, Cornell Maritime Press, New York, 1941.

SPEDDING, CHARLES T., (for many years purser of the *Aquitania*), *Reminiscences of Transatlantic Travellers*, Fisher, Unwin, London, 1926.

STANFORD, DON, *The Ile de France*, London, 1960.

STREET, JULIAN, *Ship-Bored*, New York, 1912.

Titanic Disaster, Hearings before a sub-committee of the Committee of Commerce, US Senate, Sen. Doc. 726, 62nd Congress, 2nd Session, 1912. (See also *Journal of Commerce* for report of the British inquiry.)

Titanic Passenger List. In the British Museum Reading Room, catalogue NGK 143 M.

VERNE, JULES, *A Floating City*, Scribner's Sons, New York, 1904. An account of a voyage on the *Great Eastern*.

WILKES, GEORGE, *Europe in a Hurry*, New York, 1852.

WINKLER, JOHN KENNEDY, *The Life of J. Pierpont Morgan*, Allen & Unwin, London, 1931.

WINOCOUR, JACK (ed.), *The Story of the Titanic*, Dover, New York, 1960. Reprinted eye-witness accounts of the *Titanic* sinking, including that of Lawrence Beesley, q.v.

WOON, BASIL, *The Frantic Atlantic*, Knopf, New York, 1927.

Books: Reference Works

BONSOR, N. R. P., *North Atlantic Seaway. An Illustrated History of the Passenger Services Linking the Old World with the New*, foreword by A. C. Hardy, illustrated by J. H. Isherwood, Extra Master, Stephenson, Prescot, Lancs., 1955, with supplement added 1960. Indispensable reference book, line by line and ship by ship, compiled with love and scholarship. Many photographs, and also many excellent line drawings, severe silhouettes showing the changing shape of the liner, by Mr Isherwood. A new edition of this book, with the same title but virtually rewritten by the author and with much extra material, is to be published in four volumes by David & Charles, Newton Abbot, Devon, starting with volume 1 in 1976.

GIBBS, COMMANDER C. R. VERNON, RN, *Passenger Liners of the Western Ocean: A record of the North Atlantic Steam and Motor Passenger Vessels from 1838 to the Present Day*, Staples Press, London, 1952. Another work of love, less detailed than Bonsor but more anecdotal in parts. The two works complement each other admirably.

GIBBS, COMMANDER C. R. VERNON, RN, *Western Ocean Passenger Lines and Liners 1934–1969*, Brown, Son & Ferguson, Glasgow, 1970. Brings the survey up to 1969.

Newspapers and Magazines

Some of the best material comes from this source, but is of course scattered all over the place. Both the London *Times* and the *New York Times* have indexes. The principal publications used, sometimes searched but more often dipped into, were:

IN ENGLAND: *The Times, Manchester Guardian, Daily Telegraph, Daily Mail, Daily Express, Evening Standard, Sunday Times, Spectator, Punch, Illustrated London News, Sphere, Graphic*, and the *Shipbuilder*. The special editions published by this last magazine on the launching of great ships like the *Olympic* and *Titanic* and *Queen Mary*, have been reprinted in book form by Patrick Stephens, London.

IN AMERICA: *New York Times*, New York *Herald Tribune, Chicago Tribune, Los Angeles Times, New Yorker, Life, Harper's, Scientific American*, and the *Titanic Commutator* (not a general publication but the journal of the Titanic Enthusiasts of America).

Shipboard Newspapers

These are disappointing, as they often contain very little shipboard news, but only tiny condensations of news from the outer world. The earlier ones, when voyages were longer, and before radio, are more rewarding.

Copies of the *Cunard Daily Bulletin*, published on Cunard ships, and of ship's newspapers from other lines, are at the British Museum newspaper library at Colindale under 'Misc., London. 377'. It is a small collection though. The New York Public Library has copies of some of the same, and also

of the French Line's *L'Atlantique* and of the *Hamburg American Gazette*.

House Magazines

White Star and *Cunard*, were published by the companies for their staff. *Cunard* sometimes contains delightful illustrations particularly in the Christmas numbers.

Pamphlets

Advertising pamphlets and booklets printed by the steamship companies often catch the tone of a ship most accurately, or at least the tone that the company wanted to create. There are hundreds, and a list would be useless as most libraries do not catalogue them by name or at all, but they are to be found principally in the following places:

NATIONAL MARITIME MUSEUM, GREENWICH. Pamphlets are stored in box files, apart from the main library, and given the catalogue number 321. Box 321B is foreign, i.e. other than British, companies; 321WSL contains White Star Line pamphlets; and so on. Pamphlets of the different companies are sometimes mixed up.

MARINERS MUSEUM, NEWPORT NEWS, VIRGINIA. This is a large collection, stored in filing cabinets, again under the names of the companies.

NEW YORK PUBLIC LIBRARY. Many pamphlets are mentioned in the main catalogue under the names of companies or ships. Others are not, but are obtainable in the library annex, many under the general classification TRK. The New York Public Library also has, included in the bundle of pamphlets, a collection of company handouts to the Press, giving arrival dates and passenger lists and so on.

LIVERPOOL UNIVERSITY. The Cunard Archive contains many company pamphlets.

FRENCH LINE. In 1974 the company had a rich collection of pamphlets at its Paris offices.

Manuscripts and Other Original Records

The records of most companies have vanished. I have, for instance, been able to find no single paper of the White Star Line. Much of the old Cunard archive is at Liverpool University. It includes ledgers, the chairman's letter books, minute books, and some other correspondence and is being catalogued. The French Line maintains its own plentiful archives in Paris.

ILLUSTRATIONS AND ACKNOWLEDGEMENTS

INDEX

Entries in **bold type** indicate illustrations.

MAMA
DINO

THE
VELOCIRAPTOR

THE
FARM
ANIMALS

KU-757-850

In...

Raintree is an imprint of Capstone
Global Library Limited, a company
incorporated in England and Wales
having its registered office at 264
Banbury Road, Oxford, OX2 7DY –
Registered company number: 6695582

www.raintree.co.uk
myorders@raintree.co.uk

Text and illustrations © Capstone
Global Library Limited 2018.
The moral rights of the proprietor
have been asserted.

All rights reserved. No part of this
publication may be reproduced in
any form or by any means (including
photocopying or storing it in any
medium by electronic means and
whether or not transiently or
incidentally to some other use
of this publication) without the
written permission of the copyright
owner, except in accordance with
the provisions of the Copyright,
Designs and Patents Act 1988 or
under the terms of a licence issued
by the Copyright Licensing Agency,
Saffron House, 6–10 Kirby Street,
London EC1N 8TS (www.cla.co.uk).
Applications for the copyright owner's
written permission should be addressed
to the publisher.

Designed by Hilary Wacholz
Edited by Abby Huff
Lettered by Jaymes Reed

ISBN 978 1 474 75029 5
21 20 19 18 17
10 9 8 7 6 5 4 3 2 1

British Library Cataloguing in
Publication Data: A full catalogue
record for this book is available
from the British Library.

Printed and bound in China.

FAR OUT FABLES

THE UGLY DINO HATCHLING

A GRAPHIC NOVEL

BY STEPHANIE PETERS

ILLUSTRATED BY OTIS FRAMPTON

8

Then she made an even more exciting discovery.

They're hatching! They're hatching!

CRICK CRICK CRICK CRICK CRICK CRICK

Welcome, First!

I'm first!

Wait, his *name* is First?

Three guesses what she names the others.

You're *Second!*

You're *Third!*

You're *Fourth!*

And you're...

CRIIICK

9

11

At first, Rex's strangeness wasn't a big deal.

Nighty-night, my babies.

But over time . . .

Come along, my babies!

You can do it, Rex!

His differences became harder to overlook.

BLUB
BLUB BLUB
BLUB

Almost impossible, actually.

Mother, I'm tired.

Hop on, my baby!

I'm coming on board too, Mama!

Aah!

Soon, Rex's duckling brothers stopped ignoring the differences.

The chicken crossed the road to get to the other side! Get it?

Ha ha!

I don't get it.

ROARHOROAR! HOROAR!

Whoa. Turn it down, Rex!

And ignored Rex instead.

Guys? Aren't we going to *play?*

Pretend you can't hear him.

Hear who?

Exactly!

13

They don't like me because I'm so ugly.

You're not ugly. You're just *different.*

What do you mean, *different?*

Fourth tried to explain.

There's an old saying…

If it *looks* like a duckling…

Swims like a duckling…

And *quacks* like a duckling…

Quack!

Then it's a *duckling.*

Get it?

I do.

He didn't.

TA-DA!
I *look* like a duckling.

I *swim* like a duckling. And listen to this...

QUROARK!

Oh, Rex.

15

Rex raced to show his brothers what a good duckling he was now.

Wait, Rex!

Guys, look at me. I'm just like *you!*

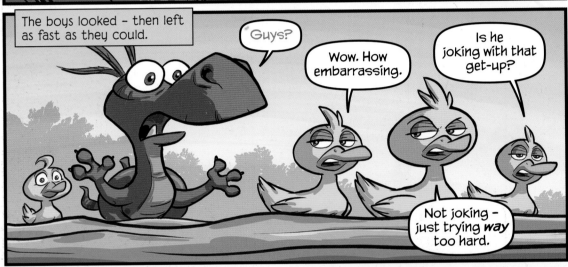

The boys looked – then left as fast as they could.

Guys?

Wow. How embarrassing.

Is he joking with that get-up?

Not joking – just trying *way* too hard.

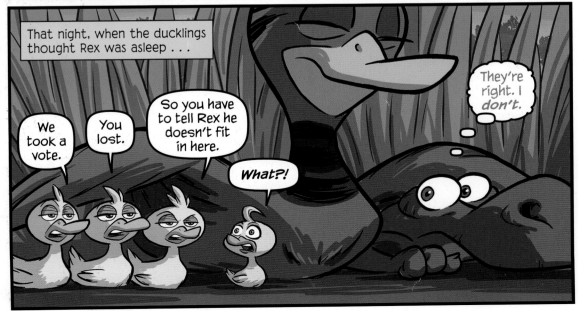

That night, when the ducklings thought Rex was asleep . . .

We took a vote.

You lost.

So you have to tell Rex he doesn't fit in here.

What?!

They're right. I *don't.*

16

21

Meanwhile, earlier that same day . . .

Mama, Rex has gone!

Oh, baby, Rex is a big boy.

I'm sure he'll return before dark.

But he didn't come back that night.

Where did you go, Rex?

Or the next day. Because he'd made a decision.

This is my home now.

Rex spent his days exploring the forest. He talked to many animals, but he didn't find any like him.

Days turned into weeks.

Although Rex missed his duck family . . .

Good night, Fourth.

He stayed out on his own.

Good night, Rex . . . *wherever* you are.

But one night, something else returned to the pond . . .

Huh? What is *that?!*

24

27

28

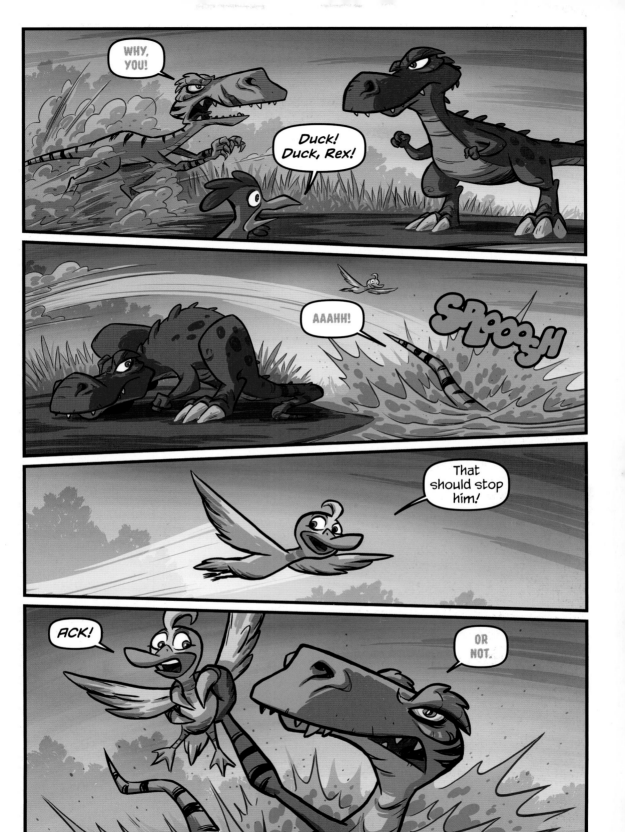

So Rex was transported far away to a different place in a different time. But every now and then . . .

He found his way back to where he first belonged.

ALL ABOUT FABLES

A fable is a short tale that teaches the reader a lesson about life, often with animal characters. At the end of a fable, there's almost always a moral (a fancy word for lesson) stated very clearly, so you don't miss it. Yes, fables can be a bit bossy. But luckily, they usually give pretty good advice. Read on to learn more about the original fable written by Danish author Hans Christian Andersen in 1843, and its moral. Can you spot any other lessons?

THE UGLY DUCKLING

One day, a swan egg rolls into a duck's nest. When all the eggs hatch, the baby swan - called a cygnet - looks a lot different from the ducklings. Although the cygnet swims better than his siblings, the farm animals tease him and call him ugly. Soon, even the mother duck says he doesn't belong. So the baby swan decides to run away. He tries living with wild ducks and then with an old lady and her pets. But he doesn't fit in. Out on his own, the cygnet nearly freezes during winter. In spring, the cygnet spots a flock of majestic swans. He worries they'll pick on him like everyone else has. But to his astonishment, they greet him with respect. Because he isn't an ugly duckling anymore. He's grown into the most beautiful swan in the entire pond.

THE MORAL

NEVER GIVE UP ON FINDING WHERE YOU BELONG
(In other words, don't change who
you are to fit in - find
where you're valued
for being YOU!)

A FAR OUT GUIDE TO THE FABLE'S JURASSIC TWISTS!

The swan egg is swapped out for a dinosaur egg that has tumbled through a time portal!

In the original, even the mother duck and siblings teased the ugly duckling. Here, Fourth encourages Rex to stay true to himself.

The ugly duckling turns into a beautiful swan, but Rex grows up to use his awesome dino abilities to rescue the farm animals.

The swan leaves the ducks of the pond far behind. Rex still visits his duck family!

VISUAL QUESTIONS

The animals judge Rex because of how he looks. Do you think that's fair? Have you ever felt like you don't fit in? Talk about your answers.

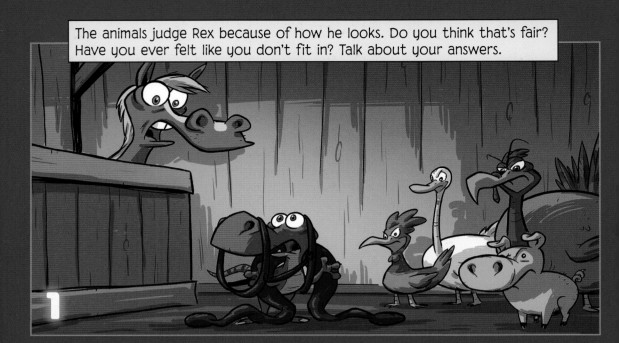

The background in this panel is orange and yellow. Why do you think the illustrator chose to do this? What feeling does it create?

Rex is teased for being different, but his differences help to save the day. In your own words, discuss how Rex uses his unique dinosaur abilities to defeat the velociraptor.

List three ways Rex tries to fit in with the ducklings and farm animals. Did you think his plans would work? Why or why not?

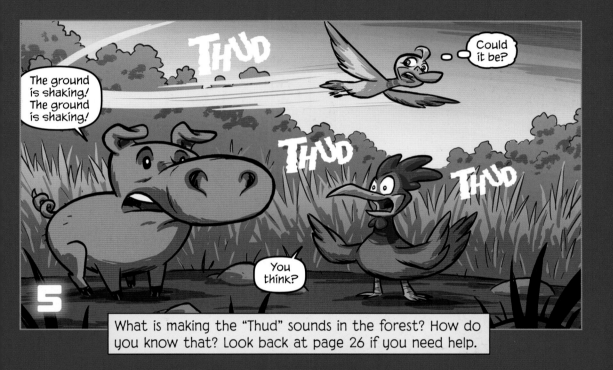

THUD

Could it be?

The ground is shaking! The ground is shaking!

You think?

What is making the "Thud" sounds in the forest? How do you know that? Look back at page 26 if you need help.

The art in graphic novels can tell you a lot about what a character is feeling or thinking. How do you think Rex feels here? Use examples from the art and text to support your answer.

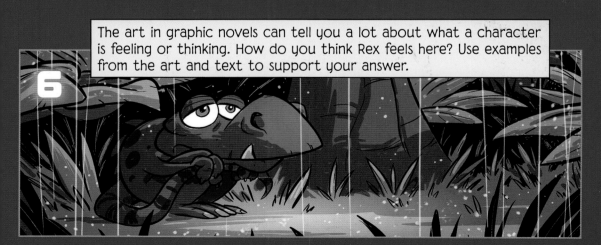

AUTHOR

Stephanie Peters worked as a children's book editor for ten years before she started writing books herself. She has since written forty books, including *Sleeping Beauty, Magic Master* and the New York Times best-seller *A Princess Primer: A Fairy Godmother's Guide to Being a Princess*. When not at her computer, Peters enjoys playing with her two children, going to the gym or working on home improvement projects with her patient and supportive husband, Daniel.

ILLUSTRATOR

Otis Frampton is a writer and artist. He is the creator of *Oddly Normal*, published by Image Comics. He is also one of the artists on the popular animated web series *How It Should Have Ended*.

GLOSSARY

decision act of making up your mind about what to do

eon long period of time that can't be measured

explore travel through a new area in order to learn or for adventure

familiar well known or easily recognized; if something *seems* familiar, you're not quite sure if you know it and can't fully remember

inherit receive something from a parent, such as looks, habits or skills

insist demand or ask in a very firm way

overlook ignore or not pay attention to something

portal large, impressive opening or entrance

poultry birds raised for their eggs and meat; chickens, turkeys, ducks and geese are poultry

precious having great importance or value

strut walk in a proud way

unique one of a kind and unlike anything else

wreck destroy or damage in a violent way

THE MORAL OF THE STORY IS... EPIC!

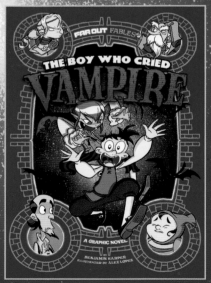

FAR OUT FABLES